Praise for ONE DAY IN SEPTEMBER

"A page turner . . . Goes somewhat further [than the documentary], offering background notes on Jewish and Palestinian history and the Black September group, and Reeve fleshes out the long aftermath of the affair, in which Israel's Mossad agents took revenge over a period lasting almost twenty years. . . . Highly skilled and detailed."
— *The New Yorker*

"The strength of Reeve's book is that it starts from the beginning. It details not only the crisis itself, but also the historical background that led to the crisis. It is an important book, a thorough primer on the origins of the Israeli-Palestinian standoff." — *Chicago Tribune*

"Simon Reeve pulls off another master stroke." — *Village Voice*

"[A] controversial, engrossing new account of the slaughter. The governments of Israel and Germany have criticized Reeve's book for exposing state secrets; he may have done so, but he avoids passing judgment on any one group. Instead, he tries to show why the countries and people involved felt compelled to act the way they did, even when their actions led to horrible consequences."
— *Time Out New York*

"Powerful . . . recounts in horrifying detail the tragedy that claimed the lives of 11 Israelis. *One Day in September* describes the savagery of the Black September Palestinian terrorists and the monumental ineptitude of the German forces that tried to rescue the hostages at Fürstenfeldbruck airfield." — *Pittsburgh Post-Gazette*

"Written with all the pace of a thriller, this is a genuinely moving account of one of the most tragic, and shameful, episodes of recent history. Excellent." — *Birmingham Post*

"Fascinating . . . a gripping account which reads like a thriller. Reeve is a very thorough investigator, and the book encompasses German archives, news programs, quotes, decisions, and international reactions." — *Jewish Book World*

"A gripping, often moving, account of the bloodiest sports day on record." — *Jewish Chronicle*

"Simon Reeve captures the essence of the slaughter. . . . *One Day in September* is the inside story told by those who were present. . . . The book is easy to read, even with obscure political and religious references."
— *Daytona Beach News-Journal*

"A splendid, disturbing and gripping account of these events and the world's reactions . . . Stands among the best of its kind."
— *Publishers Weekly* (starred review)

"A comprehensive and unsettling account . . . Reeve's book is an important one since it deals with many issues—terrorism, anti-Semitism and other forms of racism, and Middle East unrest."
— *Library Journal*

"An exhaustively-researched account of the hostage-taking drama which deteriorated into an unmitigated nightmare."
— *Canadian Jewish News*

"Brilliant investigation . . . a master class in investigative journalism."
— *International Herald Tribune*

"This astonishing record of the massacre at the Munich Olympics should be compulsory reading. . . . I read in one sitting the gripping narrative."
— *Daily Mail*, London

"His account is rounded and . . . gripping. . . . A very moving testimony."
— *Financial Times*

"Explosive."
— *Observer,* London

"In this gripping and very moving account based on newly released documents, Reeve shows how official incompetence and indifference sealed the fate of the hostages, all of whom died in a botched rescue attempt."
— *Scotland on Sunday*

"A compelling investigation . . . This book is both a journey back in time to an event many people know about—but that very few know enough about—and an excellent insight into why these terrible events happened and how the subsequent tit for tat revenge operations affected both sides in the conflict."
— *Sunday Business Post,* Ireland

ONE DAY IN SEPTEMBER

THE FULL STORY OF THE 1972 MUNICH OLYMPICS
MASSACRE AND THE ISRAELI REVENGE OPERATION
"WRATH OF GOD"

SIMON REEVE

ARCADE PUBLISHING • NEW YORK

For all the families who suffered
as a result of the events of September 5, 1972.

FIRST U.S. EDITION

Title page image courtesy of Bettmann-Corbis

ISBN 1-55970-547-7 (hc)
ISBN 1-55970-603-1 (pb)
Library of Congress Control Number 00-131704
Library of Congress Cataloging-in-Publication Data is available.

Published in the United States by Arcade Publishing, Inc., New York
Distributed by Time Warner Trade Publishing

Visit our Web site at www.arcadepub.com

10   9   8   7   6   5   4   3   2   1

Designed by API

EB

PRINTED IN THE UNITED STATES OF AMERICA

Contents

Illustrations

Photographs are from the author's collection unless otherwise credited.

Introduction

They were billed as "The Games of Peace and Joy." The 1972 Olympic Games, held in the southern German city of Munich, were to be the biggest and most expensive ever mounted, with more athletes representing more countries than at any previous sporting event.

At 3:00 P.M. on August 26, 1972, the world watched as ranks of tall Greek athletes marched into the packed Olympic Stadium, in the north of the city, to bathe in warm sunshine and thunderous applause.

The arrival in the stadium of the Greek team, representing the nation that invented the ancient Games, signalled the start of a magnificent opening ceremony for the XXth Olympiad. Teams from the rest of the world emerged from the stadium tunnel to the sound of drums and cymbals and followed the Greeks in alphabetical order. Spectators roared their approval, and banners and national flags fluttered in the light breeze. Behind the Egyptian team ("Aegypten" in German) came those from Afghanistan, Albania, Brazil: the cream of the world's athletes assembling to compete in tests of physical strength, agility, and skill.

As most of the 10,490 athletes present at the Games milled around the stadium, jostling for a better view, groups of whip-cracking Bavarian folk-dancers entertained the crowds. Next, 5,000 doves were released into the blue skies over Munich. Sixty men wearing Bavarian national costume fired antique pistols into the sky, signalling the arrival of the hallowed Olympic flame carried from the Peloponnese, the site of the ancient Olympics. With the Munich beacon lit, the Games could begin.

*

The opening ceremony was a moving experience for the West German officials who had fought tenaciously to bring the Games to Munich. Hans-Jochen Vogel, the mayor of Munich from the 1960s until just a few weeks before the Games began, was bursting with pride during the ceremony. "It was emotional," he said, "in a good sense."[1]

Bavarian officials hoped the event would confirm Germany's rehabilitation as a civilized society, expunging memories of the Second World War and the infamous 1936 Berlin Olympics, which Hitler used to glorify Nazi ideology. They invited massed ranks of the media, a greater concentration than ever before, to witness the festival of sport and the redevelopment of West Germany.

"The first thing you felt on arriving in Munich was this utter determination of the Germans, whether they be Olympic officials, policemen, journalists, or indeed the general population of Munich, to wipe away the past," said Gerald Seymour, a reporter at the Games with Independent Television News (ITN) of Britain. "We were totally overwhelmed by the sense that this was the new Germany. It was a massive attempt, and it hit you straight away, by the Germans to appear open and modern and shorn of their past. Friendliness was in overdrive."[2]

At least four thousand newspaper, magazine, and radio journalists travelled to the Bavarian capital, along with another two thousand television journalists, announcers, and crews. They fed tales of grit and courage to a television audience of nearly one billion souls in more than one hundred countries around the world. New satellite technology made it the mass-media event of the century.

Reconciliation between former enemies was a worthy goal, and the Germans worked feverishly to build an Olympic site the entire world could enjoy. A majestic Olympic Stadium was constructed on wasteland alongside a sprawling Olympic Village where the athletes would stay.

But there was no greater confirmation of Germany's rehabilitation than the presence at the Games of a delegation from Israel. The Jewish state, still struggling to forge a relationship with West Germany, sent its largest ever team of athletes and officials, several of them older Eastern Europeans still bearing physical and mental scars from Nazi concentration camps. To discourage any memories of Germany's Nazi past, the two thousand Olympic security guards were dressed in tasteful, light-blue uniforms and sent out to charm the world, armed with nothing more than walkie-talkies.

"The atmosphere was . . . to let everybody feel that Germany has changed from the time of 1936," recalls Shmuel Lalkin, the head of the Israeli delegation. "It was an open Olympic Games."[3] Across the vast Olympic site, dominated by a 950-foot-high television tower and a futuristic tented cover, a party atmosphere soon prevailed. Even entry into the Olympic Village was easy for competitors and autograph-hunters alike. "The atmosphere was . . . enjoy yourself, see that Germany is not the same as it was."[4]

However, many of the Israelis had mixed feelings about their presence in Germany. Henry Herskowitz, a competitor in the rifle shooting, felt a degree of pride that Jews were returning to raise the Israeli flag on German soil.[5] It proved the Nazis had not killed their spirit. But Jewish fears of Germany run deep, and before he left Israel, Herskowitz "had a feeling that something might happen."[6] Herskowitz was the athlete chosen to carry the Israeli flag during the opening ceremony, and in his darkest nightmares he had visions of being shot while carrying the Star of David around the Olympic Stadium.

Terror did not strike at the opening ceremony, and the sprinter Esther Shahamurov, now Roth, one of the brightest Israeli track stars, marched just a few yards behind Herskowitz, also buoyant with pride. "It is a unique feeling to march while the Israeli flag is in front . . . There are many Jews around the world; you sympathize with them and they sympathize with you. You feel that you have to represent them."[7]

For Roth, the Olympics were "better than a dream." "When I went there my eyes were opened . . . I saw people from all over the world, I didn't know where to look first." She remembers the Olympics as a feast for the eyes: so much color, so many different nationalities. "It was very beautiful, not only for athletes, but for everyone . . . You see an athlete and you can tell by his physique the sport he is in. For instance, the people who play basketball, they are so tall you can hardly stand next to them. The wrestlers, they have those ears, you can see the flesh in their ears . . . It was an amazing experience," recalled Roth.

With the ceremony over, the Games began, and for the first week they went spectacularly. Despite the problems of the world outside — the Cold War between East and West, the "hot" war in Vietnam,[8] violence in Ulster and the Middle East — Munich bore witness to the Olympic ideal.

To many of those watching the Games, it seemed that amid increasing international tension sport offered the only chance of sanity, a means of communicating with international enemies on an individual, human level. Fans celebrated the achievements of athletes like Valery Borzov, the Soviet sprinter, and the pentathlete Mary Peters, Ulster's "Golden Girl." Mark Spitz, the twenty-two-year-old American swimmer, shattered world records and won seven gold medals, while the elfin Soviet gymnast Olga Korbut won her first and thrilled the world. When Korbut finished her floor exercises with a toss of her hair and a pout, the world erupted. The teenager was the antithesis of the gray Soviet leaders paraded before the West, bouncing proof that Soviets were capable of humor. The crowd screamed for her to be given the perfect "10" mark. "I don't believe it! Give her 11!" exclaimed the American television commentator Gordon Maddux.

However, not all of the competitors enjoyed their time in Munich. Memories of the Second World War and six million exterminated Jews are etched in the Jewish psyche. Many of the Israeli athletes felt uncomfortable in Germany. Munich, after all, was close to the site of the Dachau concentration camp where at least sixty-five thousand Jews were slaughtered. Israeli athletes and officials had been forced to confront personal demons when summoning the courage to compete and work on German soil.

"All my family was exterminated in that country," said Tuvia Sokolovsky, an Israeli weightlifting trainer in the 1972 squad. "I am a Holocaust survivor. For me, Germans and Munich mean the extermination of six million Jews, including my father and his family."[9]

Sokolovsky was tormented by the past from the moment he arrived on German soil: "I had a horrible feeling as I saw in every adult German the face of the murderers of my parents."

Other Israelis felt the same, but all still competed gallantly. Esther Roth, a great hope for the 100-meter hurdles, was enrolled in the 100-meter sprint by her coach Amitzur Shapira. "I broke my personal best and I felt fast," she recalls. "In those Olympic Games, I felt as if I were a wild horse."[10] She made the sprint semifinals, but then "blew it. I missed the final by the tiniest fraction of a second," said Roth, who then began training for the semifinals of the 100-meter hurdles held a few days later, towards the end of the Games.

Success eluded the rest of the team, however, and most of the Israeli athletes were knocked out in early events. Roth's success galvanized them with pride, but most secretly longed to return home to their loved ones. Yossef Romano, a weightlifter born in Tripoli, Libya, sent messages and a cassette tape back to his wife and three daughters wishing them a happy Rosh Hashanah. Zeev Friedman, a weightlifter from Haifa, wrote postcards to his parents and sister Nina. Andre Spitzer, a fencing coach born in Romania, pumped coins into pay phones to ring his wife Ankie in Holland.

On September 4, 1972, a free day for the Israeli team, most of the athletes relaxed around the Olympic Village, then travelled into the city of Munich in the evening to see a popular play, *Fiddler on the Roof,* starring Shmuel Rodensky, "Israel's Laurence Olivier." It was a wonderful night. Esther Roth sat next to Amitzur Shapira, who had discovered her running talent when she was just fourteen and told her he would train her for the Olympics. The play was in German, but because Amitzur spoke Yiddish he could understand it. Esther listened carefully as he translated for her.

"We felt great; it was a wonderful atmosphere," remembered Roth. "I had reached the second stage, and it felt like the whole delegation had won. Everybody celebrated in the success. It was a very moving night. In the middle of the play we were invited to have a glass of wine. They took photos of me and Shmuel Rodensky. They lifted us in the air, the whole delegation."

When the play finished and the party was over, the Israelis trooped back to their rooms in the Olympic Village. Roth recalled: "When we came back to the village, Amitzur told me that in the morning we would meet in the dining room . . . And that was it. I went to sleep. I had all kinds of sporty dreams."

The Takeover

S hortly after 4 A.M. on the morning of September 5, 1972, a small gang of shadowy figures arrived on the outskirts of the Olympic Village and silently made their way to the six-foot-high perimeter fence supposed to offer protection to the thousands of athletes sleeping within.

Creeping through the darkness carrying heavy sports bags, the group made for a length of the fence near Gate 25A, which was locked at midnight but left unguarded. The thirty-five-year-old leader of the small troop, Luttif Afif, a.k.a. "Issa," had carefully chosen the point at which his men were to enter the Village.[1] On previous nights he had seen athletes climbing the fence near Gate 25A while returning drunk from late-night parties. Security was lax and none of the athletes had been stopped. Issa dressed his seven colleagues in tracksuits, reasoning that if guards saw them they would assume they were just sportsmen returning to their quarters.

Jamal Al-Gashey, at nineteen one of the youngest members of the group, remembers the tension building as they approached the fence.[2] As they drew closer they came across a small group of drunk American athletes returning to their beds by the same route.[3] "They had been forced to leave the village in secret for their night out," Al-Gashey said. "We could see they were Americans . . . and they were going to go over the [fence] as well." Issa quickly decided the foreign athletes could give his group cover if they helped each other over the fence. "We got chatting," recalled Al-Gashey, "and then we helped each other over." He lifted a member of the U.S. team up onto the fence, which was topped not by barbed wire but by small round cones, and then the American turned and helped to pull him up and over.

Several officials, including six German postmen on their way to a temporary post office in the Village Plaza, saw the groups climbing the fence with their sports bags at around 4:10 A.M.[4] But as Issa had assumed, none of the passersby challenged them because they thought the fence-climbers were just athletes returning home. "We walked for a while with the American athletes, then said goodbye," remembered Al-Gashey.[5] The group split up and stole through the sleeping Village to a drab three-story building on Connollystrasse, one of three broad pedestrianized streets, adorned with shrubbery and fountains, snaking from east to west through the Village. Even if the unarmed Olympic guards or the Munich police had been alerted, it would probably have been too late. For the eight men were heavily armed terrorists from Black September, an extremist faction within the Palestinian Liberation Organization. The *fedayeen* ("fighters for the faith") were carrying Kalashnikov assault rifles and grenades, hidden under clothing in the sports bags,[6] and they were fully prepared to fight their way to their target: 31 Connollystrasse, the building in the heart of the Olympic Village that housed the Israeli delegation to the Olympic Games. The new entrants were about to make their mark on the XXth Olympiad.

The Black September terrorists knew exactly where to go after scaling the perimeter fence. The attack had been weeks in the planning, and Issa and his deputy, "Tony" (real name, Yusuf Nazzal), worked undercover in the Olympic Village to familiarize themselves with its layout. Issa had lived in Germany for five years and attended university in Berlin. He took a job in the Village as a civil engineer. Tony, who is believed to have worked for a Munich oil company, went undercover as a cook.[7]

The temporary jobs allowed both men to roam freely through the Village. As the world revelled in sporting glories, Issa and Tony sat on a bench on Connollystrasse together and played chess in the sunshine, watching athletes coming and going from No. 31. Tony proved to be a particularly good spy. Luis Friedman, an official with the Uruguayan team, which was sharing 31 Connollystrasse with the Israelis, even found him inside the building at 8:00 A.M. on September 4. Speaking in English the Palestinian shyly told Friedman that he was a worker in the Village and that someone in the building occasionally gave him a few pieces of fruit. Friedman walked over to a crate of apples and pears sitting on a table and gave him all the fruit he could carry.

The next night Issa and Tony led their squad of terrorists quickly through the Village. They paused just around the corner from the Israeli building, changed out of their athletes' tracksuits into the clothes they would wear during the attack, and then headed towards Connollystrasse (named after the American athlete James B. Connolly, a gold-medal winner at the 1896 Olympics).

There were twenty-four separate apartments in No. 31: eleven of the apartments were spread over two floors, with an entrance on the main street and a garden at the back; the rest were on the fourth floor, which was topped by two penthouses. Twenty-one members of the Israeli delegation were housed in the duplex apartments 1–6. The block was also home to athletes and officials from Uruguay, who had the other duplex apartments, 7–10, and several more on the fourth floor, and the Hong Kong team which occupied five apartments on the fourth floor and the two penthouses. A German caretaker lived in the remaining duplex with his wife and two young children, and a steward had the remaining fourth-floor apartment.

Shortly after 4:30 A.M. the terrorists assembled at the far end of the building, opened the blue main entrance door to apartment 1, and crept into the communal foyer. Whereas the other ten duplexes opened directly onto the street, apartment 1 had a foyer with an elevator and stairs leading up to the fourth-floor and penthouse apartments and down into the lower-level streets and parking lot. The door was never locked.

"When we got to the building, the leader of the operation gave out jobs to us," Al-Gashey said. "My job was to stand guard at the entrance of the building and the others went up the steps into the building to begin the mission."[8] With Jamal guarding the entrance, the rest of the group positioned themselves outside apartment 1, home to seven Israelis, and tried to open the door with a key they had obtained during their preparations for the attack.

Inside the apartment the Israelis were fast asleep: Amitzur Shapira, athletics coach, Kehat Shorr, marksmen coach, Andre Spitzer, fencing coach, Tuvia Sokolovsky, weightlifting trainer, Jacov Springer, weight-lifting judge, and Moshe Weinberg, wrestling coach. Yossef Gutfreund, a wrestling referee, was the only one awakened by the faint sound of scratching at the door.

Gutfreund crept out of his bedroom and into the communal lounge, not wanting to wake the others. As he stood barefoot by the door, listening for a sound, it opened just a few inches. Even in the dim light, with sleep still misting his eyes, he saw the eyes of the fedayeen and the barrels of their Kalashnikov assault rifles. Sleep turned instantly to horror. *"CHEVRE TISTATRU!!"* ("Take cover, boys!!"), screamed the 6-foot, 3-inch Gutfreund, thrusting his two-hundred-ninety-pound bear-like physique against the door as the terrorists abandoned their keys and began pushing from the other side.

The apartment erupted. Tuvia Sokolovsky, who shared Gutfreund's room, jumped from his bed and ran into the communal lounge. Gutfreund was wedging the front door closed with his body.[9]

"Through the half-open door I saw a man with a black-painted face holding a weapon," said Sokolovsky.[10] "At that moment I knew I had to escape."[11]

Sokolovsky screamed to his friends in the other rooms, leapt back into his bedroom and sprinted towards the window. "I tried to open it but couldn't. I pushed it with all my force."[12]

Behind him three terrorists were desperately trying to dislodge Gutfreund and shove the door open.[13] They pushed with their hands, they braced their legs against the other side of the corridor wall, and then they stuck the barrels of two Kalashnikovs through the small opening and used them as levers in the frame. Man-mountain Gutfreund held them for at least ten seconds before they spilled into the apartment, forcing him to the ground at gunpoint.

In a blind panic Sokolovsky finally broke the window open. "It fell out and I jumped and began to run." The fedayeen ran into the bedroom behind him. "The Arab terrorists started shooting at me and I could hear the bullets flying near my ears."[14]

Sokolovsky never looked back. He ran through the small garden barefoot in his pyjamas, rounded the corner onto an offshoot of Connollystrasse, and hid behind a raised concrete flowerbed.[15]

Back in apartment 1 the terrorists pulled Gutfreund off the floor and began rounding up the other athletes. Shapira and Kehat Shorr, a Romanian who fought the Nazis during the Second World War, were both bundled out of bed. But one of the Israelis was awake and moving quickly. As Issa burst into another bedroom he was confronted by Moshe Weinberg, who grabbed a fruit knife from a bedside table and slashed at the terrorist leader, slicing through the left breast pocket of his jacket but missing his body.

Issa fell to one side, and one of the other terrorists standing behind him fired a single round from his rifle directly at Weinberg's head. The bullet tore through the side of Moshe's mouth, exiting on the other side to leave a gaping wound. The force of the bullet sent him spinning, blood pouring from the side of his face.

According to Al-Gashey, Weinberg attacked Issa "and grabbed him." "At that moment, another member of the group entered the room and opened fire on the athlete who was holding the leader and had taken his weapon."[16]

The attack was now horribly real. Blood, Jewish blood, was once again being shed on German soil.

The fedayeen pulled Weinberg off the floor and dragged him into the communal lounge. Then they pushed the other four Israelis up the stairs within apartment 1 into the bedroom of Andre Spitzer and Jacov Springer. All the Israelis were tied up tightly at their wrists and ankles with rough cord precut to the correct length.

Despite his appalling wound, Weinberg was still conscious. While Issa and two other terrorists guarded their prisoners, Tony and the rest of the Palestinian squad dragged the injured Israeli out onto Connollystrasse and began pushing and shoving him along to the next apartment — the fedayeen wanted more hostages.

Inexplicably, however, the terrorists passed apartment 2, where the lightly built Israeli fencers Dan Alon and Moshe Yehuda Weinstain, marksmen Henry Herskowitz and Zelig Shtroch, and the walker Dr. Shaul Ladany were all sleeping. Instead the fedayeen dragged Weinberg a few more yards down the pedestrianized street until he was outside apartment 3, home to six Israeli wrestlers and weightlifters.

The Village was still deathly quiet, and sleeping quietly inside No. 3 were David Berger, an American graduate of the Columbia Law School and son of a wealthy family from Cleveland; Zeev Friedman, a 5-foot, 3-inch powerhouse born in Siberia; and Eliezer Halfin, Yossef Romano, Gad Tsabari, and Mark Slavin, perhaps the most gifted of the Israeli wrestlers. The Palestinians cocked their assault rifles, opened the door, and crept inside.

Tsabari, a 5-foot, 4-inch wrestler who had finished a highly respectable twelfth in the Olympic freestyle event, had been awakened by the shot that had ripped into Moshe Weinberg (it was "something like an explosion," he said).[17] But like dozens of other athletes and officials in surrounding houses who heard that first shot, he thought he was dreaming and merely turned over in his sleep. Minutes later he heard voices outside his bedroom door. Curious but not particularly fearful, Tsabari clambered out of bed, careful not to wake his roommate, young David Berger, jumped into a pair of trousers, and sleepily opened the door to see what was going on outside.

Tsabari was confronted by a terrorist in a bright yellow sweater, pointing a gun at his friends Mark Slavin and Eliezer Halfin, who had already been captured. As soon as Tsabari emerged the Palestinian turned his gun on him. "From that moment I had to stand close to the terrorist and he ordered Slavin and Halfin to stand closely behind me." Other curious members of the Israeli team heard the commotion, and a few seconds later David Berger appeared behind Tsabari. He "made the same mistake that I did," recalled Tsabari. "I came out and so did he . . . and this is how he was also trapped."

Screaming commands at the Israelis, the terrorists thrust the barrels of their Kalashnikovs into the athletes' chests. The Israelis were pushed down the stairs to join the muscular weightlifters Yossef Romano and Zeev Friedman and poor Moshe Weinberg, clutching a scarf to the side of his face. The Palestinians had their targets. Weinberg began cleaning his wound with the scarf, then squeezed the cloth until his blood dribbled onto the shiny floor.

While one of the terrorists began checking the rooms for any other members of the Israeli team hiding in cupboards or under beds, those already captured stood half naked under wavering gun barrels. Tony bounded down the stairs from the second floor, demanding to know where the rest of the team were hiding. Nobody answered.

"Let's pounce on them!" said David Berger quickly, speaking in terse Hebrew to the other Israelis. "We have nothing to lose!" But the Palestinians were too quick. "One of the terrorists understood David Berger and put the barrel of the gun against my waist and ordered me to go in the direction of the corridor, towards the exit," Tsabari recounted.

The terrorists pushed the Israelis into a line with their hands on their heads — even Yossef Romano, on crutches after tearing a ligament in his leg during competition — and motioned them out onto Connollystrasse.

Tsabari knew the situation was desperate. The Palestinians pushed them towards apartment 1, where the other Israelis were being held, but Tsabari had no idea what was happening. The Palestinians might have been about to execute all of them, for all he knew. With David Berger's cry that they had nothing to lose still running through his mind, Tsabari decided to make a break for freedom.

As they were led down Connollystrasse and back into the foyer entrance to No. 1, Tsabari darted to one side: "Instead of going toward where the trainers were I went down the stairs."[18] "I believe it was God's hand that guided me," Tsabari has said.[19]

Tsabari shoved a terrorist blocking his path and dived down the stairs from apartment 1 towards the underground basement and Olympic parking lot, a warren beneath the athletes' accommodations. At least one of the terrorists chased after him, but the pillars in the underground parking lot offered Tsabari protection as he sped to safety. "I felt two or three rounds being shot at me. I ran for my life, zigzagging to avoid the salvo of shots. I could not believe that none of them hit me. It only lasted a few minutes but every minute was as long as the years in my life."[20]

Tsabari left chaos behind. As the wrestler made his break for freedom the badly injured Weinberg tackled one of the terrorists, a nineteen-year-old code-named "Badran" (actually Mohammed Safady), landing a massive punch in his face which knocked out several of Badran's teeth and fractured his jaw.

With a Kalashnikov trained on them from behind, Yossef Romano and David Berger could only watch helplessly as Weinberg made a grab for Badran's gun, which he had knocked to the floor. One of the terrorists firing at Tsabari spun round, drew a bead on the troublesome Israeli, and fired a burst of shots straight into his chest, peppering him with bullets. Weinberg collapsed on the ground in a bloody mess.

The Palestinians, of course, see events in a different light. Although they do not shy away from confirming details of the killing, they are adamant they wanted no loss of life. According to Abu Daoud, a Black September commander and one of the Palestinian militants who planned and organized the attack, the terrorists never had any specific instructions to open fire on the hostages.[21] However, he says, "one of the athletes, a heavily built man, tried to grab one of the guns of the [group], and so he was forced to shoot him, otherwise they would all have died. It's logical to shoot someone in self-defense."[22]

Jamal Al-Gashey appears to offer confirmation: "We never had instructions to kill anyone, either to put pressure on anyone or for any other reason."[23] However, the Palestinians had been told to shoot if they encountered any resistance,[24] and they must have known these strong, athletic Israelis would not submit willingly to an armed threat. Violence was a tragic inevitability.

After killing Weinberg the fedayeen knew the burst of shots had awakened others sleeping nearby. Lights were flickering on in rooms along Connollystrasse; curtains rustled open. The police would surely be on the scene within minutes, and the terrorists began shouting and hustling their remaining hostages at gunpoint towards the upstairs room of 31 Connollystrasse, where Gutfreund and the other athletes were already being held.

But Yossef Romano, an interior decorator who would pump iron at home in Israel for up to four hours a day, was not prepared to go quietly. Even the sight of bullets tearing into Moshe Weinberg had not quenched his fighting spirit. As Romano was pushed into the upstairs room he threw down his crutches and lunged at a terrorist, desperately trying to grab his gun and save his friends.[25] He had a Kalashnikov in his hands when a burst of fire from another Palestinian scythed into his body. Yossef, the beloved father of three young girls, fell to the floor. A second Israeli was dead.

"It was necessary and beyond anyone's control," Al-Gashey claimed. "They nearly caused the failure of the operation. They were strong athletes. The second one was another powerful athlete who attacked a member of our group and grabbed his gun, and had almost wrestled it from his hand, so we had to open fire on him as well."[26]

The four surviving Israelis from apartment 3, Berger, Friedman, Halfin, and Slavin, were tied up and herded into Andre Spitzer's bedroom, where the other athletes were being held. Yossef Romano's corpse was left on the floor in the middle of the room as a dramatic reminder to the Jews of the fate that would befall them should they try to escape. Meanwhile other members of the Israeli team in adjoining buildings who heard the shots were desperately trying to escape through the back windows. Among them was Dr. Shaul Ladany, a professor at the Graduate School of Business in Tel Aviv and noted 50-kilometer walker who as an eight-year-old had been freed from Bergen-Belsen concentration camp.

"It all happened so fast I didn't have time to think clearly," Dr. Ladany has said.[27] "I had a quick look around, saw what was happening, and made a bolt for it out the back. You don't look at people when they are shooting at you. So far as I know we had no warning that this would happen, but Jews are always wary because danger stalks them wherever they go."

Shaul Ladany ran around to the building housing the U.S. team and pounded on the door of the coaches' room on the ground floor. According to the American marathon runner Kenny Moore, who was asleep on the sixth floor, Bill Bowerman, the U.S. track coach, groggily answered. Ladany was standing before him, utterly distraught.

"Can I come in?" asked Ladany in a desperate tone.

"What for?" asked Bowerman with a tired growl.

"The Arabs are in our building," said Ladany.

"Well, push them out," replied Bowerman.

"They have guns," said Ladany, "two people are dead."[28]

His mind clearing quickly at the news, Bowerman pulled Ladany into the safety of the room and called the police.

The terrorists had wanted to capture the Israelis in apartment 2 but spotted Ladany racing away from the building and decided they were already too late. "We wanted to take [apartment 2] as well but it seemed that the people in No. 2 had heard what was going on and had escaped through the window," said Jamal Al-Gashey.[29]

But although Ladany had managed to escape, several more Israelis were still inside apartment 2, peeking out through the curtains to see what was happening. The Israelis inside had been awakened earlier during the Games by sharpshooters firing continuously into the air to celebrate their individual success, but this sounded ominously different.

Henry Herskowitz, the Israeli shooter who had carried the Israeli flag around the Olympic Stadium during the opening ceremony, awoke to one small detail in the commotion. "I heard the sound of an automatic rifle [being loaded]," he recalls. "When you put the bullets in the barrel you can hear this special sound; only this kind of rifle can make this sound. So I felt that something was wrong. I got up and looked out of the window."[30]

Herskowitz was still looking out of the window when a young Olympic Village security officer jogged down the street towards the Israeli building. A German cleaning woman on her way to work had rung the security office and reported the sound of shots just before 4:50 A.M.; the official in charge had dispatched the security officer with a walkie-talkie to check the report. The guard looked none too happy traipsing the streets in the early hours of the morning, and as he spotted Herskowitz leaning out of his window he called out to the Israeli, asking what had happened.

Herskowitz could only shrug dramatically for the officer. The German looked around but could see nothing untoward, and then, just as he was turning to leave, the front door of the Israeli delegation building opened slowly. Framed in the doorway in front of the German was an Arab armed with a Kalashnikov.

The security officer maintained his composure. "What's the meaning of this?" he barked, first in German and then in slow, steady English.[31] But the terrorist appeared almost oblivious of the presence of the German officer. The guerrilla simply swept his eyes up and down the street, turned, and disappeared back inside the building, leaving the young officer sweating outside.

The German began nervously babbling into his walkie-talkie, telling his stunned colleagues in the control room that a masked man with a machine gun was in the Israeli building. He could also see two more armed men on the first floor. The alarm was finally raised. Two more unarmed Village security officers ran down to Connollystrasse.

The first senior German official to be awakened with news of the Olympic Village attack was Manfred Schreiber, the granite-faced Munich chief of police.[32] Known as "The Sheriff" because he always got his man, Schreiber was a law graduate who proved his mettle as the head of the local detective squad, cracking a string of difficult cases, and was made the youngest police chief in Germany in November 1963.

Schreiber was contacted by telephone at home just after 5:00 A.M., within ten minutes of the first contact between the fedayeen and the German security officer. He immediately ordered the area around the Israeli building cordoned off and the Olympic Village sealed, then rang Bruno Merck, the Bavarian minister of the interior, and tersely apprised him of the situation. Schreiber dressed quickly, left his wife and two young daughters asleep in bed, and raced to the Village, his car's siren blaring and blue lights flashing through the night.

As Schreiber drove, German phone lines began to hum. Merck telephoned Hans-Dietrich Genscher, his counterpart in the federal government. The news "hit me like a big blow," Genscher said. "It meant that Jews in Germany were again in danger."[33] Genscher immediately rang German Chancellor Willy Brandt and Walter Scheel, the foreign minister. Scheel woke up his senior civil servant, Paul Frank, and he contacted Eliashiv Ben Horin, the Israeli ambassador in Bonn. By 5:40 A.M. the ambassador had contacted senior figures in the Israeli government, and officials across Bonn and Israel began tumbling out of bed to learn of the crisis. Golda Meir, the Israeli prime minister, was awakened at her official residence at Ramban Street in Jerusalem by her military secretary, General Israel Lior. Her officials soon discovered who was holding the sons of Israel.

At 5:10 A.M. a Munich police officer, sent to Connollystrasse on Schreiber's orders, walked down the center of the street to reach the Israeli quarters, his arms slightly raised to indicate he was unarmed. As he stared up at the three-story building looking for signs of life, a terrorist appeared at a window on the second floor and threw two pieces of paper down onto the pavement. They bore Black September's ultimatum. The police officer scurried off clutching the pages.

Within fifteen minutes, around 5:25 A.M., another more senior German police officer appeared in front of the Israeli building demanding to know what was going on. The Germans simply could not believe someone was trying to spoil their Games. Wearing a light safari suit, and with boot polish darkening his face, neck, and hands, Issa emerged from the front door to talk briefly with the officer. Other fedayeen covered both men with their machine guns from upstairs windows.

The Munich Olympics were so ordered, so efficient, that the officer might have thought he could simply command the gunmen to leave the building and surrender. But the Palestinians were desperate men, and Issa decided to prove their determination to the world. He motioned over his shoulder, and the virtually naked, bloodied corpse of Moshe Weinberg was brought out and unceremoniously dumped in front of the aghast police officer.

Weinberg had suffered horrific injuries. The side of his face had been shot away and his chest blown open. His blood formed a dark shroud around his body.

"He was naked . . . blood was all around him," said Shmuel Lalkin, the head of the Israeli delegation at the Munich Olympics.[34] Lalkin had been asleep in apartment 5, just a few yards from apartment 1, when the first shots were fired. He woke, walked to his window, and glanced up and down the street outside. Seeing nothing, he went back to bed, only to be awakened later by more shots. "I was looking again, and then I realized . . . Weinberg had been thrown out of the door onto the pavement." His body was lying less than twenty yards from Lalkin's window.

In apartment 2, Henry Herskowitz was also watching Weinberg in horror.[35] Herskowitz and his roommates had barricaded their front door as protection against the terrorists but could still peek out through the window. "I looked at his color and he didn't make any signs of life," he said. The police officer hollered into his radio for help, and at 5:30 A.M. two Red Cross paramedics parked their ambulance on the roadway under the Israeli building. They jogged up the stairs onto Connollystrasse and ran over to Weinberg, bravely ignoring the armed terrorists posturing by the entrance to apartment 1. The medics knelt by Weinberg's body and checked his pulse: there was no hope.

"Two people from the Red Cross came and they did this sign with their hands and I understood, he was dead," Herskowitz remembered. "I said to my roommates, 'We must leave the flat.' We went downstairs to the other side of the building. Each flat had a little garden. We went out from there and ran to the other side of the road."[36] Outside the police were beginning to swarm around the building; the two paramedics stretchered Weinberg's body away.

Shmuel Lalkin, meanwhile, ran downstairs to his small office after seeing Weinberg pushed into the street and began telephoning Olympic and Israeli officials and journalists to tell them what had happened.[37] The officials immediately telephoned Israel and briefed senior government officials, while the journalists ran down into the Olympic Village. By the time Manfred Schreiber and several dozen armed German police arrived, between 5:30 and 5:45 A.M., Israeli journalists were already on the scene inside the police cordon trying to find out what was happening.

As Schreiber raced towards the Village, Walther Tröger, the youthful mayor of the Olympic Village and the general secretary of the West German National Olympic Committee, was also alerted to news of the attack.[38] "We were woken up by the police banging on our door at 5:30 A.M.," said Tröger. "My wife answered the door and called me. They [the police] said there was terrorist activity in the Village involving the Israelis. There was an order from the terrorists saying that as it happened in the Village, they wanted the Village mayor to be included in the negotiations. They would not accept police unless accompanied by me."[39] "I had no time for shock . . . because I was involved nearly from the beginning on," said Tröger.[40] He dressed quickly and ran down to the scene.

Schreiber arrived around the same time as Tröger, and the two men were shown the pieces of paper the terrorists had thrown out of the window. The demands were clear: the terrorists wanted the release of 234 prisoners held in Israeli jails and two from German prisons — Andreas Baader and Ulrike Meinhof, leaders of the infamous Baader–Meinhof terrorist gang. It was a straight, if unequal, exchange of souls, and the deadline was 9:00 A.M. Unless the Israeli leadership was prepared to release scores of hardened Palestinian terrorists, the Black September guerrillas would start executing their hostages.

German police officers now poured into the Olympic Village. The attack was confirmed as a terrorist incident and Schreiber formally alerted the government in Bonn and the army just after 5:30 A.M. Further reinforcements soon arrived: marksmen with bulletproof vests, submachine guns, and rifles with telescopic sights. Swarming into Connollystrasse, they climbed onto roofs overlooking No. 31 and waited.

Schreiber, Tröger, and other senior German officials immediately convened a crisis meeting in a room at the Olympic administration building to the east of the Village to decide how they should respond to the attack. Schreiber's first priority was to open a channel of communication with the terrorists. One of his officers, a young policewoman named Frau Lautebach, was already down in Connollystrasse trying to make contact with the terrorists, but she would soon need to be replaced by a more experienced officer.[41]

Annaliese Graes, a forty-two-year-old policewoman from Essen who had volunteered to work as an Olympic security guard, offered to act as the intermediary. It was a brave decision, but Graes was perfect for the job: she had a mature, easy manner that her superiors hoped would put the terrorists at ease.

At 8:10 A.M. Annaliese Graes began her long walk from the Olympic administration building, past the police cordons, down the middle of Connollystrasse, under the curious gaze of athletes still in their rooms, and along to No. 31. She stopped a short distance from the building and began telling Frau Lautebach she was taking over.

While she was talking, Issa appeared at the front door of No. 31. He lingered for a moment, perhaps bemused by the sight of the two women — Graes, resplendent in a light-blue Olympic security uniform — standing before him unarmed.

Graes was a fiery sort. "What kind of rubbish is this?" she immediately demanded of the terrorist.

"This has nothing to do with you or Germany," said Issa, startled by her tone. He spoke fluent German (with a French accent, according to Graes) and began to explain his demands.

"We can do nothing about freeing all those political prisoners you want from Israel," Graes told Issa. "We can only transmit your terms. Why not give us conditions that are possible for us to meet?"[42]

Issa smiled wanly. He was in no mood to barter. "Free all those prisoners," he said simply, "or all the hostages will die."

Apart from the appearance of Graes, there was silence and little action on Connollystrasse between 6:00 and 8:15 A.M. Issa or Tony occasionally appeared outside the front door to glance up and down the street, and the terrorists would periodically glance out of the upper windows and along the walkways to make sure the Germans were not launching a surprise attack. But the astonishing scenes in No. 31 did not disturb the rest of the Village. The German officials simply threw a cordon around the building and the rest of the Village woke and began preparing for the Games, ignorant of the siege. At 8:00 A.M., the day's events started on schedule with the Grand Prix de Dressage.

The scene in Connollystrasse at 8:15 A.M. is perhaps best described by Wolfgang Gitter, an East German journalist who managed to sneak into the room of the East German weightlifters, directly opposite the Israeli delegation. About fifteen yards away, "five armed men are smiling at [Gitter]," according to his chronology of events, since found in the files of the East German secret police, the dreaded Stasi, which had dozens of agents at the Olympics.[43]

At the entrance to the building, his face still darkened with boot polish, stood Issa in a linen suit and white hat, occasionally smoking a cigarette.[44] At the window on the second floor was another man with a dark-gray broad-rimmed hat, large sunglasses, and a red-patterned shirt open at the front to reveal a gold chain. This was Tony, the Black September second-in-command, nicknamed the "Cowboy."

"Eventually, another younger man with curly black hair and red shirt appears at the door to the balcony on the third floor and a similarly dressed man with a revolver. Also a person with a dark-blue shirt is seen partly in the stairwell and also in the room on the second floor."[45] When other East Germans began photographing the house, "the Cowboy winks and touches his revolver without actually drawing it. 'I don't like that,' he says, but he gives them to understand that the DDR [East German] team has nothing to fear," reads the Stasi report.

Although there was little activity on Connollystrasse, the Olympic Village administration building G-1 was a scene of frenetic activity from 6:00 A.M. onwards. At 7:00 A.M. Hans-Dietrich Genscher, the German federal interior minister, was flown to Munich with Ulrich Wegener, his aide-de-camp, who was acting as the liaison officer between Genscher and the German federal border guards (Bundesgrenzschutz).[46]

Dozens, then hundreds of journalists and television reporters also began flocking to the administration center. The press had only sparse details, but everyone there knew it was a critical moment in history: a terrorist attack at the Olympic Games? Most of those present could hardly believe it was possible. Was nothing sacred? Reports of the attack began leading television and radio news broadcasts around the world.

At 7:15 A.M. senior German officials met in the basement of the Olympic administrative tower G-1. Those present included Schreiber, Tröger, Genscher, Hans-Jochen Vogel (vice president of the Organizing Committee and the former mayor of Munich), Willi Daume (head of the National Olympic Committee for Germany and the de facto head of German amateur athletics), and Bavarian interior minister Bruno Merck.

Although Hans-Dietrich Genscher was the most senior official or politician present, the peculiarities of the postwar German constitution ensured that the crisis would remain an exclusively Bavarian affair. Genscher could only offer advice and help to the state officials.

After agreeing that the initial response to the crisis should be negotiation rather than force, the officials jointly agreed that a crisis committee (*Krisenstat*) would be set up immediately under Bruno Merck in Walther Tröger's offices on the fourth floor of G-1. Manfred Schreiber announced he had called in a high-tech police communications van and would have it parked close to Connollystrasse for use as a forward command post. Junior officials scurried off to make the arrangements.

Then the latest news from Bonn arrived. German Foreign Ministry officials had been making a series of frantic phone calls seeking the Israeli response to the terrorist demands. The initial response was not positive: the Israeli government would not be blackmailed by Black September. They would brook no deals with terrorists.

All present at that meeting in G-1 knew they had a frantic race against time to get the hostages released. The 9:00 A.M. deadline loomed large.

Shmuel Lalkin stayed quietly in his room for an hour and a half after the initial attack, first watching as Moshe Weinberg's body was dumped on the street and then monitoring the movement of the ter-rorists. At about 6:30 A.M. he left his room and was shepherded by the German police to the office of Walther Tröger, where he imme-diately went back on the phone, this time to Israel. "I had a straight line to the government of Israel, to the prime minister," said Lalkin.[47]

Lalkin knew the terrorists had thrown a list of demands out of the window, and he knew his comrades were in a perilous situation. Israeli Prime Minister Golda Meir had announced many times that she would not countenance discussions with terrorists. "This was the main policy . . . not to give in to the terrorist, not to surrender to them."[48]

It was a torturous time for the entire Israeli delegation. Gad Tsabari, the wrestler, was still in shock when he was taken to the Olympic administration building to be debriefed by officials. After escaping Connollystrasse, he had sprinted to the fence of the Olympic Village, about 70 yards away from the Israeli building, jumped over, and run into the Olympic press center.[49]

Initially he had been ignored: "For twenty seconds no one took any notice of me, they were just laughing and joking around." Tsabari pulled one of the journalists outside, stood by the perimeter fence with him, and explained "calmly" who he was and what had happened. "And that's how the story, the drama, started."

A Munich police officer arrived to take him under protective armed guard to the administration block. "There was a woman who spoke German and Hebrew and I sketched on maps for five hours what exactly happened, where I'd put myself, who was injured, what kind of people, how many terrorists," Tsabari remembered.[50] The Germans gave him clothes, beach shoes, and a shirt belonging to a German policeman "that was as big as a dress on me" and then took him to an office where he waited with other members of the Israeli delegation for more news of his friends.

Word of the attack was spreading among the other Israeli ath-letes and officials. Esther Roth was asleep in the women's section of the Olympic Village when she heard a knock on her door.[51] "I was sure that people were coming to wake me up to take part in the Games," said Roth. Earlier in the Olympics two Americans had overslept when one of their officials used an out-of-date schedule, enabling the Russian sprinter Valery Borzov to win the event. Roth was afraid of being late for a competition. "I immediately dressed and said 'just wait a second.' I opened the door and Shlomit Nir the swimmer and another person [were in the corridor]. She told me that a group of terrorists had penetrated the Israeli dorms. We had to pack our stuff and leave the place. I didn't know what to do. I was shocked, I was very frightened."

Roth packed quickly and was taken to the administration building where Lalkin and Tsabari were waiting. "I remember the feeling," she said. "We felt as if there were terrorists in every building, and they all wanted to hurt us. We were afraid to move from one building to another." The other members of the delegation were already hearing rumors that one and possibly two of their friends had been killed. "They didn't say his name and I thought maybe it was my trainer. It was a very bad feeling." The Israeli athletes who had escaped began arriving. "They were only wearing their underwear. And they were all panicking," Roth recalled. The Israelis sat together in a large room, watching television, listening to the radio for the latest news of events, and comforting each other as the 9:00 A.M. deadline approached. "I remember the tension," said Roth. "We didn't know what to do with ourselves."

Black September

The Black September faction was virtually unknown to the Western world before the attack at Munich elevated it to global infamy. But Munich was not Black September's first appearance on the international stage. The group had emerged on November 28, 1971, with an attack on Wasfi Tell, the fifty-two-year-old prime minister of Jordan.

Tell was in Egypt, returning to his room at the Cairo Sheraton Hotel after enjoying a lavish lunch hosted by Abdul Khalek Hassouna, secretary general of the Arab League. He slid out of his armored limousine, returned the salute of the doorman, and strolled through the hotel door into the foyer.

"I saw him coming from his car," said Essat Rabah, a Black September commando waiting with a small assassination team in the lobby of the Sheraton, "and when he opened the door I fired the five shots in my pistol into him."[1] Tell reached into his jacket for his own gun, but fell backwards and died on the marble floor.

Monzer Khalifa, one of Rabah's backup team, promptly bent down and licked up some of the blood pouring from Tell's chest wounds. "I am proud! Finally I have done it," proclaimed Khalifa after the group was arrested by Egyptian police. "We have been after him for six months. We have taken our revenge on a traitor. We wanted to have him for breakfast but we had him for lunch instead."

It was a well-planned attack. Khalifa and Rabah had flown in from Beirut and sat calmly in the lobby eating sandwiches and drinking Coca-Cola, waiting for Tell. As the killers fled and their victim died on the floor, Tell's wife hugged his body. "Are you happy, Arabs?" she screamed after them. "Palestine is finished! Arabs are sons of bitches!"[2]

Governments in the Middle East initially thought the murder was an isolated attack by a small group of young fanatics who would soon disappear. They were wrong. Many of Black September's guerrillas were certainly young, but they had no intention of slipping into obscurity. Within three weeks of the death of Wasfi Tell, Black September shifted their attention to London and a close supporter of Jordan's King Hussein, Zaid el Rifai, the Jordanian ambassador there.

In another brazen attack a gunman standing on a traffic island at the junction of Campden Hill Road and Duchess of Bedford's Walk in Kensington pulled a Sten gun from under his raincoat and machine-gunned the ambassador's Daimler as it drove past on the way to the Jordanian embassy. "I couldn't believe it," said William Parsons, an Electricity Board worker who watched the attack. "He levelled it at hip height, pulled the trigger, and loosed off about thirty rounds. It was like a scene from a Chicago gangster film."[3]

Bullets sliced through the car, into el Rifai's right hand, and smashed out the windows, and the vehicle ploughed into a wall beside the road. The gunman dived into a getaway car and escaped. Miraculously, el Rifai survived. From their headquarters in Beirut, Black September claimed responsibility.

The West typically views such barbarous attacks with disgust, and the perpetrators as "evil terrorists." But the roots of the anger and frustration that gave birth to Black September, and led to the assassination of Wasfi Tell and the attack in Munich, run deep, back through centuries, to the very heart of the dispute between the Israelis and the Palestinians. It is impossible to comprehend either the anguish felt in Israel when Black September occupied 31 Connollystrasse or the desperation of the Munich attackers without understanding the tragic history of both sides.

Any chronicle of their story must go back several thousand years, to when King David (reigned circa 1000–962 B.C.) defeated neighboring tribes and fellow Jews, conquered Jerusalem, and first made the neutral city his capital.[4] Jews lived in the region for another one thousand years until they were suppressed and then forcibly dispersed by the Romans. According to some accounts, more than half a million people were killed by the Romans and nearly a thousand villages were destroyed after Jews revolted at a ban on circumcision and plans to build a Roman colony on the site of Jerusalem in A.D. 132. Some Jews went east and south, but the majority trekked north into Western and Eastern Europe. They formed the Jewish Diaspora, a victimized people bound by religion and history. Expelled from England in 1290, from France in 1306, from Spain in 1492,[5] many Jews were abused wherever they settled. While families survived on stories of their past and the glories of Jerusalem — the capital of a land that much of the Jewish Diaspora viewed as their home — other peoples had made that territory their own.

Roman conquest of Palestine was followed by the birth of the Prophet Muhammad in 570 A.D. and the founding of Islam. Muslim Arabs burst across the world map in the seventh century, erupting out of the Arabian peninsula and forging a vast empire stretching from modern-day India to Spain and southern France.[6] By the time the Christian Crusaders arrived in the Holy Land, the Arabs were living in a golden age of discovery, science, and the arts.

The two sides battled for nearly two hundred years before the Christians were finally defeated. After a period of Egyptian rule and Mongol invasion, Palestine fell to the Ottoman Turks, who arrived in the early sixteenth century, eventually capturing all but the desert heartlands of Saudi Arabia. The Palestinian Arabs were enervated by centuries of Turkish rule. For a period, when Napoleon Bonaparte arrived in Cairo in 1798 with a small army of scholars, Arabs began to rediscover and revive their history and identity. But the rest of Europe followed Napoleon, and there was little unity or pan-Arab na-

tionalism to prevent foreign powers waltzing into the region and taking control. Arab rulers enjoyed retaining power over their small fief-
doms and eagerly signed lucrative trading deals with Western
companies. The Arabs were slow to realize that their lands were
falling under the influence of European merchants and governments.
Worse was to come.

Amid rampant anti-Semitism across Europe and Russia, the end
of the nineteenth century saw the founding of Zionism, a movement
that sought the creation of a Jewish state, a place where Jews would
be free of oppression. The first meeting of the International Congress of Zionists was held in Basel, Switzerland, in 1897, and it soon
became clear that, although other sites were considered, including
Libya, Uganda, and Argentina, the Zionists wanted to return to
Palestine and build a Jewish state, their "promised land."[7]

Initially most Arabs failed to take Zionism seriously; before
1880 Palestine was home to fewer than twenty-five thousand Jews,
with the vast majority in Jerusalem. But wealthy Jewish businessmen
began campaigning hard to establish a Jewish state in Palestine, and
they found a receptive audience in Washington and Europe.[8] By
1914 there were approximately eighty-five thousand Jews in Palestine
(with thirteen thousand settlers on forty-three Jewish agricultural
settlements), although this number was almost halved during the First
World War.

On November 2, 1917, Arthur Balfour, the British foreign secretary, formally agreed to support the creation of a Jewish state in a
117-word letter to Lord Rothschild, the head of the British branch
of the international Jewish banking family.[9] In Arab eyes "the Balfour
Declaration" was a complete betrayal. The First World War was raging, and under Colonel T. E. Lawrence (Lawrence of Arabia) many
Arabs had been battling for Britain against the Turks, believing their
actions would lead to independence.

Palestine came under British administration after the end of the
war, and Arab discontent rumbled on as Jewish immigrants continued to arrive. Arab terrorists soon began attacking Jewish settlements,
and Jews living in other Arab states were also terrorized and murdered.

By the start of the Second World War in 1939, many Arab leaders saw the possibility of a German victory as a potential boost to their national aspirations. Most Zionists, by contrast, immediately sided with the Allies and began planning how an Allied victory could increase their chances of creating a new Jewish state. Emerging Jewish terrorist groups, however, began harrying the British (who had in 1939 imposed immigration and land purchase limits to pacify the Arabs) and the Arabs, even as Zionist political leaders campaigned for statehood.

As news of increasing anti-Semitic attacks in Europe reached the free world, the Zionist campaign became a more desperate quest. In Germany Jews were forced to wear the notorious "Jude" yellow star beginning in 1941 and in France in 1942. Jewish ghettos were cleared, and the first news of Nazi pogroms reached the free world. Then rumors began of even greater evil, of unimaginable horror: of concentration camps, barbed wire, and the gas, now known to be Zyklon B (five kilograms of which could kill 1,500 people), first used on humans at Auschwitz in August 1941. By the end of the war Jews around the world knew that "civilized" Europeans had tried to annihilate them. By then nothing could have stopped their desire for a place of safety from persecution.

The world learned too late of the Holocaust, but deeply troubled by the Jewish suffering and the vast numbers of European Jews displaced by the Second World War, American President Harry Truman finally began backing the concept of a Jewish nation. In 1947, with Britain exhausted and unable to resolve the intercommunal tensions, the problem was referred to the new United Nations.

Palestinians now began suffering in their homeland. Zionists forced tens of thousands of Arabs — families who had been living in the region for centuries — to flee their homes. Both sides were responsible for terrible atrocities. On the night of April 9, 1948, members of the Jewish guerrilla splinter group Irgun attacked the village of Dier Yassin, a major stronghold in the Arab blockade of Jerusalem and a base for Arab soldiers and civilians, and murdered an estimated 254 Arabs, including women and children as well as opposition guerrillas. The Jewish leadership roundly denounced and condemned the killings, but the attack has echoed down the decades. Even as Jews mourn those who have died since in scores of Arab terrorist attacks, so the Palestinians still remember the innocent of Deir Yassin.

It was not the only Zionist terrorist attack designed to drive out the British and Palestinians. After issuing several telephone warnings, Jews also blew up the King David Hotel in Jerusalem (home to the British military command), booby-trapped the dead bodies of two British army sergeants they had hung in an orange grove, and murdered dozens of innocent Arabs. The terrorist attacks were at least partly successful: the British mandate was withdrawn and the state of Israel was proclaimed in May 1948. A minority of Palestinians founded their own terror groups, but most were terrified by the violence that followed. More than seven hundred thousand Palestinians left the new state of Israel, despite pleas from some Jews that they should stay. Ironically, the Grand Mufti of Jerusalem also encouraged Palestinians to flee to neighboring states. Many did so thinking they would swell the ranks of Arab armies who would then return to Israel and push the Jews into the sea. This vow was never fulfilled.

"In retrospect, I think my compatriots were wrong to have believed the Arab regimes and in any case to have left the field open to the Jewish colonizers," Abu Iyad, a founder of Black September, wrote several decades later.[10] "They should have stood their ground, whatever the cost. The Zionists could never have exterminated them to the last man."

Although British indecision, and the resulting failure to halt a sudden and major Jewish immigration to the region after the First World War, had been a contributing factor, it was the Holocaust that ultimately led to the birth of Israel. Some radical Zionists believed they were superior in both intellect and religion to the Palestinians, but the vast majority of Jews who flocked to the region were simply trying to escape annihilation in Europe. Centuries of oppression had culminated in the most clinical, carefully managed genocide in human history. The six million dead haunted and inspired Zionists to battle ferociously for the creation of Israel.

America and the Soviet Union recognized the new state within two days, but neighboring Arab countries launched an invasion and

Arab armed groups inside Palestine attacked Jewish traffic and villages. The Palestinian Arabs fought hard for the land they considered their own, but they lacked the fervor of Zionists, who desperately wanted a country where Jews could be free from persecution. As the Arab–Israeli war began to go badly for the Arabs many of the Palestinian-Arab leaders retreated into exile outside the region. But no such option was open to the hundreds of thousands of homeless Arab civilians, who found themselves herded into refugee camps by neighboring Arab goverments.

Confining the Palestinians to camps actually suited many regional governments. Although they could have easily, and comfortably, been absorbed into the nations surrounding Israel, political leaders in those countries were concerned about the impact of tens of thousands of Palestinians on their fragile nations. They also knew that it would discourage the Palestinians from leading the fight against the Israelis. Far better to keep them in squalor near their homeland and foster their fighting spirit. And so Palestinian resentment festered.

Yasser Arafat, the leader of the modern Palestine Liberation Organization, and the man ultimately responsible for the creation of Black September and the Munich attack, was born in Cairo in 1929, the child of middle-class Palestinian parents. He lost his mother while still a child, rebelled against authority, and by the tender age of fifteen was gun-running for gangs of Arab peasants fighting the Haganah, the Stern Gang, and other Jewish militants. By 1947–48 Arafat was fighting as a lowly guerrilla, but after the birth of Israel he returned to Cairo to complete his studies and became a prominent activist for Palestinian rights.

While the United Nations and many countries accepted or welcomed the founding of Israel, Arabs vowed to continue the war and destroy the new Jewish state. However, it took time for Arafat and other Palestinians to realize they would be fighting a solitary war. King Farouk of Egypt sent guerrillas (who used the name fedayeen) into Israel on raiding missions after 1949; Gamal Abdul Nasser increased Egyptian support for the raids when he took power; and the Syrians were also actively funding guerrilla operations against the Israeli state. But these raids were hardly likely to drive the Israelis into the sea. Cattle were killed, crops were damaged, and Israeli settlers were murdered. But by the mid-1950s Arafat and other Palestinian activists had realized the guerrilla operations of Egypt and Syria were self-serving — aimed not at the creation of a Palestinian state, but at the preservation of the regional status quo.

In 1955 Arafat founded an engineering firm in Kuwait, and with the money he earned he began working among the thousands of young Palestinians studying in Germany, securing donations and recruiting for Fatah, an organization he had established to harness the anger of young militants in Palestinian refugee camps.

Arafat was soon shuttling between Germany (particularly the University of Stuttgart, the hub of Palestinian activity in Europe), Algeria (where he helped to organize military training camps for recruits to Fatah), and Kuwait (where the pockets of well-paid Palestinian expatriate workers were shaken for cash "for the struggle back home").

A Palestinian resistance movement slowly emerged.[12] Ahmed Shukairy, a Palestinian lawyer, proposed the formation of a Palestinian government in exile, and in May 1964 the Palestine Liberation Organization (PLO) was launched, with Shukairy later appointed as its head. Fatah was first heard of in January 1965, when a rucksack containing ten sticks of gelignite and a detonator was spotted floating in a canal in the Beit Netofa Valley in the Lower Galilee.[13] Although the bomb was defused, Israeli trackers realized the attackers had crossed the River Jordan into Israel. Two days later Fatah claimed responsibility and a new chapter was opened in the history of the Middle East.

Fatah launched occasional strikes against Israel from bases in the Gaza Strip until February 1966, when the left-wing Syrian Ba'athist party seized power in Damascus. Among the Ba'athists' avowed aims was the liberation of Palestine, and Arafat quickly persuaded Syrian intelligence officers to allow Fatah to open training camps in Syria. While Shukairy was restricted by his Egyptian controllers to making aggressive speeches against Israel, the Syrians gave Fatah a free rein.

The guerrillas launched scores of cross-border raids. Israeli military and political leaders, incensed by these incursions, began making speeches during April and May 1967 in which the Syrian government read warnings of an Israeli invasion.

The Soviets gave Damascus intelligence that Israeli troops were massing on the border (they were not), and Syria appealed to Egypt for military support. Nasser marched his troops into the Sinai Desert south of Israel in a show of support, and the Strait of Tiran was then closed on May 22, denying Israel access to the Red Sea.

Israelis felt that the very future of their nation was at stake. This period, from May 23 to June 4, is now known as the Hamtana, the "waiting period," as Israelis listened to broadcasts of the intensely charismatic Nasser rousing his people to battle against the Jews. The Israelis thought they were about to be annihilated by the Arabs, but Jews were not to be driven away again. They would no longer go quietly into the night.

On June 1, 1967, General Moshe Dayan was appointed Israeli minister of defense in a Government of National Unity, and on June 5 he ordered lightning strikes against Israel's Arab neighbors. Israeli planes flew in low across the sea and within the space of a few hours destroyed seventeen Egyptian airfields and half the country's air force before turning to decimate the Syrian and Jordanian military.[14] On June 6 and 7, Israeli tanks and armored brigades swept into Syria's Golan Heights, Jordan's West Bank, and Egypt's Sinai. By the time a United Nations–sponsored ceasefire stopped the war on June 10, Israel had captured an Arab area four times its own size; by taking the West Bank and Gaza Strip the 2.4 million Israelis had increased the Arab population of their country from a pre-1967 population of approximately 400,000 to at least 1.4 million.

Israel immediately began celebrating the end of the "Six Day War" and a spectacular victory. The emotional importance of the war is difficult to overestimate. Israeli Jews felt they had been oppressed for centuries, but in 1967 the tiny new state defeated its neighbors in battle; it gave many Israelis a new sense of pride and power. The Arabs, by contrast, were left with a humiliating defeat. Israel lost 778 troops and 61 tanks, while more than 1,000 Syrian soldiers and some

10,000 Egyptian troops died, many of thirst. Arab nations lost 700 tanks, and Egypt alone lost more than 360 fighter aircraft and 69 bombers.[15]

But nowhere was the disaster felt more keenly than in Palestinian refugee camps, which were swamped by another 150,000 desperate souls. Yasser Arafat acted quickly to prevent a collapse in morale, ordering a series of Fatah raids inside Israel and the newly occupied territories. Recruits queued to join Fatah, and Arab governments began donating huge quantities of weapons and money to the Palestinian struggle to assuage the humiliation of the war. When Israel failed to withdraw from land captured during the Six Day War, support for Fatah grew still further.

By early 1968 Fatah guerrillas were launching regular raids against Israel, and on March 18, two children were killed and twenty-eight injured when a Fatah landmine wrecked their bus. This was more than Israel could stand. An armored column was sent to attack the main Fatah base at Karameh, across the border in Jordan. Leaflets were dropped over the region warning civilians to leave before troops attacked, but the advance notice gave the Fatah guerrillas time to prepare for the assault. Under Arafat's direct command a handful of Fatah fighters resolved to fight to the last man. None of the Palestinians believed they could win, and Arafat's friend and colleague Abu Jihad was sent to Damascus to reorganize Palestinian resistance after Fatah's likely obliteration.

On the morning of March 21, 1968, vicious street-fighting erupted between the Palestinian guerrillas and some of the fifteen thousand crack Israeli troops who had entered Jordan. The Palestinians, knowing they could be facing extermination, were ferocious in their desperation. Young boys carrying dynamite martyred themselves against Israeli tanks, halting them in their tracks and forcing their Israeli crews to flee for safety. Fatah guerrillas battled for every inch of land.

At least one hundred fifty Palestinian and Jordanian fighters were killed in the battle and their fortified houses were destroyed; twenty Israelis were killed and another seventy wounded, but the advancing Jordanian army drove the Israelis back across the border. For Palestinians it was perhaps the most important battle of the century. In the Arab world and among Fatah supporters, Karameh (which means "dignity") was seen as a huge victory for the Palestinian movement, and for Arafat in particular. The Israelis were not invincible; they could be defeated. Money flowed into Fatah's coffers and the ranks of Arafat's supporters swelled again with new legions of fighters.

"When I was young, in the 1960s, there was an optimistic feeling about the prospect for the liberation of Palestine, partly helped by the speeches of Nasser," recalls Jamal Al-Gashey. "Secret Palestinian organizations were formed such as Fatah in 1965. Their first military operations inspired hope and encouragement that we would be able to liberate Palestine and return to houses and be finished with the wretchedness and humiliation. The disaster of the 1967 war was a major catastrophe for us, but after the Battle of Karameh in Jordan in '68, which was the first defeat for the Israeli army by Palestinian freedom fighters, we became very optimistic. Tens of thousands of young people joined the revolution in Jordan because we were convinced that Palestine could only be liberated by its children, certainly not by the Arab leaders."[16]

Al-Gashey joined Fatah as soon as a recruiting office was opened in his refugee camp. "I joined Fatah immediately and held a gun for the first time, and was trained to use it. For the first time, I felt proud and felt that my existence and my life had a meaning, that I was not just a wretched refugee, but a revolutionary fighting for a cause."

With recruits such as Al-Gashey, Fatah attacks on Israel increased. But they were often ineffective. Guerrillas in the Gaza Strip seemed more concerned with enforcing their control over other Palestinians, while on the border with Jordan Israeli patrols had a fearsome reputation. Fedayeen were often spotted soon after entering the country, then hunted down and killed. Many guerrillas were so terrified of crossing into Israel they would let off a round of bullets from the Jordanian side of the border and then return to their bases claiming to have fought a major battle with Israeli troops.

By July 1968 Arafat had brought other Palestine militant groups under his broad umbrella and managed to oust Ahmed Shukairy as leader of the PLO at the Palestine National Congress meeting in Cairo. At the following Congress meetings in February and June 1969, Arafat's leadership was extended and he took control of a joint Fatah-PLO as its new chairman and head of an eleven-member committee responsible for organizing all operations against Israel.

With a strong mandate from his colleagues and Palestinian activists, Arafat set about building more Fatah bases in Jordan, including clinics, orphanages, schools, training camps, and refugee centers. The Palestinians began treating their Jordanian hosts with a degree of contempt, swaggering around Amman, armed to the teeth. Jordan's King Hussein realized his guests were gradually building "a state within a state" that threatened his kingdom.

Arafat was determined that Fatah and other Palestinian guerrillas would wage what he perceived as a legitimate military war against the state of Israel, mainly from bases in Jordan. Events, however, conspired against him.

George Habash, the Marxist leader of the Popular Front for the Liberation of Palestine (PFLP), decided to pursue a terrorist agenda and refused to join with Arafat. On July 23, 1968, guerrillas from the PFLP began a series of actions by taking over an El Al flight from Rome to Tel Aviv and forcing the pilot on to Algiers, where the Israeli passengers were promptly imprisoned. On December 26 that same year, a small PFLP unit shot up another El Al jet leaving Athens airport, killing one passenger, a retired Israeli naval officer, and injuring several others on the flight.

The Athens attack prompted Israeli retaliation against Lebanon, which the Israelis accused of harboring and helping terrorists, and thirteen Arab jets were destroyed in a raid by helicopter commandos on Beirut airport. Still the PFLP attacks continued. Leila Khaled, a young guerrilla who found international fame because of her commitment and good looks, led a PFLP team that hijacked a TWA jet to Damascus on August 29, 1969. Five El Al offices were attacked in Europe and the Middle East by a group of terrorists, including "Lion Cubs": three terrorists aged fourteen and fifteen years old.[17]

On February 10, 1970, a grenade attack on an airline bus in Munich killed one passenger and seriously injured eleven others, including Hannah Marron, a popular Israeli actress. Seven elderly Jews died in a fire in the Jewish Home for the Aged in the same city, and on February 22 a Swissair plane flying to Tel Aviv was blown out of the sky, with the loss of forty-seven passengers and crew (including fifteen Israelis).[18] International anger at the atrocities was mounting, but George Habash was defiant: "Our struggle has barely begun, the worst is yet to come. The prospect of triggering a third world war doesn't bother us. The world has been using us and has forgotten us. It is time they realized we exist. It is time they stopped exploiting us. Whatever the price, we'll continue our struggle."[19]

In Jordan King Hussein was fearful of the increasing strength of the Palestinians and tired of the international opprobrium heaped upon him as their host. He began marshalling his forces, waiting for an excuse to eject or crush the guerrillas, and soon he had it. On September 6, 1970, the PFLP attacked four airliners around the world. Two planes, belonging to TWA and Swissair, were hijacked and flown to a disused former Royal Air Force airfield in Jordan called Dawson's Field, where the passengers were held hostage. A Pan Am jet was hijacked and flown to Cairo. The passengers escaped down emergency chutes and the terrorists then blew up the plane.

The fourth attack, on an El Al jet, was led by Leila Khaled and another terrorist called Patrick Arguello, a Nicaraguan-American supporter of the PFLP. But when the two drew their guns while flying over the English Channel, a specially trained squad of El Al security officers (known as the "007 Squad") shot down Arguello and captured Khaled.[20] El Al pilots have strict instructions to fly directly back to Israel in such situations, but Captain Uri Bar-Lev, fearing for the life of steward Shlomo Vider who had been shot five times by Arguello in the attack, quickly landed at Heathrow Airport on the outskirts of London. Khaled was arrested and taken to Ealing police station.

Three days later a BOAC VC-10 flying from Bahrain to London was hijacked by PFLP terrorists to trade for Khaled's release and flown to join the other two jets held at Dawson's Field in Jordan.

The 425 hostages were soon sweating it out under the desert sun. Khaled was swiftly released by the British authorities — they had little choice with hundreds of lives at stake — and all but forty of the hostages were then set free by the PFLP.

King Hussein and his proud Bedouin soldiers had had enough. Jordanian army chiefs begged Hussein to allow them to wipe out the Palestinian guerrillas within the kingdom. The king later spoke of meeting one tank commander who had a bra tied to his radio aerial; when the king asked why he was told: "Because we are like cowardly women!"

When Hussein returned to his palace he discovered the PFLP had blown up the jets parked at Dawson's Field in front of the massed ranks of the world's media. Field Marshal Habes al-Majali was appointed as military governor, and a massive strike was ordered on the Palestinian guerrillas. On the morning of September 17, 1970, tanks and armored cars rolled onto the streets of Amman and a twenty-four-hour curfew was imposed. Battle commenced.

Palestinian guerrilla positions, and even those positions merely suspected of hiding guerrillas, were shelled mercilessly. In support of Arafat, the Syrians sent tanks into Jordan and Hussein's fighters promptly attacked them from the air. Thousands of Israeli soldiers and scores of tanks were sent to the border in preparation for a full-scale invasion of Jordan should the Palestinians gain the upper hand, and at least twelve thousand American paratroopers and the powerful American Sixth Fleet were put on standby to intervene. Arafat begged Iraq and Egypt for military support, Soviet forces mobilized, and the region teetered on the brink of a massive war.

The Palestinians fought ferociously, but the Jordanian army was well trained, well equipped, and determined to prevail. In the slaughter that followed at least four thousand fedayeen were killed. The Palestinians called it Black September.

Arafat and the entire Palestine liberation movement felt completely betrayed by the Jordanian attacks. They had lost their homeland to the Zionists, and now their brother Arabs had turned on them.

As Bedouin troops continued to mop up resistance in Palestinian strongholds, some Fatah militants fled to Syria, but most moved en masse to southern Lebanon, where the government gave them control over more than a dozen refugee camps and bases in the Ar-koub, on Lebanon's southeastern border with Israel.

In Jordan one of Arafat's most competent and aggressive deputies, Abu Ali Iyad, was captured by King Hussein's forces and tortured and killed — in a final indignity his body was dragged through villages behind a tank. The Palestinian movement was in tat-ters, its people seemingly destined for a permanent existence in squalid refugee camps. Younger Palestinians began migrating to the extremist PFLP.

Arafat knew Fatah could not afford to keep losing supporters. He seems to have felt that he had no choice but to give tacit approval to the use of blatant terrorism. His men, from the bottom to the top, were racked by low morale and anger at world indifference to their plight. Unless he was seen to be taking action against the Israeli state, no matter how desperate the attack, Arafat would lose control of the PLO. But Arab governments refused to allow the PLO to launch strikes against Israel from their territory for fear of incurring Israeli wrath and international opprobrium. So with Arafat's implicit bless-ing, a new group was formed that would launch terrorist attacks and conduct assassinations, principally abroad. By keeping its leadership secret and separating its hierarchy from Fatah, Arafat hoped to main-tain "plausible deniability" should the new group's actions cause em-barrassment to Fatah or its wealthy Arab backers.

The name of the group was soon to echo around Europe and the Middle East. In memory of the Jordanian attacks the previous year it bore the evocative and sinister name of Black September.

"After what happened to the Palestinian resistance in Jordan in September and our expulsion from the whole country in 1971, there was renewed evidence of the futility of the Palestinian leadership," confirms Abu Daoud, a tall lean man who had been the commander of Fatah forces in Jordan.[21] "There was a need to find a meaningful way of pursuing the struggle." Daoud and a few other senior Pales-tinians "decided to form a group with no link to Fatah. The group would take a role in drawing attention to the significance of the struggle and then return to the mother organization, Fatah. So we set up an organization called Black September."

According to Abu Daoud, Black September was independent from Fatah in both "its decisions" and "its finance." "It was separate from Fatah so that Fatah and the PLO would not have to carry opprobrium for our operations. The group, as individuals and as a leadership, was responsible for its own successes and failures without compromising the legitimate leadership of the Palestinian people [the PLO]." Essentially, said Abu Daoud, "there is no such thing as Black September. Fatah announces its operations under this name so that Fatah will not appear as the direct executor of the operations."[22] Abu Iyad, the de facto leader of Black September, offers confirmation: "There was not an organization. There was a cause, Black September. It was a Palestinian state of mind."[23]

Abu Iyad, a schoolteacher born in Jaffa in 1933, was regarded as something of a "dove" within Fatah. But after the Jordanian treachery he became an aggressive militant. Under Iyad's command a support structure for Black September was formed from the remnants of Jihaz el Razd, the intelligence arm of Fatah, which was comprised largely of well-educated, elegant young men and women, many of whom studied at the American University in Beirut. As his deputy Iyad chose a handsome and charming womanizer called Ali Hassan Salameh. The son of Sheikh Hassan Salameh, a legendary fighter against the Israelis killed in 1948, Ali Hassan bore his father's name with pride.[24]

As well as Abu Daoud, Iyad recruited Ahmed Afghani (a.k.a. Abu Motassin) to look after the group's finances and supplies; an engineer called Ghazi el Husseini to develop or obtain sophisticated weaponry and equipment; and Fakhri al Umari, a talented guerrilla, as head of the so-called special services division of Black September — the operational wing responsible for terrorist attacks.

These militants were the elite of the Palestinian liberation movement. Salameh, Abu Daoud, and Umari were among a handful of Fatah fighters sent on a special intelligence course in Cairo in 1968, where they learned the craft of urban terrorism. They soon made their presence known with the murder of Wasfi Tell in Cairo and the assassination attempt on the Jordanian ambassador to London.

From the start of 1972, Black September began forcing itself onto the world stage. On February 6, five Jordanians who had been accused of collaborating with Israel were murdered in Bruehl, near Cologne in Germany; on the same day oil tanks belonging to Gulf Oil were destroyed in Holland. Two days later the Hamburg factory of a firm making engines for Israel was destroyed, and then on February 22 Black September operatives damaged the Esso Oil pipeline near the same city.

The group's first attempt to launch a terrorist "spectacular" came in early May 1972. The four terrorists involved — "Major" Ahmed Mousa Awad, "Lieutenant" Abdel Aziz el Atrash, Therese Halsa, and Rima Tannous — spent three days in Brussels, sharing bedrooms, indulging in plenty of shopping, dining at expensive restaurants, and dancing together in the evenings.[25] It was a curious way of preparing for a major terrorist strike, but then they were a curious group of terrorists. Halsa, a nineteen-year-old nursing student born into a middle-class family near Nazareth, had joined Fatah the previous year in Jordan, after a lifetime spent living under Israeli rule. Tannous, twenty-one, was an orphan educated by nuns who had been working as a nurse in Amman.[26]

On May 8 the four terrorists, speaking a little Hebrew and carrying forged Israeli passports as well as guns and grenades, boarded Sabena flight 571 from Brussels to Tel Aviv. The two women later claimed they only knew the two men as "Yosef" and "Zechariah," and had not known their eventual destination was Israel until the plane left Vienna on the second leg of its flight.

As Captain Reginald Levy, a British Jew, flew the plane over Belgrade toward the Holy Land, the four Black September terrorists struck, hijacking the flight, with its eighty-seven passengers and ten crew members, wielding guns and grenades. Levy warned Tel Aviv airport, the flight's original destination, that he was bringing the plane in to land and that the hijackers wanted more than two hundred of their compatriots released from Israeli jails.

General Moshe Dayan, the Israeli hero of the 1967 war, arranged for a hand-picked group of special forces to meet the plane when it landed. A member of the ground crew sauntered over to the plane and let the air out of its tires and drained its hydraulics. The hijackers were therefore stuck at the airport.

Negotiations went on for more than twenty hours, although the Israelis never had any intention of releasing a single prisoner: they were just stalling for time while their special forces prepared an assault on the Sabena plane by practicing on another Boeing 707 parked at another airport. When the soldiers managed to get the speed of their assault down to below ninety seconds, they were sent into action.

Dressed in the white overalls of the ground crew, the soldiers approached the jet and then suddenly attacked. "It all happened at once," said one passenger. "Suddenly the doors were torn open and the Israelis were in the plane firing everywhere and shouting, 'Lie down, lie down, it's all over!' "[27]

One male terrorist was shot between the eyes by an Israeli who emerged from an escape hatch. The other was killed by a couple of shots from a pistol. Therese Halsa was wounded, and Rima Tannous was flattened on the floor under a burly soldier. One passenger, twenty-two-year-old Miriam Anderson, was fatally wounded and died later in the hospital. Two of the Israeli assault team were also injured, but the operation was an overwhelming success for the Israelis. And it had come in the nick of time.

Captain Levy later described how close the hostages had been to killing everyone: "The Arabs were getting very agitated because the Israelis would not hand over the fedayeen. They were all carrying grenades and they decided to blow us all to kingdom come, themselves included."[28] Halsa and Tannous had been crying and kissing the two male terrorists goodbye as the Israeli attack started.

The Sabena operation was a spectacular failure for Black September. Not only did the Israelis con the terrorists and force them to delay their deadlines, but they then used force to storm the plane and killed or captured all four guerrillas. Senior Palestinian leaders decided that only more attacks could restore their reputation and maintain morale in the refugee camps. As the Israelis were celebrating the military skill of their elite soldiers, Abu Iyad and Fuad Shemali of Black September are understood to have travelled to a major terrorist convention hosted by George Habash in the Baddawi refugee camp in Lebanon.

It was an extraordinary meeting. Representatives of the Irish Republican Army turned up, as did the Japanese Red Army and Germany's Baader–Meinhof gang. The talks culminated in an agreement that some of the groups would help or "represent" each other in attacks within their own territories. So the Baader–Meinhof gang would attack targets in Germany on behalf of the Palestinians. At least that was the theory. The first attack to result from this new spirit of international terrorist cooperation was a sickening massacre in Israel by members of the Japanese Red Army.

The men, Kozo Okamoto, Takeshi Okidoro, and Yasuiki Yashuda, had been indoctrinated in Japan with tales of the Palestinian struggle and had travelled to Beirut several months previously to prepare for a future, unspecified terrorist attack. All three had been taken to Port Said and trained by Palestinian guerrillas in the use of explosives, grenades, and Kalashnikov assault rifles.[29]

Carrying forged passports the three budding killers flew from Beirut to Paris on May 22 and then travelled on to Rome, where they checked into a hotel often used by Arab visitors to the city. On May 30 the three men took a taxi to Leonardo da Vinci Airport to catch Air France flight 132 to Tel Aviv and checked their baggage — containing a small arsenal of weapons — into the hold of the plane.

It was an uneventful flight, and when they landed in Israel at Tel Aviv's Lod Airport the three men calmly disembarked and waited for their baggage in the arrivals area with the other passengers. Across the hall were a group of pilgrims from Puerto Rico, gathering their bags for a package holiday in the Holy Land. Professor Aharon Katchalsky, one of the world's leading physicists, was waiting for his luggage.

The terrorists calmly picked three fiberglass suitcases from the conveyor belt and put them carefully on the ground. They bent down, opened the cases, and produced Czech-made VZT-58 submachine guns and a quantity of fragmentation grenades. Without a word they stood up and simply opened fire on the other passengers. The carnage was appalling: twenty-four people, most of them Puerto Rican pilgrims, died in the hail of bullets and another seventy-eight were injured. Professor Katchalsky was among the dead. Within two minutes the floor of the hall was awash with blood.

In the mayhem Yashuda was accidentally riddled with bullets fired by one of his comrades and Okidoro detonated a grenade next to his head. After emptying every bullet from his gun into the crowd, Okamoto ran outside onto the airport tarmac and tried to blow up a parked jet with a grenade. He was tackled around the neck by Hannan Claude Zeiton, an El Al official, and then arrested by the police.

The massacre at Lod Airport sent shock waves around the world, and Palestinian guerrillas continued to mount more terrorist attacks. On August 5, 1972, a mixed Black September group of Arabs, at least one Italian, and a couple of Frenchmen destroyed a major oil terminal at Trieste, starting a two-day fire that incinerated millions of gallons of oil. Just eleven days later two young English women on holiday in Italy were befriended by two Palestinians who invited them to Israel. The women agreed, and the men — Adnam Ali Hasham and Ahmed Zaid — gave them a tape recorder as a gift. Just as they were about to leave, the Arabs announced they needed to make a short trip to Tehran, but would meet up with the women in Israel. The two women boarded an El Al 707 for the short flight, and thankfully packed the tape recorder, complete with a small bomb and barometric pressure detonator, in their luggage which was stored in the armored hold of the plane. When it exploded the hold contained the blast and the plane landed safely in Israel.

It was amid this period of rampaging Palestinian terrorism that Israel prepared to send its athletes to the Olympics in Munich, due to start at the beginning of September, and the Palestinians began planning their attack.

The origins of the plot have always been vague, but they can now be traced back to the beginning of July 1972, and a café terrace in the picturesque Piazza della Rotonda in Rome.

At the time Abu Daoud was staying in an apartment in the Eternal City and waiting for the arrival of Black September commander Abu Iyad, who was due to meet extreme right-wing groups in the north of the country. On July 13, Iyad finally arrived in Rome with his colleague Fakhri al Umari, and within a few days the three men met for a coffee.

Sitting in the sun outside the café, enjoying the atmosphere of Rome and flicking through European and Arab newspapers, the Palestinians spotted a small article about the forthcoming Munich Olympics, which were then less than two months away. The International Olympic Committee had just confirmed its refusal to allow a Palestinian delegation to take part in the Games.

"At the beginning of 1972, the PLO sent an official letter to the Olympic Committee proposing that a team of Palestinian athletes participate in the games," recalled Abu Iyad later. "Since no reply was received, a second letter was sent, which also evoked nothing more than a scornful silence. It was clear that for this honorable institution which claims to be apolitical, we didn't exist or, worse, didn't deserve to exist."[30]

The three terrorists were furious at the snub. After reading details in the newspaper, Fakhri al Umari turned to his colleagues and told them that the Palestinians should still try to take part in the Olympics.

But what, queried Abu Iyad, could they do?

It was then that al Umari, apparently spontaneously, suggested kidnapping some Israeli athletes and holding them hostage.

Abu Iyad, while initially skeptical of the idea, warmed to it quickly. The three men chatted away, building mutual confidence for such a breathtaking assault, before Abu Iyad proposed that they should kidnap as many Israeli athletes and officials as possible and ransom them off in exchange for their imprisoned colleagues. The fate of the Israeli team was sealed.

Abu Daoud was due to go to Sofia, Bulgaria, to try and obtain some silenced submachine guns for Fatah, and it was decided that he would pass through Munich on the way there and initiate plans for the attack.

One afternoon in mid-July 1972, Abu Daoud arrived in Munich, bought a detailed street map, and collected information on hotels and flights into and out of the city. To the north of Munich he found the site of the Olympic Park, which required little more than finishing touches before the start of the Games. After a quick look around Abu Daoud left Munich the same day and went on to Bulgaria to purchase arms for Fatah.[31]

Abu Iyad, meanwhile, was already organizing a commando team. The operation, he later claimed, was "meticulously planned." "The two commando leaders . . . were tried militants who had fought in Amman in September 1970 and at the battle of Jerash and Ajlun in July 1971," wrote Iyad.[32]

As commander of the attack Iyad and Ali Hassan Salameh chose Luttif Afif ("Issa"), a Palestinian militant born in Nazareth. Issa's mother, ironically, was Jewish; his father was a wealthy Christian Arab businessman, and he had three other brothers, all of whom were in Black September and two of whom were in Israeli jails.[33]

In 1958 he had moved to Germany to study engineering, learned the language, and then moved to France to work.[34] He enjoyed his time in Europe, but joined Fatah in 1966, possibly while in Germany, and returned to the Middle East to fight several battles against Israeli soldiers. By the early 1970s, however, he was living in Berlin and was engaged to be married to a young German woman.

Issa seemed to be the perfect choice to command the action. "Tony" (Yasuf Nazzal), a committed fedayeen who had also studied in Germany, was a good candidate for deputy commander. The two men were immediately dispatched to Munich to begin preparing for the attack and familiarizing themselves with the layout of the Olympic Village.

Choosing the leaders was relatively easy for Iyad.[35] Selecting the foot soldiers was harder. Initially some fifty young fedayeen between seventeen and twenty years old were selected for intensive training. "They all came from refugee camps in Lebanon, Syria, and especially Jordan, and all came from poor families," said Iyad. Most of them, according to Iyad, were motivated by a determination to see members of their families released from Israeli jails. "They knew nothing of the operation that some of them would ultimately be selected to carry out, but all burned with impatience to be among the lucky ones chosen."[36]

Eventually, from a shortlist of around twelve, six youngsters were selected for the operation: Afif Ahmed Hamid, Khalid Jawad, Ahmed Chic Thaa, nineteen-year-old Mohammed Safady, Adnan Al-Gashey (twenty-seven years old), and his nineteen-year-old nephew Jamal Al-Gashey.

Jamal was an archetypal recruit for Fatah, having experienced the harsh realities of refugee life from the moment he was born: "I am a member of a Palestinian family which was exiled by the Zionist gangs in '48 from our village in Galilee in Palestine. My family moved from camp to camp and finally settled in Chatila [refugee camp]."[37] Al-Gashey claims he was born in the mid-1950s "into conditions of great poverty" and grew up in a refugee house "made of sheets of tin." Even to this day, his family in the camp "suffer from extreme cold in the winter and stifling heat in the summer."

He remembers his formative years with anger. "For years we were reliant on food aid from UNRWA [the United Nations Relief and Works Agency for Palestine Refugees], but the amounts were small, which sometimes meant that ten days after distribution, we would be living on one meal a day so that the parcels would last until the end of the month." Clothes were made out of relief aid sacks; shoes from old rubber tires.

"I was raised on my family's stories about Palestine, the paradise we were driven from, about how the Jews had stolen our land and expelled us from it, how the Arab leaders had betrayed us. When I was growing up, I thought that there was no future for us unless we returned to Palestine, and that if we didn't return, I would spend my whole life as a refugee deprived of any kind of human rights."[38]

According to Abu Daoud, all eight terrorists selected for the operation had suffered at the hands of the Israelis: "They were people who had left their homes in '48, forced to flee, and then languished in the Lebanese camps since then. They were people whose houses were now the homes of Polish, French, and American Jews who had replaced them in their own country, living as citizens there without any right to."[39] All the young guerrillas, or "shabab,"[40] were determined "to fight for their land firstly, secondly for their dignity, and thirdly for their right to a decent life."

Several of the terrorists grew up near each other in Chatila refugee camp and even played together on the same soccer team (Khalid Jawad, in particular, was a soccer-mad youngster, according to his brothers Adel and Mahmoud).[41] But although the fedayeen chosen for the attack were all children of the camps, the reason most were selected seems to have been their previous familiarity with Germany. Ahmed Chic Thaa had lived in Berlin before the attack and was married to a German woman. Khalid Jawad had lived in Germany for two years with his brother Farud, before Black September recruited him for the attack.[42] Afif Ahmed Hamid, who joined Fatah in 1968, had lived and studied in Germany for more than a year before returning to Lebanon in 1971.[43]

Adnan Al-Gashey does not appear to have spent time living in Germany, but he was resourceful, reliable, and committed. A former student of nursing in Tripoli, he won a scholarship to study chemistry at the American University in Beirut.[44] "He was like a lot of other young men, sure of himself, ambitious; he loved life," said his wife.

The six fedayeen chosen for the operation were told to prepare to fly to Libya for final training. Their families were kept in the dark about their objective. Hajja Hamid, Afif's mother, knew only that he was going to Germany.[45]

"Where are you going in Germany?" she asked her son one day.

"I am going to study and then come back," he lied.

"So how long will you be gone?" said Hajja.

"Two months, two and a half months or so," he replied.

Security was so tight that Mahmoud Mohammad Jawad, the brother of Khalid, had even less of an idea what was going on: "One day, [Khalid] said, 'I'm going to play football in Syria.' He was gone for a week or two, and when he came back, he had marks from carrying a pack as part of his training. We asked him where he had been and he said he had been playing football. Then he said, 'Don't tell anyone.' A couple of weeks later, they went to Libya. We knew something was up. So we followed the news. Someone else who knew about the operation said, 'Don't worry, it'll all be fine.'"[46]

A month before the start of the Games, the six men flew to

Tripoli. "The leadership sent us to Libya to undergo special training, and they told us about it without saying what the training was for," said Jamal Al-Gashey. "In Libya we got about a month's advanced military training and special attention was paid to jumping exercises, off high walls. We guessed that this was special training for infiltrating Israeli military bases. As I later found out, we did this exercise because part of the plan was to enter the Olympic Village by jumping off a high wall."[47]

Nothing was left to chance. Abu Iyad and Abu Daoud drew up two communiqués that were to be given to the German police during the operation. The first one, typed in English, demanded the release of Palestinian and other terrorist prisoners. The second, handwritten in German by a bilingual Palestinian student using a ballpoint pen, granted an extension of their planned deadline and demanded planes to fly the hostages and terrorists out of Germany.

The two men also gave the attack a code name. It was to be known as Operation Iqrit and Biri'm, the names of two ancient Arab Christian villages in northern Israel that had been evacuated by the Israeli army in 1948, because of "security concerns." Arab families were forced to leave homes their ancestors had lived in for generations and told they would be allowed to return within two weeks. Decades later, the Palestinians were still waiting. Whereas most Israelis knew little of the tragedy, for Arabs it remained a festering sore.[48]

Although preparations for the Munich operation were going smoothly, Abu Daoud was still worried about how the guns needed for the attack would be smuggled into Germany. Abu Iyad told him not to worry; he would take care of it personally.

After flying to Damascus to briefly visit his wife and children, Daoud travelled to Tunis around August 17 or 18 for a round of meetings with Yasser Arafat, Abu Iyad, Abu Youssef, and several other senior members of Fatah. Daoud refuses to disclose exactly what was discussed at the meetings, but after two days in Tunis it was time for him to return to Munich for final preparations. As he was leaving the luxurious villa where the Fatah group was staying — the property of Mohammed Masmoudi, the head of the Tunisian diplomatic service — Daoud had to interrupt Arafat, Abu Iyad, and Abu Youssef's conversation (they were busy discussing an assassination attempt on the life of Morocco's King Hassan II). Each man apparently took Abu Daoud in his arms and embraced him.

There can be little doubt that Arafat knew of the planned assault on the Israeli team.[49] Although Abu Daoud did not personally discuss details of the Munich operation with the PLO leader, Arafat knew the reason for his departure.[50]

Flying a circuitous route, Abu Daoud returned to Munich to prepare for the arrival of the weapons to be used in the planned attack. The Olympics were now less than a week away.

Daoud spent a nervous few days in Munich, waiting for Abu Iyad to contact him. Eventually Daoud was told Iyad would be arriving in Frankfurt on a flight from Algiers via Paris on August 24. Abu Daoud left Munich and travelled 198 miles northwest to meet his colleague.

Iyad arrived at the airport travelling with another man and a woman, and together the three put their suitcases on the same baggage cart and headed towards Customs. Iyad strolled forward with a confident gait, but the man with him kept looking furtively at the Customs officers and bumped his cart into other passengers. "There was an extremely tense moment getting the weapons into Germany," admitted Iyad. As the three terrorists walked through the arrivals hall, a Customs officer pointed at one of the suitcases and demanded it be opened.

Fortunately for the fedayeen it was the only one of the three that did not contain weapons; it was packed to bursting with lingerie and women's clothing. As the nervous Palestinian began spreading out frilly underpants on the bench in front of the German official, his female conspirator, who was pretending to be his wife, looked on indignantly. The embarrassed Customs officer had soon seen enough. He waved the Palestinians through and out onto German soil. The guns had arrived.

By August 26, the opening day of the Games, the nervous Palestinian had brought ten grenades into Munich in his hand luggage. Abu Daoud stored them along with the guns in separate lockers at Munich railway station. All was set. Daoud sat back in his hotel to watch the opening ceremony and wait for the arrival of the final five members of the Black September commando unit.

On August 31, 1972, Jamal Al-Gashey flew to Rome from Libya with his Uncle Adnan and Afif Ahmed Hamid.[51] From there they took a train to Munich, met the others in the main station, retrieved the weapons they would use from the storage lockers, and checked into rooms at a small hotel.[52] The other three junior members of the unit travelled to Munich via Belgrade.

Jamal claims that at this point he was still unsure of the target, although it was impossible to move around Munich without being aware of the Games. For the next few days and nights the terrorists relaxed and prepared for their attack. Jamal even bought tickets to the Olympics and went to see two volleyball games.[53]

On the night of September 4, as the Israeli team watched *Fiddler on the Roof* and celebrated with the actor Shmuel Rodensky, the Palestinian team met at a restaurant in the Munich railway station for dinner to receive final instructions on Operation Iqrit and Biri'm from the Black September commanders Ali Hassan Salameh and Abu Daoud. The six junior members apparently had still not been told details of the action.

"I first knew the night of the operation, a few hours before it started," Jamal Al-Gashey asserted.[54] According to Al-Gashey the railway station meeting was the first time he had met all of the other terrorists involved in the operation. "I knew some of them . . . we lived in [Palestinian refugee] camps together and were from the same organizations . . . We got to know each other during training in Libya; we were all alike, children of the refugee camps with a shared cause and a shared aim."

In the dim light of the restaurant, one of the Palestinian commanders sketched out details of the operation and assigned each member of the terrorist unit their individual tasks. "Personally, I felt pride and joy," remembered Al-Gashey. "My dream of taking part in an operation against the Israelis was coming true."

It was to be an audacious attack, as Al-Gashey related: "The final instructions were to take control of the Israeli athletes and negotiate for the release of Palestinian prisoners from Israeli prisons. This was to last no longer than twenty-four hours, which was the limit that was put on [our] physical and psychological ability to keep control of a situation. At the end of that time, if there was no agreement from the Israelis, we were to ask for a plane to take us and the hostages to an Arab country."

After details of the attack were issued, money, passports "and anything else that showed our identity" were taken from the terrorists. The fedayeen left the railway station and walked back to their hotel.

Al-Gashey claims he felt no fear: "I was just young, full of enthusiasm and drive, and the idea of Palestine and returning there was all that controlled my thinking and my being. We knew that achieving our objective would cost lives, but since the day we joined up we had been aware that there was a possibility of martyrdom at any time in the name of Palestine. We were not afraid, but we felt the apprehension that a person feels when embarking on an important job, the fear of failure."

It was already early morning by the time the terrorists were ready to leave their hotel in the center of Munich for the attack, their bags packed and prepared. Esther Roth and the other Israeli athletes were sound asleep, dreaming of sports victories, when the men from Black September quietly slipped out of their hotel, jumped into two waiting taxis, and drove off towards the Olympic Village.[55]

3
Negotiations

*T*he Black September terrorists may have spent weeks planning their assault on 31 Connollystrasse, but their initial deadline of 9:00 A.M. for the release of their comrades from Israel and German jails was hopelessly unrealistic.

The Palestinian attack on the Munich Olympics was such a shock to the administration in Bonn that it took several hours for the full machinery of government to swing into action. By 8:45 A.M., with just fifteen minutes to go before the first executions were due to begin, no progress had been made at resolving the crisis. The senior German officials in the Olympic Village decided they had to speak to the terrorists in person and plead with them to delay the deadline to give the Israeli and German governments more time to act. Perhaps, thought some of the officials, the Palestinians could be reasoned with.

Annaliese Graes, the female police officer acting as intermediary, was ordered to ask the terrorist leader, Issa, if he would meet with a small delegation of senior German, Olympic, and foreign officials. Issa agreed, and Manfred Schreiber, Walther Tröger, and A. D. Touny, an Egyptian member of the International Olympic Committee, slowly approached the Israeli building. It was obvious to all the officials that the Palestinians were in total control of the situation.

"On the second-floor balcony was a man wearing a balaclava and pointing a submachine gun towards us, towards me!" said Schreiber, the Munich police chief.[1] As they tentatively approached the door of 31 Connollystrasse, Issa emerged and the negotiations began.

"He expressed his demands in a staccato manner; [of] was very cool and very determined, almost fanatical in his convictions," according to Schreiber. "His voice sounded harsh, metallic. He expressed his demands in a forceful manner and at times sounded like [one of] those people who aren't completely anchored in reality or totally aware."

There was little scope for discussion or negotiation. "It was as if he was reeling off what he said, having rehearsed it all beforehand," Schreiber said.

The atmosphere between the men was incredibly tense. "There were always two or three machine guns pointing on me and the leader of the terrorists always had a hand grenade in his hands," said Walther Tröger.[2]

The key to finding a successful resolution, the Germans had thought, was to get Touny to talk to Issa. Arab to Arab, perhaps he could find a solution. Touny moved closer and began talking quietly to Issa, explaining that his demands were being considered in Tel Aviv and Bonn, but that the Israelis and Germans needed more time to locate and then free all the hostages. Without any sign of disappointment or anger, Issa, who had been expecting such delaying tactics, agreed to extend his deadline to noon.[3] At a stroke, the immediate threat to the remaining Israeli hostages was lifted.

As the small group stood outside the Israeli building, Schreiber began a close examination of Issa. The German officer was used to dealing with dangerous and desperate criminals, and he actually began considering whether he might be able to grab Issa and take *him* hostage.

"I assessed the distance between the next corner and the gunman on the balcony and realized that he was pointing the gun downwards, in our direction. Out of the corner of my eye I glanced towards the left in the direction of the corner and had the impression that I'd be able to drag him along for two to three meters." But

Schreiber took too long formulating his plan. "My intention was to put my arms round him and then drag him round the corner, thereby obtaining a hostage. He realized that something was afoot and brought his hands round to the front to show that he was holding a hand grenade, and that his thumb was inserted in the ring-pull."

"If you lay a hand on me," threatened Issa, moving his hand forward, "I'll blow us both up!"

Schreiber immediately abandoned his plan: "That was my first failed attempt."[4] The incident was to set the pattern for a day of tense negotiations and abject police failure.

At the same time as Manfred Schreiber began negotiating for the lives of the Israeli hostages, their families and relatives across Europe and the Middle East were waking to the news from Munich. Ankie Spitzer, the wife of fencing master Andre, was awakened just after 8:00 A.M. in her parents' house in the Dutch village of Helvoirt. The first reports of shootings were coming through. Around 9:30 A.M. an official rang from Munich with devastating news: Andre was among the hostages.

Andre was born in Transylvania, Romania, but after his father died when he was eleven he moved to Israel with his mother.[5] He served his time as a conscript in the Israeli army and then went to the Israeli National Sports Academy to study fencing, his favorite sport. The director of the Academy spotted the young Romanian's natural skill with a foil and sent him to Holland to perfect his fencing skills. There, Ankie became one of his pupils.

"I didn't know he was from Israel at all. He spoke Dutch but with a slight accent, so I thought maybe he was from Eastern Europe or something." Andre was a charmer. He became first her fencing master, and then her lover. "Being the person that he was, it was hard not to fall in love with him."

Ankie converted to Judaism and the couple married, with a crowd of Andre's new friends turning out to celebrate. She recalled: "I felt a bit bad for him because I thought, here I have all my friends and all my family and everything, all my relatives, and here is Andre who has been only two years in Holland, he probably had nobody coming to our wedding from his side." Her fears were unfounded. Most of the guests at the wedding were there because of their friendship with the groom. "He had a very special character and it was very easy to get along with him. Because of his sense of humor he made numerous friends in a very short time in Holland."

Ankie, a vivacious free spirit, returned with Andre to Israel and the couple moved to the north, on the border with Lebanon, where Spitzer founded the Israeli fencing academy in a group of derelict buildings. It was a tough, hard life, 30 miles from the nearest town, with a five o'clock curfew because of roving bandits. For a young girl from Holland more used to concerts and the theater, it was a different world. "We had to leave afterwards because it became too dangerous, but the year that we lived there was the most beautiful and most wonderful year of my life."

As they struggled with life in the bandit zone, Andre was preparing for the Munich Olympics. It was, says Ankie, "his dream," capped just a month before the start by the birth of the couple's first child, a beautiful baby girl they named Anouk. Occasionally Ankie would query his dedication to sport. "What is so important to you about the Olympics?" she would ask.

His answers came from the heart: "The idea of the Olympics," Andre told Ankie, "is the fact that you can forget that you're two nations, or two warring nations, and you can come together in sport, and through sport find the good in each other and make friendships, forge relationships, and find brotherhood with each other. That appeals to me greatly." The Olympics, says Ankie, were "everything for Andre."

Ankie was so proud of her husband for making it to the Munich Games that she desperately wanted to accompany him to Germany. "Financially it was difficult for me to go there because we were a young couple with a baby girl, but we decided that it was more important for us to be together than to save some more pennies, so we decided to spend whatever we had on this trip."

The Israeli delegation left for Munich on a special communal passport, and on the same day Ankie flew to Holland with their baby. Ankie's idea was that her parents would look after Anouk while she travelled on to Munich to see Andre, but Anouk began an incessant bout of crying that lasted for twenty-four hours.

Such was the baby's distress that Ankie's brother, a Dutch pediatrician, suggested she take Anouk into the hospital for a few days for a checkup. "So I was in a dilemma: am I going to stay with the baby in Holland or am I going to go to Munich to join Andre?"

"You can easily go to Munich," her brother reassured her, "because we're just giving her a checkup. You'll make Andre very worried if you don't go."

Ankie decided to make the trip. Short of money, she hitchhiked from Holland to Munich, arriving in the German city the same day and meeting Andre in the Olympic Village. The sexes were segregated in the Village, so the Spitzers decided to rent a room together in a small hotel nearby. Being on the wrong side of the perimeter fence posed few problems: although Ankie did not have an official pass for the Village, security was so lax she simply walked in through one of the unguarded exits.

It was a blissful time for Ankie, marred only by her concerns about Anouk. She decided against telling her husband their baby was in the hospital because she knew he would have dropped everything and rushed to Holland. "And he was not in Munich to do that. He was in Munich to be with his fencers and to be part of the Olympic group."

Ankie bore the burden alone, calling her parents every day to check on Anouk's condition, which slowly improved. Her secrecy ensured the couple's enjoyment of their time in Munich, with Andre in his element as a participant in a uniquely international event. He was a man who passionately believed the Olympics could break down national barriers, and after one of his competitions he spotted members of the Lebanese team and told Ankie he was going to go and say hello to them.

Ankie had immediate reservations. "I said to him, 'Are you out of your mind?! They're from Lebanon!' Israel was in a state of war with Lebanon at the time."

"Ankie," said Andre calmly, "that's exactly what the Olympics are all about. Here I can go to them, I can talk to them, I can ask them how they are. That's exactly what the Olympics are all about."

"So he went . . . towards this Lebanese team, and . . . he asked them, 'How were your results?' and 'I'm from Israel and how did it go?' And to my amazement, I saw that the [Lebanese] responded and they shook hands with him and they talked to him and they asked him about his results. I'll never forget, when he turned around and came back towards me with this huge smile on his face. 'You see!' said Andre excitedly. 'This is what I was dreaming about, I knew it was going to happen.'"

Andre had soon finished all his competitions at the Games. The results, in Ankie's own words, were not "earth shattering," but for Israel they were extremely good. Her husband enjoyed himself so much in Germany that he suggested they stay on for another week and travel around the region to do some sightseeing. Ankie decided it was time to tell him Anouk had been ill. It was, she said, as if "a bomb dropped on his head."

Andre immediately went to see the head of the Israeli delegation and was given permission to take a few days off. The couple raced to the Munich station, took a train most of the way back to Holland, and then hitchhiked the final leg of the journey.

"We got back to Holland the next morning and went immediately to the hospital," Ankie said. Doctors told her that Anouk was fine and that her crying may have been caused by tension, but they wanted to keep her in the hospital under observation as long as possible. The Spitzers sat with Anouk for the rest of the day, watching over their tiny child.

The following day, September 4, Andre had to return to Germany and was due to catch a 10:00 A.M. train from Den Bosch. But as the couple drove to the station Andre suddenly decided he had to see his daughter one last time. "I just want to give Anouk a quick kiss," he told his wife.

"I was very impatient because I was afraid he would miss the train." But Andre ran into the hospital, grabbed his daughter, kissed her, and raced back out. "I was still in the car waiting for him," she adds. The delay meant that Andre missed his train. "I was desperate because I thought he's going to get in trouble when he gets back to Munich."

"Let's try the other train station, about thirty miles onwards," Ankie told her husband. The young Dutchwoman "stepped on the gas" and raced to the next station in Eindhoven in southeast Holland.

The train was already in the station, and Andre jumped on without a ticket. As Ankie ran alongside the train, Andre opened the window and shouted to her: "Ankie, I'm going to call you tonight when I get back to Munich!"

"Okay!" shouted Ankie in response as the train picked up speed. "Call me and I'll take care of Anouk!" Ankie watched as the train disappeared into the distance. "And he left," she adds simply. It was her final parting from her beloved Andre.

Ankie Spitzer went back to the hospital to see Anouk, and then home to wait for her husband's call. At around midnight he rang from the Olympic Village. The lanky fencing master was on his way to 31 Connollystrasse to check his bedroom, which he had not been using because he had been staying with Ankie in their hotel room.

"Nobody is here," Andre told his wife.

"Where are they?" she asked.

"I'm going to see," said Andre.

The couple kept talking for a few more minutes, and then Andre realized he was running out of money.

"Ankie, I only have fifty pfennigs left," said Andre, "so we have to talk quick."

"So we talked quick, quick, quick," remembers Ankie, "and he said, 'I'm going to call you tomorrow to let you know when the whole delegation is arriving back in Israel, because I want to get there before you so I can wait for you and the baby, to help when you arrive.' So we still talked and he said, 'I love you,' and the money was finished, the coins were done . . . and that was the last time I spoke to him. That was the last time I heard his voice."

Four hours later Black September arrived at 31 Connollystrasse and took Andre hostage. "My parents came to wake me up, and they said,

'Ankie, how many athletes are there in the Israeli delegation?' I had just opened my eyes and I said, 'I don't know. I think maybe twenty, twenty-five. I don't know.'"

Ankie's parents had heard news of the attack on the radio. The media already knew that one of the Israelis had been killed. Rumors were flying around the Village; initially the press thought the victim was the Israeli boxing coach.

"Who is the boxing coach?" asked Ankie's parents.

"There is no boxing coach," replied Ankie. "Israel did not send any boxers. Why are you asking me this at seven o'clock in the morning?" Her parents quickly explained what they had heard. "I jumped out of my bed and I thought if it is not the boxing coach then what coach is it? Maybe it's Andre."

Cold fear swept through Ankie. The family switched on their radio and television to begin a desperate vigil. "I waited and at nine o'clock in the morning I found out that Andre was one of the hostages. I was devastated. Devastated to know that this peace-loving person, that they just took him hostage . . . that they robbed him of his freedom. I sat in front of the television and had on the German station and the Dutch station and the radio and I never moved from my spot."

Dozens of relatives experienced that same desperate fear on the morning of September 5. In Israel, in a smattering of homes across the fledgling state, the horror was mixed with disbelief: not in Germany, not Jews, not again.

Relatives reacted differently to the news. Some wanted to be surrounded by friends and family. Others just wanted to be alone with their thoughts. Miriam Gutfreund, the wife of Yossef, the wrestling referee, walked to the Western Wall in Jerusalem to pray. Judith, the couple's daughter, dismissed the gossip of schoolmates that her father had been killed. "He's too big to be killed," she retorted and rushed home to tape news reports for her father to enjoy when he returned.[6]

Ilana Romano, the young wife of the weightlifter Yossef, was asleep in bed when she was awakened by a pounding on her door at around 9:00 A.M.[7] Her neighbor had been listening to the radio and was first to break the appalling news. Ilana recalled: "I turned on the radio and I heard that a group of terrorists had entered the Olympic Village. They had murdered an athlete and taken hostages."

The young woman was thrown into hysterics, a terror made worse, perhaps, because she had not wanted her husband to travel to Munich. "Throughout his training for the Olympic Games I had fears, a very bad feeling. The closer we got to the Olympics I said, 'Yosse, you know what? I am very afraid. I have a bad feeling concerning the Olympic Games.'"

Yossef would simply turn to her, a broad smile creasing his face, and say: "Ilana, come on, stop it. Don't put pressure on yourself. The Germans, they think about everything. Nothing will happen, don't worry. I'm telling you everything will be okay."

But Ilana did worry, every time Yossef left the house to train for the competition. Like other wives of members of the Israeli delegation, Ilana was a young woman, struggling to bring up the couple's children while her husband built up his muscles.

The two of them had met on the beach. Yossef Romano was the local superhero, all brawn and muscle coupled with a winning personality. "He was very strong and he had this smile on his face, he always had a smile on his face. When I first saw him [I said], 'Wow!' And when he first opened his mouth he was so gentle. It was so easy to fall in love with the man."

Their marriage still came as something of a surprise. Her parents were about to emigrate from Israel to Italy, and Ilana announced she wanted to stay behind. "No way, you're not going to stay here by yourself," said her parents.

"What are you talking about? We're getting married," Yossef told them indignantly.

"I didn't even have time to think," recalled Ilana. "It was simple true love."

She married a sports fanatic. While Ilana was giving birth to their first child, Yossef was away pumping iron at a competition. "He used to promise me that this [competition] would be the last," she says with a wry smile. Then came the Olympics.

Yossef had trained hard, but he was no match for the top athletes of nations many times larger than tiny Israel. He enjoyed his competitions, but on September 3 Yossef rang Ilana from Munich to tell her he had injured himself and would be returning home in two days with one of the team doctors for an operation on his leg. "Don't worry. Everything is fine. I miss you. How are the children? I want to come back home."

"That was his last telephone call," said Ilana. "It was very moving."

Ilana did not hear from Yossef the next day, and on the 5th she expected a telegram or a call to let her know when he would be home. Instead the news from Munich came via her neighbor: the Israeli building had been invaded.

"I rang up the Olympic Committee in hysterics and asked what had happened," recalled Ilana. They told her not to panic, but when an official mentioned that the attack had started several hours earlier, Ilana became even more frightened. "Four or five hours later and Yosse didn't call?" she remembered thinking. "It didn't seem reasonable. Yosse didn't call. And Yosse knows that I worry."

Ilana instinctively knew something terrible had happened. She made desperate calls to friends and officials within Israel, but nobody seemed to know what was going on in Munich. Then, finally, she heard on the news that Yossef was one of the hostages, and her world fell apart. "I understood Yossef. I knew his character — he wouldn't be treated like cattle. He would do something; I was worried his chances were slim. The devil inside me told me that there was no chance."

Yossef Romano was a Jew from the younger generation, a generation with no personal memory of the Holocaust but with intimate knowledge of its obscene consequences. Other, older members of the Israeli delegation had personal memories and nightmares to battle against during the Olympics.

Jacov Springer, a weightlifting referee captured in apartment 1 within moments of the terrorist attack, was born in Poland in 1921 into one of the most populous branches of the Jewish Diaspora.[8] When war came his family thought they would have nothing to fear from the Nazis. They were not an alien race, they kept telling themselves; they even spoke German. The Nazis would leave them alone.

Springer's family wanted to stay in Poland during the war, but something inside Jacov told him it was time to leave the country. If his parents would not join him, he would have to go alone. At the age of eighteen, as German forces began their race through Europe at the outbreak of war, Jacov fled Poland for Russia. "No one from the family wanted to hear about it. So they stayed in Poland and he was the only one that ran away," said his son Alex. Jacov's entire family — "his brother, sisters, and parents" — was killed in Poland; Jacov alone survived.

After the war, Jacov battled against the demons and the nightmares. He met Rosa — who became his wife — in Moscow in 1946, then returned to Poland to study at the Academy of Sports. "He was the only Jew who went to this Academy," said Rosa. "When he graduated he got a very distinguished position in the ministry of sports. He was responsible for athletes, and he did that for many years."

Finally in 1957, the Springers and their two young children emigrated to Israel, where Jacov began teaching weightlifting. Jacov established the sport in Israel and is still remembered as its father there. "There was nothing like that in Israel," recalls Rosa Springer. "He organized courses for judges, and he was an international judge." Although Israel was not invited to the 1964 Olympic Games, Jacov Springer was asked to attend and judge competitions. Jacov also attended the Games in 1968.

Then came Munich. Deciding whether to go to Munich was an intensely painful choice for Jacov. Germans had wiped out his entire family. He could never forget and never forgive. Even twenty-five years after the end of the war, Jacov would not use electronic appliances that had been made in Germany.

Yet although he was unhappy about going to Germany, "on the other hand he probably looked at it as part of his duty," thinks Mayo. "It was a peak in his career. Of course it wasn't easy for him to step on German land. I assume when he stepped on German land, representing the sport . . . he wanted to say, 'I'm coming back, and look, I survived and I've beaten you!'"

Rosa Springer still has a postcard Jacov sent her during the final days of the Olympics. "He wrote exactly when he was coming back and he mentioned the flight number; it was right before the Jewish New Year. He sent us regards and wishes." Because Jacov went to Munich as a judge, he was allowed to stay outside the Village in a hotel; instead he chose to be with his friends in the Israeli team on Connollystrasse. It was a decision that was to prove fatal.

As relatives wept at news of the crisis in Munich, Manfred Schreiber and Walther Tröger were still trying to establish a telephone link to 31 Connollystrasse and negotiate directly with the terrorists. The entire German government finally seemed to swing into action behind them in a desperate bid to prevent more Jewish blood being shed on German soil. German Chancellor Willy Brandt summoned his cabinet for an emergency meeting as Schreiber telephoned the terrorists and offered them an "unlimited amount of money" for the release of the hostages. As ministers sped to the cabinet meeting in Bonn the terrorists rejected the offer, as well as another suggesting that German officials be substituted for the Israeli hostages.

All the terrorists wanted, they claimed, was the release of their "brothers." One of these was Kozo Okamoto, the Japanese terrorist sentenced to life imprisonment for his part in the massacre at Lod Airport that May. Also on the list were the two Arab nurses who had been captured when the Israelis successfully rescued the Sabena airliner hijacked the same month. With the addition of those three names, the list was identical to that carried by the Sabena hijackers. They had also threatened to kill their hostages unless Israel released scores of prisoners.

By 10:00 A.M. the noon deadline loomed, and gaining more time was of paramount importance. The German politicians and policemen therefore tried desperately to reason with the Palestinians, imploring them to surrender. "At this time, we were, I think, a little bit naïve," admitted Ulrich Wegener, the founding father of the elite German antiterrorist squad GSG-9, who was then working as Hans-Dietrich Genscher's aide-de-camp. "Also the ministers, they were thinking that they could talk to [the terrorists] and really, they thought that they could convince them to let the people go, let the Israelis go. But there was no way, you know. Their demands were very clear."[9]

But still the talking went on. "We discussed of course [the Palestinian] issue," recalled Walther Tröger. "I have some understanding for the situation, as I have for all minorities who are under pressure, and we discussed it and I said, 'Listen, why don't you give up.'"[10] Issa, however, was having none of it. "He said, 'We are dead anyway, either we will be killed here, or if we go out and give up without having hostages . . . we will be killed where we go,' that was his expression. They were desperate, they were like kamikaze." Issa seemed to be suggesting that if the terrorists did not go through with their attack, or surrendered, other Palestinian terrorists would track them down and kill them for their "cowardice."

The mayor of the Olympic Village tried a different tack, discussing the whole issue of Palestine. "When I was with Issa we were not only negotiating how to handle this, we . . . were also going into the background of the whole thing, and I asked, 'Why are you doing it?'" Issa actually apologized to Tröger, saying the Germans had produced an excellent Olympic Games, but it offered the Palestinians a showcase where they could bring their grievance to the millions watching on television around the world.

Despite the situation, Tröger found himself drawn to the terrorist leader. The German thought Issa was probably an intelligent and reasonable man. "I didn't like him of course because of what he was doing, but I could have liked him [if I had] met him elsewhere." Issa might have been holding a hand grenade, but he did not even strike Tröger as being a violent man. He was, says Tröger, a markedly different character from the rest of the gang, which was comprised — in the eyes of the German — of "gallow birds." Issa, however, "was different."

Annaliese Graes, who also chatted with Issa during the negotiations, found the terrorist leader more peculiar. He told her he had worked in the Olympic Village Milk Bar, and described how he had enjoyed dancing around in front of the bar (she didn't believe him).[11]

Issa talked about his background and his life, explaining that his mother was Jewish and his father was a wealthy Christian Arab businessman. He explained that he had worked in France for several years, and kept dropping the phrase "oo-la-la" into their conversations.

The banter was not entirely one-way. Annaliese berated Issa for his actions, telling him terrorism was not the way to achieve his goals. The Palestinian responded by saying he was fed up with the pace of negotiations in the Middle East. Two of his brothers were in Israeli jails, he said. They lived in appalling conditions and had nothing to do all day but play chess in their minds. He wanted them released and was prepared to kill to achieve his aim.

Graes was not afraid of Issa ("He was always polite and correct," she said), but she repeatedly asked him not to wave his hand grenade around in front of her. Issa laughed. "You have nothing to fear from me," he told her.

Issa may have been an eccentric terrorist, but he was also stubborn and defiant. All attempts to persuade him to surrender failed, and by 10:00 A.M. the German officials in Munich were scrabbling around, desperately trying to devise ways of resolving the crisis.

Panic was spreading through the government in Bonn at the realization that neither the Palestinians nor the Israelis were prepared to give way. Frantic calls to Israel failed to provide a solution. The Germans wanted to compromise with the terrorists, but Golda Meir, the Israeli prime minister, was adamant there would be no deal. Meir was a tough politician, a woman who had survived a terrifying childhood in Kiev, Russia, hiding from gangs that roamed the streets hunting for "Christ killers."[12]

However, she was also the archetypal caring "Jewish mother" — a woman with a nation as her brood. Yet still she refused to budge. "If we should give in, then no Israeli anywhere in the world can feel that his life is safe," she said.[13] She instructed Eliashiv Ben Horin, her ambassador to Bonn, to tell the West German government it would have to resolve the problem on its own.

Meir prepared a statement for the Knesset, the Israeli parliament, which though in recess had reconvened to confirm the appointment of a new justice minister, and delivered a brief ten-minute address, agreed to by her Cabinet, in a low, quiet voice, stating simply that the Arabs had threatened to kill the hostages and commit suicide unless more than two hundred prisoners in Israeli jails were freed.

Then she named those taken hostage: David Berger, weight-lifter; Zeev Friedman, weightlifter; Yossef Gutfreund, wrestling referee; Eliezer Halfin, wrestler; Yossef Romano, weightlifter; Amitzur Shapira, athletics coach; Kehat Shorr, marksmanship coach; Mark Slavin, wrestler; Andre Spitzer, fencing coach; Jacov Springer, weightlifting referee; Moshe Weinberg, wrestling coach. Across Israel, and in the U. S. where David Berger's parents lived, their families wept.

At 11:15 A.M. Manfred Schreiber was told that the Israeli government had given its final and absolute refusal of the terrorists' conditions to the German government.[14] Meir had passed responsibility for the safety of her athletes over to the Germans.

"The Israeli government, even Golda Meir herself, had informed us that we were free to say whatever we wished, negotiate in any way that we saw fit . . . but that we should, however, be aware of one thing: they were not going to release those two hundred prisoners," recounts Manfred Schreiber. "We regarded their decision as being both binding and persuasive and we felt that we had, therefore, to act in accordance with it."[15]

However, apart from realizing they had to withhold the news from Issa, the officials in Munich had few ideas how to resolve the crisis[16] and had already started to panic. East German journalists watching events in Connollystrasse from their national team building on the other side of the road recorded a chronology of events that was recently uncovered in the files of the Stasi. At 11:00 A.M., they wrote that the Munich police "appear more hysterical than in control."[17]

Some senior observers have alleged that the chain of command began to collapse, with officials failing to think of even the most basic considerations. According to Ulrich Wegener it was not until between 10:00 and 11:00 A.M. that he was asked to get hold of helicopters, in case they were needed by the police, and fly Eliashiv Ben Horin down from Bonn to Munich. Wegener took no chances, calling in a full squadron of helicopters, and then leaving Munich to collect the ambassador.[18]

The Germans also called in Magdi Gohary, an Egyptian adviser to the Arab League, who had lived in Germany for the previous twelve years, and asked for his help in negotiating with the terrorists. He was contacted that morning by the standing crisis committee, part of the German Foreign Ministry, and asked to go to the Olympic Village.[19] "Half an hour later I was picked up by police cars with howling sirens and we went to the council office of the Olympic Village," he said. He was immediately asked to help translate and explain nuances of the leaflet the terrorists had thrown to the German police, but even his linguistic skills and intimate knowledge of the Middle East failed to shed light on some inscriptions and abbreviations. Initially nobody realized the signature at the bottom of the page — "I.B.S.O." — stood for International Black September Organization.

In a bid to break the deadlock Gohary bravely volunteered to talk to the terrorists and made the long walk down Connollystrasse to appeal to them to surrender. "I told [Issa] that this attack would have negative effects [for the Palestinians] . . . no matter what the ending would be. I also wanted to tell them that a fulfilment of their demands seemed impossible to me, for political reasons. In my opinion Golda Meir would in no way fulfill these demands, namely freeing x number of Palestinian hostages, because it would go directly against the whole political strategy of the Israelis at that time. It would have created a precedent and so shifted the balance of power to the side of the Palestinians." Controversially, Gohary believes "the Israelis would rather have accepted their whole athletic team being killed than letting this happen," although there is no concrete evidence to support his claim.

Issa was skeptical. "He didn't seem to trust me a lot — an Egyptian wanting to mediate, they surely thought I was an agent of the German authorities or something." Gohary struggled against Issa's suspicion. "My overall impression was that they really believed in the possibility of having their demands carried out, something I still cannot understand." For the Israeli government to give in was "99.9 percent impossible . . . This made the case very complicated." Gohary made no headway with Issa.

Schreiber and the other senior German officials left Connollystrasse, dejected by their failure to resolve the crisis peacefully, and walked briskly to the Olympic administration offices to discuss the deteriorating situation with other members of the crisis committee. The Germans were running out of nonviolent options, and Schreiber began considering more direct ways of ending the siege. The Munich police had been analyzing how to assault the house and rescue the Israelis since 8:45 A.M., when Georg Wolf, the Munich deputy chief of police, was given an order to begin preparations to free the hostages with an armed police operation.[20]

Wolf had bad news for the crisis committee. After his initial study he had concluded that an attack would be extremely dangerous, because the terrorists were too numerous and too well armed.

But the Germans were coming under pressure from Avery Brundage, the American head of the International Olympic Committee (IOC), to resolve the crisis by whatever means necessary. Brundage reminded the officials assembled in the administration building that as a former resident of Chicago he knew how to deal with dangerous criminals; he also suggested contacting the Chicago police department and asking for some fast-acting knockout gas, which could quickly disable all the terrorists and save the hostages.

His suggestion excited the Germans, who called Chicago to inquire further. But Brundage's memory must have been playing tricks on him: the American police had no knowledge of the miraculous gas.[21] German officials used the Foreign Ministry in Bonn to contact other governments around the world in the desperate hope they might have developed such a gas. But it simply did not exist. They would have to find another way of saving the Israelis.

While the Bavarian officials considered how to wrest the Israeli hostages from their captors on Connollystrasse, the Olympic Games continued. Television images of the crisis were interspersed with coverage of the dressage event, with horses and riders trotting daintily in pursuit of medals, while more than thirty-five hundred spectators roared for the German volleyball team in their battle against the all-conquering Japanese.

The contrast sickened many viewers. Hostages were being held at gunpoint just a stone's throw from the Olympic Stadium, and several commentators began asking why the Games were continuing under such appalling circumstances.

In Israel there was fury. Golda Meir told the Knesset in unequivocal terms that the Games should be immediately suspended: "It is inconceivable that Olympic competitions should continue while Israeli sportsmen are threatened with murder." Olympic officials had been discussing the possibility for several hours when they heard of her request; the Games were finally suspended with the reluctant agreement of Avery Brundage.

At a packed press conference that afternoon, Hans Klein, the chief press spokesman of the Olympic Organizing Committee, read a statement from Brundage and Willi Daume, president of the Organizing Committee: "The Olympic peace has been broken by an act of assassination by criminal terrorists. The whole civilized world condemns this barbaric crime, this horror. With deep respect for the victims and as a sign of sympathy with the hostages not yet released, this afternoon's sports events are being cancelled. The IOC and the Organizing Committee will hold services in commemoration of the victims in a ceremony which will take place tomorrow, September 6, 1972, at 10:00 A.M. in the Olympic Stadium. This ceremony will demonstrate that the Olympic idea is stronger than terror or violence."

But the Olympic "idea" was not stronger than terrorism. A few Palestinians had managed to disrupt the most important sporting event in history. Although German officials offered words of reassurance, the American swimmer Mark Spitz, the golden boy of the Games, was packing his bags. As a prominent Jew, Spitz was considered a potential target for more Arab attacks. He left Munich for London, guarded by three armed German bodyguards.

Spitz left behind an Olympic Village descending into surreal —

and tragic — farce. The crisis quickly became a spectator event to rival the sporting competitions. Thousands of people gathered at the edges of the Olympic Village, peering into the athletes' quarters for a glimpse of the excitement. While Jews were being threatened with death, children who had climbed unimpeded over the Olympic fence roamed the Village hunting for autographs and sucking candies in the shape of Waldi, the dachshund mascot for the Games.

Journalists allowed near the besieged block were staggered by the indifference of most athletes and spectators to the events in Connollystrasse. "It seemed like people having a noisy picnic in a churchyard. There was something unpleasant, selfish, slightly obscene about the atmosphere in the rest of the Village," said ITN reporter Gerald Seymour.[22] Within sight of No. 31 athletes were cuddling and petting on the grass, swapping name tags and telephone numbers, limbering up, and even sunbathing. Two of their fellow athletes had been shot, and another nine were under threat of imminent death, but some athletes cared little; a few were heard expressing concern that the siege could mean a delay or cancellation of the Games.

At 11:30 A.M., as rumors began circulating among the crowds that the Israelis were refusing to accede to the terrorists' demands, many athletes were openly furious. "Golda Meir, holding the fucking world to ransom again!" one Irish athlete shouted. Meanwhile a terrorist sitting on the balcony of the third floor waved at the athletes, a machine gun cradled between his legs.

Yet inside 31 Connollystrasse the situation could hardly have been worse for the nine Israeli athletes still alive. Shackled and tethered, they were being held at gunpoint around Yossef Romano's mutilated corpse, which the terrorists left in the middle of the room as a warning against further escape attempts.

Jamal Al-Gashey, meanwhile, was on his "guard duty," standing at the bottom of the stairs near the communal entrance to 31 Connollystrasse. With the noon deadline rapidly approaching, he was relieved from his post by another terrorist and went inside to stretch his legs and see what was happening.[23] "I went into one of the rooms and found one of our group sitting on the floor with the Israelis around him, and his gun was next to him propped up against the wall." The room was squalid. Blood was splattered across the wall. Yossef Romano was lying dead on the floor under a sheet. Clothes and bedding were scattered to the sides. The Israelis were trying to keep calm.

"I'm sure you're not going to kill us," one of them said to Al-Gashey, "because one of us complained he was cold and one of you gave him a jacket."

The Israeli spoke to Al-Gashey in Arabic. Then he turned to his friends and told them that the Palestinians were not going to kill them, just exchange them for prisoners.

Al-Gashey claimed that the Israeli then turned back to another terrorist and, in an astonishing attempt to keep up the spirits of the other hostages, suggested in Arabic, "Let's tell jokes." But as the Israeli began a comedy sketch, Issa came into the room and put a stop to the growing repartee. He "told us to stop telling jokes and return to our posts," said Al-Gashey. "I think he wanted to avoid there being any familiarity which might be exploited by the athletes in order to overpower us and escape."

Communication between the two groups was in fact rare, Al-Gashey recalled. "Most of the time, the athletes stayed in the place we put them and we stayed in our posts. Every now and then they asked us if there were any developments and the leader would give them general answers. He was not giving them details of the operation." The conversation witnessed by Al-Gashey was one of the few moments of positive communication between the two groups. For the rest of the time the Israelis must have been racked by unimaginable terror.

There were scores of witnesses to the extraordinary scenes on Connollystrasse that sunny day in Munich. From the balcony of their sixth-floor apartment near the Israeli building, a group of American athletes spent all day watching the drama unfold and praying for a peaceful resolution. Kenny Moore, Frank Shorter, Jon Anderson,

Mike Manley, Steve Savage, and Dave Wottle had all been awake since Shaul Ladany had banged on their door after his escape from the Israeli building hours earlier.[24]

The Americans took turns keeping vigil on the terrace all day, nervously plucking seeds from a fennel plant that grew there and grinding them into their palms. "We could see tanks, troops, and emergency vehicles assembling 150 yards away," recalls Moore. The wait was agonizing.

"Imagine how it must be for them in there," said Frank Shorter to the other athletes. "Some maniac with a machine gun saying, 'Let's kill 'em now,' and another one saying, 'No, let's wait awhile.' How long could you stand that?"

Other appalled spectators were also drawn to the balconies overlooking the Israeli team quarters, including representatives of the world's media, gathering for what would become the most widely watched terrorist attack in history. On the balcony of the Puerto Rican team was Gerald Seymour and two members of his crew. It was, he says, "very quiet . . . looking down into that little walkway. In a sense you were looking down into the cockpit of world events. Of that year, of that decade, maybe of that quarter-century."[25]

Among other reporters inside the police cordon was Peter Jennings, the now famous anchorman who was then working as the Middle East correspondent for ABC News. Ironically, Roone Arledge, the executive producer of ABC Sports, had invited Jennings to Munich for "a rest from Middle East politics."[26]

After hearing the first reports of the siege, Jennings grabbed a Telefunken walkie-talkie and ran to the Olympic Village. He managed to slip past security barriers and dodged into the Italian headquarters on the third floor of the building opposite the Israeli delegation. "The Italians were very receptive and let me get close enough to look over the balcony and in fact look right down on 31."[27]

Roone Arledge, meanwhile, had decided to get the sports broadcaster Jim McKay to "anchor" the breaking news story from the ABC studio. McKay was swimming when the call came. He hurriedly put his clothes on over his swimming trunks, thinking he would be back in the pool quickly. "A day later when he finally got back to his hotel room, he changed clothes and realized he still had his swimming trunks on underneath," said Arledge.[28]

TV stations around the globe had paid ABC to cover the Games on their behalf, and as the world began tuning in to the pictures from Munich, Peter Jennings began broadcasting his commentary via walkie-talkie from the isolation of the Italian balcony. He had the perfect vantage point from which to track the unfolding crisis, and with three years' experience reporting from the Middle East he was just the man for ABC to have on the spot. "I kept saying to people, well, you know there's nothing in the Palestinian nature which suggests they're going to murder these people," he said.[29]

Backing up Jennings's commentary were pictures from a television camera ABC had placed on top of the Olympic TV tower, a 950-foot-high edifice that dominated the Village. Arledge's prime objective was simply to keep the camera pointing at 31 Connollystrasse in case something happened.[30]

"I didn't dare ever move that camera," he admitted. "We just stayed right on that shot. And it just went on and on and on."[31] His decision meant the entire Munich crisis was played out like a real-life soap opera on television screens across the globe.

As the world watched and waited, the minutes ticked away towards noon, the second deadline the Palestinians had set for the release of prisoners from Israeli jails.

Operation 4 Sunshine

*W*ith less than fifteen minutes remaining before the noon dead-line, Manfred Schreiber walked briskly down Connollystrasse towards the Israeli building accompanied by A. D. Touny. Theirs was a desperate mission. The two men had to persuade Issa, who was al-ready wary of any trickery, to extend his deadline by several hours. The fate of the Israelis hinged on their powers of persuasion.

Annaliese Graes, the intermediary, was waiting for the two offi-cials outside the blue front door of 31 Connollystrasse. She called in-side and Issa emerged with a confident swagger to hear their pleas. He had applied more boot polish to his face as a bizarre form of dis-guise and seemed almost to be enjoying himself. Tony stood guard behind him on the street, a ludicrous, sinister figure with lifts in his heels, two grenades and a pistol on his belt, and his finger on the trig-ger of a Kalashnikov assault rifle. Another terrorist monitored the group with a gun from the second floor.

Schreiber spoke first, in urgent tones, explaining to the Pales-tinian that it was simply impossible for the Israelis to locate all the prisoners he had demanded within the space of a few hours. The Is-raelis were trying to comply with the demands, said Schreiber, but the terrorists had to extend their deadline.

Walther Tröger, a man Issa seemed to trust, had arrived just as

Schreiber began his pitch. The Village mayor stood quietly in the background as Touny delivered his own short speech, explaining to Issa that telephone connections with Tel Aviv were poor, and there were problems gathering together the entire Israeli cabinet, the only political body with the power to decide the fate of the Palestinian prisoners.

Issa, a dispossessed soul who now had the entire world watching his every movement, savored his moment of supreme power. He talked briefly with the other terrorists and then issued his judgement: the deadline would be extended to 1:00 P.M. If progress was not made by then, he said, two of the hostages would be executed.

Manfred Schreiber was desperate to get an extension of at least a few hours, but realized Issa was growing tired of his attempts at mediation. Schreiber says he told Issa "in a very theatrical way" that he would get two senior members of the German and Bavarian governments to talk to him. "He should at least listen to these gentlemen," reasoned the police chief.[1] Schreiber and Touny scuttled back down Connollystrasse to find the two Germans the police chief had in mind: Hans-Dietrich Genscher, the German interior minister, and Bruno Merck, the Bavarian interior minister.

Issa was certainly weary of negotiating with the fierce Munich police chief. He told Annaliese Graes that if the 1:00 P.M. deadline passed he wanted the press to come and take a statement from him and then witness the execution of two of the hostages. The two Israelis would be killed in front of the building "so the entire world could see."[2]

Then Issa disappeared into No. 31, holding two fingers up to the watching world. Most onlookers thought he was making a V for victory sign, but he was actually warning that two Israelis would die.

Back in the G-1 administration building, Genscher and Merck had been closely monitoring the situation from within the crisis management offices when Schreiber returned and asked them to talk with the terrorists. Both men readily agreed and walked down Connollystrasse. Issa proved receptive to their pleas, perhaps flattered by the attention of such top-level negotiators.

However, Ulrich Wegener believes it was a serious mistake for such senior officials to conduct negotiations. "It was another mistake, in my view," he said. "Because that was the end of the chain of command." Wegener is scathing of many — perhaps even most — aspects of the German response to the Palestinian attack. He points out that negotiations should always be conducted by a subordinate officer. "And then he could always say, 'Well, I cannot decide this, but I have to ask somebody, one of my supervisors,' and this could go on, go on, go on, and so you can gain time — very important."[3]

But with the new 1:00 P.M. deadline closing in, the Germans felt they had little choice but to wheel in senior negotiators. Genscher towered over Issa as both Germans pleaded with the terrorist for more time.

It was the moment for a dramatic gesture: "When it was clear to me that negotiations with the terrorists served no purpose, I offered myself as a hostage to the terrorists," said Genscher.[4] It was an unprecedented move by a German politician, but it was no spur-of-the-moment decision. Genscher had been considering whether to offer himself for several hours. "I had thought about it in the hours before, again and again," he revealed. He had even phoned his mother and daughter so he could hear their voices in case his offer was accepted and he was then killed.

"I implored him time and again," Genscher said. "You know what happened to Jews in the Third Reich," he told Issa, "and you have to understand that this cannot happen in Germany [again]. For this reason I beg you to do this exchange."[5]

The Germans were so desperate for a peaceful resolution that both Walther Tröger and Hans-Jochen Vogel offered to change places with the Israeli hostages, all to no avail.[6]

"The leader refused constantly," said Genscher.[7] Issa was not interested in taking any of the Germans hostage. He had been given his orders by the Black September commanders and he was sticking to them.[8]

Tröger remembered: "They said, 'No way, we have nothing to do with you, we are only dealing with Israelis,' and they did not accept it."[9] He modestly dismisses any suggestion of bravery. The Israelis "were my guests, and I wished to do everything in order to get them free."[10]

Involving the senior Germans was a dangerous gamble, but Genscher and Merck did persuade Issa to extend the deadline to 3:00 P.M. Manfred Schreiber, who was standing in the background while Genscher talked to Issa, admits the negotiations were "pretty tough": "I was . . . of the firm conviction that if I had just personally gone on negotiating . . . the assassins would have killed [two more hostages]."[11]

But for reasons that now baffle Magdi Gohary, the Black September guerrillas actually seem to have believed Genscher and Merck when they said the Israeli government was obeying their commands. By 12:57 P.M. the situation in Connollystrasse was relaxed enough for Annaliese Graes to pause and drink a can of Coca-Cola outside the Israeli house.

This modest success galvanized the government in Bonn. Chancellor Willy Brandt, who had been chairing cabinet discussions, cut short his meeting and flew to Munich to monitor further negotiations. Although the Bavarian authorities were still in charge of the situation in the Olympic Village, Brandt ordered his officials in the Foreign Ministry to issue an urgent appeal to the heads of state and governments of Arab countries to do everything in their power to secure the release of the hostages.[12]

The increasing German confidence was not mirrored in Israel. Golda Meir's government were convinced that the terrorists meant business and would not willingly allow any of the hostages to survive. Lacking complete confidence in the ability of the German authorities to save Jewish lives, Meir and her ministers ordered an elite Israeli army unit, the Sayeret Matkal, also known simply as "The Unit," to prepare to fly to Germany to assist in a hostage rescue operation. Several dozen men were put on standby.

The men of Sayeret Matkal are the cream of the Israeli forces. Highly secretive, The Unit was inspired by the British Special Air Services and founded in the 1960s by a legendary soldier named Avraham Arnan. Sayeret Matkal soldiers, who limit their identification to small gold pins worn anonymously inside the shirt lapel,[13]

were among the few who could understand something of the torment the Israeli athletes were going through: during training for The
Unit soldiers would be kidnapped — sometimes while on leave,
walking along the street in civilian clothes — and then subjected to a
harsh interrogation, as if they were in the hands of Arab commandos.[14] When the call came through at the squad's headquarters to start
preparations for a flight to Munich, the soldiers had been watching
developments throughout the day and knew the enormity of their
task.

Muki Betser was a platoon commander in the secretive squad at
the time: "Ehud Barak [the future Israeli prime minister] was the
commander of The Unit. A special force was selected and we were
supposed to fly to Munich in order to release the hostages. We waited
for a few hours; we arranged the equipment, we collected information, passports, and civilian clothes, and basically we were waiting for
developments [in Munich]."[15]

According to Betser, however, the squad knew there could be
problems that might prevent their deployment in Munich. "We knew
that a political problem might occur, that the Germans could refuse to
bring us in to do the operation instead of them." The Israelis were
even unsure whether the Germans had a special antiterrorist squad
similar to Sayeret Matkal. "At this time the topic was new in Germany . . . We didn't know exactly whether they had a special force . . .
We were hoping that if we got there and studied the object and came
up with a good plan we'd be able to conduct a successful operation."

Betser and the other soldiers waited the whole day. "We were
hoping to get a positive answer and be able to fly over there and conduct this mission. Hours passed, then we realized that the chances
were slim."

The call ordering them into action never came. Although the
Germans did not have a counterterrorist force, the German government rejected the Israeli offer of help, saying "their security forces
would handle the problem," according to Betser.[16] The Sayeret
Matkal team, at that time one of the few military units in the world
trained in counterterrorism tactics and hostage rescue, never left
Israel.

Several German politicians and Bavarian officials have since denied that Israel ever offered to help, but Muki Betser is adamant: "Our unit for freeing hostages was ready for action. But the German government refused permission."[17]

Zvi Zamir, the head of the Israeli secret service, Mossad, also remembers Golda Meir telling him and several cabinet colleagues that Willy Brandt had refused to allow an Israeli team to assist in rescuing the hostages: "There was a discussion at the cabinet and . . . the general feeling was that if the German army or whoever are capable of doing it well in Germany there is no necessity to send the Israeli team. And the feeling was that Chancellor Brandt feels that this is Germany's obligation, its part of hosting the Olympics in Germany proving that this Olympic gathering is well defended and well run. And as a result the decision was to wait and see what the Germans are doing."[18]

The Israelis could do little but let the Germans try to save their athletes. When the Israeli cabinet discussions finished and the meeting broke up, Zvi Zamir returned to his office in Tel Aviv to talk with senior Mossad officials who were monitoring the situation in Munich. He had only been back a few minutes when he received a phone call telling him that Moshe Dayan, the legendary Israeli minister of defense and architect of the nation's victory in the 1967 Six Day War, had decided to fly to Germany to monitor the situation in Munich and coordinate the Israeli response.

Dayan wanted Zamir to travel with him to Munich, along with Victor Cohen, an agent of the General Security Services ("Shin Bet," or "SHABEK"), the internal intelligence service. Cohen, who spoke fluent Arabic, had worked with Moshe Dayan just a few weeks previously, when he had negotiated with the Black September terrorists who had hijacked the Sabena plane. Dayan wanted his expertise and steady nerves.[19]

Initially, the plan was for Zamir, Cohen, and Moshe Dayan to travel to Munich together as a high-level delegation to negotiate with the Arabs and Germans and monitor any plan for a counterterrorist strike. But when the three men met at the airport in the early afternoon, Dayan and Cohen became concerned at the number of journalists milling around. Dayan was a revered figure among Israelis, but Arabs despised him, and the three men agreed that if the Black September guerrillas in Munich knew of his presence it might encourage them to behave even more aggressively. "At the last moment I thought that it wouldn't be wise for Dayan to travel with us," said Cohen. "General Dayan accepted my idea, and he said: 'Okay, you are going to fly only with General Zamir.'"

Dayan spoke to Golda Meir on the telephone, and she agreed that Zamir and Cohen should fly to Munich anyway. According to Zamir: "I said, 'The ambassador is there,' but [Golda Meir] said, 'Well . . . if you are there you will see what the Germans are doing. It's important that we shall be there and see . . . how they rescue our team.' They insisted that I be present."[20] Cohen and Zamir left for Munich together.

By 2:00 P.M. the situation in Munich was tense. The hostages were getting hungry, and the terrorists demanded food ("enough for twenty people").[21] "We will not be eating," Issa told Graes.[22] The terrorists knew the Germans might try to lace any food or drink with drugs, so they had brought their own supplies.

The demand gave the Germans a chance to implement one of their more pathetic rescue plans. At 2:18 P.M. Manfred Schreiber and Walther Tröger appeared with two police officers, ludicrously disguised as chefs in white overalls, carrying four large boxes of food. One of the chefs was the leader of a Munich police "attack team" that Schreiber thought might be used in any assault on the building, and he was hoping the guerrillas would be unable to carry all the boxes themselves and would request the help of the "chefs," enabling them to enter and assess the situation inside. "This is why we distributed the food to at least four baskets, so that we needed as many people as possible to carry it," said Schreiber.[23] It was a pitiful attempt at subterfuge, and the terrorists were too canny. Schreiber and Tröger took yogurts from the boxes and ate them to prove the food was not poisoned,[24] then Issa slowly carried each box inside, one by one.

The food seems to have briefly alleviated the tension in the street. At 2:40 P.M., notes the Stasi chronology of events, "the guerrillas are a picture of contentment and self-importance. On the second floor one of them is leaning out of the window, sunning himself, chain-smoking and observing the street. At the entrance to No. 31 there is a cigarette machine. One of the guards, in light-blue uniform, uses the vending machine — they can move freely about the area without any interference."[25]

The clocks ticked on, and with fifteen minutes to go before the 3:00 P.M. deadline Genscher, Schreiber, and Merck took another long walk down to the Israeli building to beg for an extension of the deadline and the lives of the Israeli hostages. It must have been a shocking task for the German officials, negotiating for the lives of the Israelis. One wrong word, one sentence misinterpreted, and the fedayeen had shown themselves only too willing to murder the captives.

But Bruno Merck decided to be bold. The Israelis, he told Issa, had still not managed to gather together all the files on the prisoners. "We still have nothing definite," he said. "If you want to murder the Israelis you are holding, we can do nothing to stop you. Whether you shoot one or several five minutes from now, nothing will be changed."

Issa was livid. He threatened to shoot one of the hostages within five minutes. "Do you think that between the life of a Jew and the freedom of our brothers who are Israeli prisoners, we would hesitate?" he said furiously.[26]

Merck begged him to wait for a few moments, and strode back down the street. Schreiber and Genscher stood by Issa's side, fuming silently.

Within two minutes Merck had returned, followed by Mahmoud Mestiri, the Tunisian ambassador to West Germany, and Mohammed Khadif, the head of the Arab League in Bonn. It was their turn to beg Issa. Give the Israelis more time, implored Mestiri; show the world that Palestinians are not eager to kill. It was a crucial intervention. Issa paused to consider, then agreed to extend his deadline to 5:00 P.M. Yet he was under no illusions; Issa knew he was being conned.

The terrorists "were getting more and more nervous," confirmed Walther Tröger, "and they certainly knew that time was against them, and they knew or guessed that running out of time was an attempt of the other side — of our side — to get better prepared for a final decision."[27] Issa even told Annaliese Graes he did not trust Schreiber and thought the Germans were "playing" with him.[28]

The Black September leader was gradually beginning to realize the Israelis had no intention of releasing their prisoners. It was a bitter blow. In their own way the Israeli government had proved just as fanatical as the terrorists. The Germans were stalling, and Issa knew his men could only remain alert for a finite length of time.

But what could he do? The Black September commando knew he could not keep control of 31 Connollystrasse for a prolonged period; the Germans would eventually storm the building, and then the attack would have failed.

According to Abu Iyad, one possible solution was offered by "an Arab embassy" that managed to get a proposal through to the Palestinians, which could have formed the basis for a secret agreement between all sides. "The Israeli hostages would be freed and replaced by German volunteers, who would be taken by the fedayeen to an Arab country," Iyad has said.[29] As part of the deal, he claims, "two or three months later," Israel would discreetly release some fifty prisoners. According to Iyad, a number of other countries were prepared to act as guarantors to the agreement.

It remains unclear how far the proposal from the Arab embassy progressed, and officials and politicians involved in the negotiations now deny all knowledge. Abu Iyad, however, described the proposal as "tempting," and says it had the advantage of satisfying the Palestinians while still proving face-saving for Golda Meir's government.

While many scenarios had been considered by the Black September leadership during their preparations for the attack, this proposal seems to have surprised Issa. According to Abu Iyad, he decided to check whether the proposal was agreeable to senior Black September officials and called the phone number of a militant, code-named "Talal," in Tunisia.[30]

"Unfortunately for everyone concerned, the Talal in question had been detained at the Tunis airport, having failed to procure a visa in advance," wrote Abu Iyad.[31] By an extraordinary coincidence, the man who answered the telephone in Tunis also happened to be named Talal. "An incredible misunderstanding took place when [Issa] telephoned." The wrong Talal could not understand why someone was calling from Munich and talking in riddles, and Issa was astonished to be talking to a Talal he did not know and who did not understand the code words being used.

Issa knew the telephone he was using would have been bugged by the Germans, so he gave up on the call, then rang back a little later. The wrong Talal again picked up the phone, at which point Issa gave up. He told the Arab diplomat who had suggested the proposal that it had been rejected.

Jamal Al-Gashey was a junior foot soldier in the attack, but he still remembers the various attempts at mediation: "Arab embassies were mediating, and one of them informed us that Israel was refusing to release any Palestinian prisoners and that they were firm about this, and that instead they were offering us $9,000,000 and safe passage to release the hostages . . . We refused that offer, because the purpose of our mission was to fight for the rights of our people and raise the profile of our cause, not to make money."[32]

Although Issa grew increasingly nervous between 3:00 and 5:00 P.M., outwardly the terrorists displayed their customary confidence. At 4:15 P.M. the Stasi record of events notes that the "Cowboy" on the first floor of the Israeli building "laughs and holds his fists up high — he is obviously trying to show that they feel they are on the way to victory. Then he makes the V for victory sign with both hands."[33]

The terrorists knew the eyes of the world were upon them. People were transfixed by the events in Munich, and it must have given the fedayeen confidence: they were already achieving their aim of publicizing the Palestinian cause around the globe. Even around Connollystrasse the crowd was vast — estimated at seventy-five to eighty thousand by 4:20 P.M. — munching on sauerkraut and frankfurters as they watched the drama unfold.

Inside the building Issa was not so confident. As the "Cowboy" postured on the second floor, Issa was deciding what to do with his hostages. At some point he must have talked with the Israelis, because about this same time Annaliese Graes claims one or more of the hostages suggested the entire group should fly to Cairo and try to resolve the deadlock from the Egyptian capital.[34]

At 4:35 P.M., Genscher, Schreiber, Tröger, Merck, and several other German officials walked back down Connollystrasse to No. 31. Annaliese Graes asked Issa to come outside, and the Germans began their now familiar attempts to persuade Issa to lengthen his deadline — this time beyond 5:00 P.M.

Bruno Merck spoke first, explaining to Issa that the Israeli government still had not given its final response to his demands. There were some in the cabinet who still needed to be persuaded. They needed more time, he said.

Issa knew the Germans were lying. "You're not going to trick us!" he shouted, stabbing at the officials with his finger. "You're trying to play around with us!"[35]

But the Germans were also growing weary. Hans-Dietrich Genscher cut in. "Germany is doing all it can," he insisted.[36] "All of your demands that we could reasonably meet have been met. We are ready to listen to any further demands you have."[37]

Issa paused. He was impossible to read: incendiary one moment, passive the next. Now he concealed his irritation, reached into his pocket for a cigarette, lit it, and took a long, slow drag. "Wait a minute," he told the officials in German, and strode back into the building.

Within two minutes Issa reappeared. The situation had changed, he told the German officials. The terrorists were fed up with the deadlock, said Issa, who then claimed one of the hostages had suggested that the entire group should fly to Cairo and resolve the crisis from there. Issa liked the idea. He demanded two planes and said they should be ready to fly within an hour.

German officials claim Issa then told them that if Israel did not release its prisoners and fly them to Egypt to meet Black September at the airport, all of the hostages would be executed.

Crucially, however, Annaliese Graes, who was standing close by, later stated that Issa told the Germans that he and another terrorist were prepared to be held in a German prison as "exchange hostages" to make sure everything went smoothly after the rest of the terrorists and hostages were flown out.[38] The Black September leader was apparently trying to avoid bloodshed.

But the Germans were aghast at the suggestion. They knew that Israel would never allow its citizens to be flown out of Germany by terrorists. Flustered, the officials tried to change Issa's mind. Every option was considered, according to Manfred Schreiber.

"We made all kinds of offers," claims Schreiber. "We offered money, we attempted any manner of exchanges; we also said, for tactical reasons, that they could leave Germany on the condition that they leave the hostages behind."[39] The attempts to resolve the situation even included the Germans offering themselves as hostages again. Genscher said that "he would be prepared to accompany them on the flight, on the condition that they leave the hostages behind."[40] Others also offered themselves as hostages: Schreiber, Tröger, Merck, ten West German Olympic Games organizers; even Peter Brandt, the son of the German Chancellor, took the extraordinary step of offering himself as a hostage in place of the Israelis.[41] But all offers of a swap were refused.

Next Genscher tried a more direct tack, warning Issa it would be difficult to find two planes with volunteer pilots in the time frame demanded. Issa finally settled for a single plane, which the Germans agreed would be made ready for him by 7:00 P.M.

Genscher, Merck, Schreiber, and Tröger moved slightly away from Issa for a brief conference. One thing was certain, they all agreed, the German government could never allow the Israelis to be forcefully abducted from Germany.

The group turned back and told Issa "that as far as we were concerned, it was inconceivable that, remembering what had happened in 1945, Israeli hostages could once again be removed from German soil by force," recalls Manfred Schreiber.[42]

The Germans told Issa they would only agree to his plan if they could see and speak with the hostages. Officials have since claimed they wanted to know whether the hostages were still alive and also to ask if they would agree to leave Germany with the terrorists. However, Annaliese Graes stated later that the real reason the Germans wanted to see the hostages was because they did not believe Issa's claim that it was the Israelis who had suggested the flight to Cairo.[43]

Issa considered their demand for a moment, then agreed. He signalled to the second floor, shouted in Arabic, and then Andre Spitzer, who spoke fluent German, was pushed to the window on the second floor of the apartment building. With his hands tied firmly behind his back, Spitzer was a proud but gaunt figure. Kehat Shorr stood solemnly behind him. A short, moving conversation began between Spitzer and the German politicians and policemen below.

In Holland Spitzer's wife Ankie was glued to the live television coverage: "I suddenly saw that the window of the apartment where they were kept hostage was opened and I saw Andre in front of the window, his hands bound behind his back, and they asked him questions. I could of course not hear what he was asking but I heard afterwards from Dr. Genscher what was the conversation."[44]

"Good day, gentlemen," said Spitzer politely.

"Is everybody okay? What is the situation with all the other hostages," Genscher asked Spitzer.

"Everybody is okay, except for one," Andre began saying, refusing to be cowed by the terrifying situation. But one of the terrorists whacked him with a gun butt to shut him up. When he was allowed to speak again it was to make a more cryptic comment: "All the hostages who survived the dawn attack are alive and in fair condition."

Genscher shouted back to Spitzer, desperate to offer him some reassurance, some vestige of hope: "We are doing everything we can to get you released!"

Spitzer began to express his gratitude, but the terrorists hauled him roughly back into the room, out of sight of the officials and television viewers.

Ankie Spitzer recalls: "Andre obviously tried to answer . . . I saw that he was not allowed to say . . . He got hit with the butt of the rifle of one of the Palestinians . . . and pushed away and they closed the curtains. That was the last time really that I saw him 'face to face.' It was terrible."[45]

1 A happy group photograph, taken just days before the Black
   September attack, of most members of the 1972 Israeli Olympic
   Squad.

1 Shaul Ladany, athlete
2 Shmuel Lalkin, head of
  delegation
3 Kehat Shorr, marksman
4 Mark Slavin, wrestler
5 Zelig Shtroch, marksman
6 Andre Spitzer, fencing coach
7 Esther Shahamurov,
  hurdler/sprinter
8 Yitzhak Caspi, deputy leader
  of the delegation
9 Dan Alon, fencer
10 Gad Tsabari, wrestler

11 Eliezer Halfin, wrestler
12 Shlomit Nir, swimmer
13 Henry Herskowitz, marksman
14 Yitzhak Fuchs, team chairman
15 Yossef Romano, weightlifter
16 Dr. Kurt Weil
17 Amitzur Shapira, athletics coach
18 Tuvia Sokolovsky, weightlifting
   coach
19 Zeev Friedman, weightlifter
20 Jacov Springer, weightlifting judge
21 David Berger, weightlifter
22 Moshe Weinberg, wrestling coach

2 Yossef Gutfreund,
   the 6-foot, 5-inch
   Israeli wrestling ref-
   eree. He wedged his
   290-pound bear of a
   physique against the
   door to 31 Connolly-
   strasse when the ter-
   rorists first attacked,
   giving several of his
   comrades a few pre-
   cious seconds in
   which to escape.

3 Andre Spitzer, Israeli fencing coach, and his new bride Ankie on their wedding day. "Being the person that he was, it was hard not to fall in love with him," said Ankie.

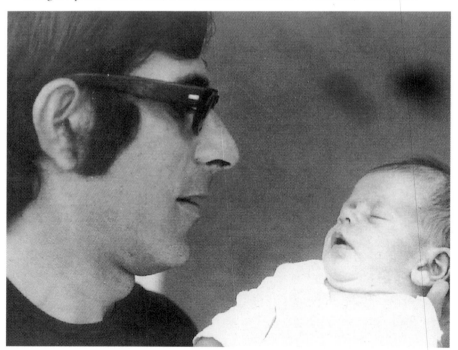

4 Andre Spitzer and his beloved baby Anouk, born just before the start of the Munich Olympics.

5 Jacov Springer. Born in Poland, he fled the country during the Second World War but later returned and eventually became an official in the Sports Ministry. He emigrated to Israel in 1957.

6 Yossef Romano, an Israeli weightlifter born in Tripoli, Libya. He injured himself during competitions and was on crutches when Black September attacked.

7 Jacov Springer and Yossef Romano, weightlifting judge and weightlifter. Jacov, whose family perished in the Holocaust, fought personal demons to compete on German soil. Yossef's wife had a premonition that something terrible would happen in Munich.

8 The vast Olympic Village, constructed to house more than 10,000 athletes for the 1972 Games.

9 The Star of David is carried into the Olympic Stadium during the opening ceremony of the Munich Games.

10 On the night before the terrorist attack many of the Israeli delegation went to a performance of *Fiddler on the Roof* in the center of Munich. This photograph was taken just a few hours prior to the assault.

11 The Israeli wrestling team and its coach. From left: Gad Tsabari (who escaped during the Black September attack on 31 Connollystrasse), young Mark Slavin, Moshe Weinberg (coach), and Eliezer Halfin.

12 The conditions that led to the creation of Black September: the Nahr-el-Bared camp near Lebanon, home to 6,000 Palestinian refugees in 1952. Most of the refugees had left their homes in Palestine voluntarily after the birth of the state of Israel in 1948, but many were forcibly ejected.

13 Conditions in early Palestinian refugee camps were appalling. This was the first school in the Jalazone camp in the West Bank in the early 1950s.

14

15

16

17

18

14 Jamal Al-Gashey at 19, one of the three Black September survivors of the Munich attack, in a photograph taken after his arrest. He is the only one of the attackers still alive.

15 Nineteen-year-old Mohammed Safady, another survivor, in a photograph taken after his capture by the Munich police. He was later killed by Israeli agents as part of a covert revenge mission, "Operation Wrath of God."

16 Adnan Al-Gashey, the third Black September survivor of the Munich attack, in a photograph taken after his safe return. He was also killed by Israeli agents.

17 Afif Ahmed Hamid, who told his mother Hajja before the attack that he was going to Germany to study.

18 Khalid Jawad, a soccer-loving youngster who lived in Germany for two years before the Black September assault on the Israeli team.

19 The squad of Black September
    terrorists poured into the Israeli
    building in the early hours of the
    morning as the athletes slept.
    This picture, taken on September 5,
    1972, shows the silhouette of a
    German police officer outside
    31 Connollystrasse.

20 Hundreds of German police and border guards were bussed into the Olympic Village in
    a desperate attempt to contain the crisis.

The Germans were far from satisfied. Genscher told Issa he wanted the terrorists to give the German officials access to the hostages, so they could speak with them properly. Only then, Issa was told, would they allow the terrorists and hostages to leave German soil.

Issa had little choice. It was 5:00 P.M., and after nearly ten hours of negotiations he must have realized his men would soon be tired and frazzled. His best option was to take the entire group to a friendly Middle East state and either continue the talks or kill all the Israelis and escape.

"Mr Genscher said he wished to have a direct discussion with the Israeli hostages," recalls Walther Tröger, "then Mr Schreiber said he wished to accompany him and they said 'No, you are policemen, you are not allowed to enter.'" Instead Tröger volunteered. "I said, 'All right, then it's me.'"[46]

Issa agreed to allow Genscher and Tröger in, and at 5:05 P.M. the two men walked through the blue door into the Israeli building. "We went up the stairs and through the corridors and at last we arrived at the room," said Genscher. Two terrorists with submachine guns were guarding the room and opened the door to reveal a scene of carnage.[47]

Lying prostrate in the middle of the room was Yossef Romano's corpse. He had been shot in the groin, creating a gruesome injury that led his widow Ilana to believe he was tortured.[48] Man-mountain Gutfreund was bound to a chair and the eight remaining hostages were lined up on beds on either side, their arms bound. Bullet holes marked the walls and blood soaked the floor. The smell was appalling. "It was a terrible impression, I must say," Tröger remembered. "The wall was full of blood in that room."

As the two Germans entered, aghast at what they were witnessing, the nine hostages looked up, their eyes betraying desperate optimism. Genscher said: "This picture of the room . . . will stay with me as long as I live. I will never forget those faces, full of fear, and yet full of hope."

The Germans began a halting discussion in English with the Israeli hostages, with Tröger translating. Genscher recalled: "I introduced myself to them as the minister of the interior and assured them that I would do anything that I could to help them." Then he asked the hostages politely whether they were being treated well and if they were hungry.[49]

"They said they were treated well," said Tröger.[50] However, "the discussion was absolutely overshadowed by the very depressed mood of the hostages." The hostages feared two things, he believes. The first, of course, was the terrorists, who had already shown a willingness to murder their friends, but the second was a police assault on the building, which the athletes thought would result in their deaths. When Tröger and Genscher asked if they were prepared to be flown out of the country, subject to stringent guarantees of their safety, the athletes readily agreed.

Tröger recalls that the men "were very depressed and fearful." "They certainly knew they were kind of soldiers, Israelis representing their country . . . and they had to keep in mind the benefit and the future of their country as well, but they wished to come to a conclusion that might save their lives." He adds: "But they were not very hopeful in that respect."

Then, grim-faced, the two Germans were forced out of the building, leaving the Jews to their fate. Genscher was deeply moved by what he saw ("Genscher was of course depressed, as I was," said Tröger afterwards): "I went out and begged again to be taken as a hostage."[51]

Ulrich Wegener, Genscher's aide-de-camp, was surprised by the pained expression on the German politician's face when he returned: "He was shocked about the whole situation inside the building. He was very depressed after he came back. I still remember it. He said, 'They mean business, no question, you know. They are serious.' He was sure they were fanatics; and they were, of course they were — they were serious, no question."[52]

The German officials returned to their crisis center and immediately began planning what to do next. The first priority was to debrief Genscher and Tröger.

Manfred Schreiber and other German police officials waiting outside had asked Genscher and Tröger to note where the hostages were being held and exactly who was guarding them.

Schreiber explained: "We wanted an accurate idea of the Israelis' mental state, we wanted reliable information as to how many hostages there were, we wanted to establish how many perpetrators there had been, what the overall condition of the house was, whether there would be a favorable opportunity for an attack inside the house."[53]

The most important fact to establish was the number of terrorists. All day there had been speculation about how many Palestinians were ranged against the massed ranks of Munich police camping outside 31 Connollystrasse. Establishing a precise figure was crucial if an assault was to be launched against the terrorists inside or outside the building. Crucially, the two German officials appear to have told Schreiber they had seen only four, perhaps five terrorists. The crisis committee took this information as a definitive statement, and the police later relied on it when preparing to rescue the hostages.

Genscher and Tröger had other news to impart upon their return: they had seen the bloodied corpse lying in the middle of the room. Careful scrutiny of team photographs taken earlier in the competition confirmed it was Yossef Romano.

Back in Israel, Ilana Romano's final torment was beginning. A policeman arrived at her house with a member of the Olympic Committee. The news of Yossef's murder had finally filtered through from Munich.[54]

"Yossef is in bad shape," the officer told Ilana.

She knew he was preparing her for the worst. Ilana looked him straight in the eye and said simply, "You are going to tell me the truth."

There could be no further denial. "You are right, Ilana," said the officer quietly, "the truth is horrible. Yossef was murdered. In the morning. Moshe then Yossef."

"Did Yossef suffer?" Ilana asked quietly.

She recalls: "He said 'No,'" but she did not believe him "even for a minute." She went into shock, and a doctor appeared at her house to administer Valium and injections. She spent the next twenty-four hours under heavy sedation.

Genscher and Tröger also had news for Ankie Spitzer. Andre had given Genscher a message for his wife, and the German foreign minister was desperate to pass it on. Eliashiv Ben Horin, the Israeli ambassador to West Germany, personally rang Ankie with the news.

"Andre gave the message that I should not be worried about the outcome of the whole ordeal," Ankie Spitzer revealed, "that he knew that in the end it would finish peacefully and that we would be together again. And then looking back at it we would laugh about it maybe, about this whole idiotic thing."[55]

"I was amazed," she added, "because here he is being kept hostage and he tells me not to worry." Andre finished his message by sending his love to Ankie and daughter Anouk.

Inside No. 31 Issa was preparing his men to leave just as Ankie was receiving the news from Munich. Before the operation the leaders of Black September had given the squad a list of countries they should try to reach with their hostages if the Israelis would not agree to their demands. First on the list was Egypt, "and if that was not possible, Morocco," said Jamal Al-Gashey. "The idea was to go to a big, influential Arab country with good relations with the West, so that later talks could be held with the West, which in turn has good relations with Israel, to achieve the release of the Palestinian prisoners from the Israeli jails."[56]

The Germans had no intention of allowing the terrorists to leave the country with their hostages; the Israeli government had strictly forbidden it. However, several of the German officials lied to Issa and told him they would begin planning his route out of the country. Issa seems to have believed their offers of safe passage. "Genscher . . . made guarantees that the German government would allow us to leave Germany with the hostages and take them to an Arab country," claimed Al-Gashey.[57] According to Walther Tröger, the Germans were adamant the terrorists could not be allowed to take the Israelis out of the country: "we would try to give the impression

to the terrorists that we'd let them fly out but try everything to then
kill them or bring them into prison before they could leave the country."[58] The Germans finally began their first serious attempt to rescue
the Israelis using force.

Plans for an assault on 31 Connollystrasse had been under way
even before Genscher and Tröger reentered the Israeli building. By
4:50 P.M., about ten minutes before Andre Spitzer was first brought
to the window to talk to Genscher, dozens of German officers had
put on sports tracksuits and crept onto roofs overlooking Connollystrasse in preparation for a possible assault on the house. The
news from Genscher and Tröger that there were a maximum of
five terrorists inside was a decisive piece of intelligence. A group of
Munich police officers were briefed on the layout of ventilation
shafts and told to sneak in through the shafts and kill or capture the
terrorists.

The selection process for this most hazardous of tasks was rudi-
mentary: "They selected them, asked them, have you shot a gun or
whatever? That was it, they had no training, nothing," said Ulrich
Wegener.[59]

Heinz Hohensinn, a thirty-year-old police Kriminalober-
inspektor (superintendent detective), was one of the officers charged
with launching the assault. A senior member of the Munich Sonderfahndung (Special Search Group), more used to fighting organized
crime, Hohensinn had been at Connollystrasse from about 7:00 A.M.
He recalls: "We, that is, the Special Search Group, were considered to
be the best-qualified unit to solve the issue, because we were trained
in hand-to-hand combat."[60] Together with twelve colleagues from
the group, he climbed up onto the roof adjoining and above 31 Connollystrasse in preparation for the assault, which was given the optimistic code name Operation Sunshine. "We were equipped with
training suits, armored vests, machine guns, and our regular re-
volvers. The aim of the action was to attack after getting the keyword
"Sonnenschein" ["Sunshine"], announced by the inspector. Then we
would have to enter the ventilation shafts and free the hostages. We
had already unscrewed the covers of the ventilation shafts."

The team had spent several hours obtaining and then studying

the plans of the building. "But we didn't know about the exact position of the terrorists in the building. We had plans about the position
of the ventilation shafts, we knew where to come out down there,
but we wouldn't know the position of the enemy at that moment."

Hohensinn and the other officers were deeply skeptical about
their chances of success. The men had agreed, he says, to do "whatever we could do to save the Israelis, the completely innocent athletes, and to minimize the amount of bloodshed," but he believes "it
would surely have been a suicide mission for us."

Peter Jennings of ABC television remembers watching from the
balcony of the Italian delegation opposite the Israeli building as the
Germans moved into place: "I remember when the Germans looked
like they were going to bring a commando team in and try to get into
31 from the top; I remember feeling very strongly that this might end
badly."[61]

It was an extraordinarily tense period. Thousands of spectators,
watching the police from a hillock just outside the perimeter fence,
grew agitated; some began shouting their support for the officers,
while others were heard yelling tactical advice as if they were watching a sports event ("Get down! Get down!"). Pressed against the
fence, a tearful group of young Jewish protesters holding banners de-
crying the hostage-taking began singing "We Shall Overcome" and
the Israeli national anthem *Hatikvah* ("Hope" in Hebrew).

But there were many more spectators watching the police prepare their assault. Dozens of television crews had their cameras
trained on the policemen. "They had exactly the right angle to film
us standing there ready to storm the building," said Heinz Hohensinn.[62]

Finally a German commander realized that television viewers
could see the police team moving into place and averted a disaster.
"We waited and waited on the roof," recalled Hohensinn, but the
code word was not given, "because — as we found out later — on
the building of the then East Germans there was a camera team that
filmed and broadcast live the events on the roof, including how we
were standing there, having already removed the ventilation shaft
covers, and ready to enter into the building to start the attack . . .

The pictures had already been broadcast all over the world, including my home, where my wife saw me anxiously sitting and climbing the roof."

The terrorists had also been watching events unfolding around them. Issa stopped planning how his men would fly out of the country and was seen scanning the roof, while the head of another terrorist kept appearing out of a window below Hohensinn to check if any officers could be seen.

Issa ran downstairs to the front door and screamed at the officials outside that unless the police were withdrawn immediately he would personally kill two of the hostages. "Later we discovered of course that there had been a TV in each of the athletes' rooms and that the terrorists had been able to follow the events on the roof live on screen," said Hohensinn.

Schreiber had no choice but to comply. At 6:10 P.M. the marksmen began to descend. Hohensinn said: "We weren't informed about the actual state of negotiations when we were on the roof. We were only told via radio to leave the roof immediately. Thank God the whole thing was cancelled, because there would have been disastrous consequences for us . . . I am happy and thankful to God that we never got the code word *Sonnenschein* because if we had I'm not quite sure if I would sit here today. We saw the whole thing as a suicide mission. We were not trained at all in fighting terrorists."[63]

As soon as Hohensinn and the other German officers were removed from the roofs above the Israeli building, the terrorists began to relax. The change of mood was palpable. Within a few minutes Issa was out front chatting with Graes. He gave her a cigarette and the two chatted amicably for ten minutes, then Issa wolfed down a banana and offered another to Graes.

"He eats a banana and gives her one," reads the Stasi's record of events. "When they've finished they throw the skins onto the stairs but the Leader goes in, picks them up, and takes them away."[64] For those watching it was a bizarre sight.

It was only after the failure of Operation Sunshine that the police conceded a rescue assault within the Israeli building was impossible.

The Arabs were too well entrenched. The building was a maze of corridors, any one of which could have concealed a bomb or a heavily armed terrorist. Termination of the siege would have to occur when the Palestinians were outside the house,[65] so the Munich police instead began concocting a plan to launch an assault on the terrorists as they transferred from the Olympic Village to the plane they had demanded.

However, the German government in Bonn was still desperate to avoid any further bloodshed. Chancellor Brandt decided to make one last bid for a peaceful solution and tried to ring the Egyptian leader, President Sadat, to broker a deal that could have resulted in freedom for the hostages and escape for the terrorists.[66] Sadat would not even answer the phone, and Brandt was left talking to the Egyptian prime minister, Aziz Sidky. "I tried to impress upon him that it was in our common interest to resolve the problem without further loss of life," wrote Brandt later. "I asked whether the aircraft the terrorists had demanded for themselves and their hostages could land in Cairo. Couldn't they be separated from their prisoners at the Egyptian capital? Sidky would not entertain the idea. In vain did I point out that further grave damage would be inflicted on the Arab cause. I was flatly informed that Cairo wanted nothing to do with 'those people.'"[67]

Aziz Sidky gives a completely different version of events. Sidky has claimed that Brandt asked him to give an absolute guarantee that if the hostages were flown to Cairo they would not be harmed. Sidky told Brandt that he could not offer an absolute guarantee (after all, he had no control over Black September), but would do his utmost to ensure the safety of the hostages. Sidky's failure to offer the impossible — a guarantee of safety — meant that the Germans could not allow the Israelis to leave. German officials then tried to exaggerate the potential threat to the hostages if they had been flown to Egypt, possibly to avoid embarrassing the Israeli government, which vetoed any suggestion that the athletes should be transferred to Cairo. A senior German politician later said that if the Israelis had gone to Cairo it would have been "certain death" for them. "How does he dare to say that the Egyptian government would allow the hostages to be massacred?" protests Sidky furiously. "Every sensible human would realize that he's wrong. If I accept to help, then I do it to rescue people's lives and not to kill hostages. We wanted to rescue the lives of the hostages. The fact is that the German government took another way. Everyone had to die, so they could get rid of the problem."[68]

Egyptian adviser Magdi Gohary also claims he has been told the Egyptian government "would have been willing to allow the Palestinian terrorists and their hostages to land in Cairo, and they would try to separate them in order to send the hostages unharmed back to Israel. This plan was not carried out." Gohary believes that Brandt asked the Egyptian government for ironclad guarantees that the hostages would not be harmed, an impossible demand. "You can only promise to do your best, but not that everything will happen as you planned it," said Gohary. Sadat was said to be so annoyed by the debacle that he even delayed, and nearly postponed, the ceremony of inauguration for the new German ambassador to Egypt.

In any event, Brandt's failure to obtain Egyptian help, and Sadat's refusal to even consider resolving the situation, meant the crisis was moving inexorably towards violent confrontation.[69]

Senior officials now privately admit this was when they became convinced it would be virtually impossible for the crisis to end without bloodshed. It was an agonizing time for the Israeli delegation, who all feared the worst. "We didn't know anything," said Esther Roth. "We got different messages at the time. We didn't know what was true and what was false."[70] German officials had gathered the Israelis together in one room and given them extra food and clothes, a television set, and a Hebrew translator. The anguish of the relatives was even worse. Scattered around the world, they could only wait for news. "I heard about the developments the whole day," said Ankie Spitzer.[71] She remembers that the hardest part of waiting, the torture, were the ultimatums. First 9:00 A.M., then noon, and all the time the families thought the terrorists were "going to start to systematically kill the Israelis." "And then noon passed and the ultimatum passed.

So then they put an ultimatum at three o'clock in the afternoon and then at five o'clock in the afternoon, and then at seven. And that was the hardest part of waiting, to see if they're going to do something . . . if they're going to shoot one Israeli after the other." As the minutes ticked by towards yet another deadline, she said, "it was like dying a little bit."

The Deception

By 6:00 P.M. plans to rescue the Israelis outside the Olympic Village were at an advanced stage. Initially the crisis committee decided to transfer the terrorists and hostages to the main Munich airport at Riem and then launch a rescue assault as the group approached an aircraft.

Walther Tröger disagreed vociferously: "I said, 'Well, isn't that crazy. We have another airport that isn't public . . . Fürstenfeld-bruck.'"[1]

For most of the year Fürstenfeldbruck was a quiet Luftwaffe base, but during the legendary annual Munich Beer Festival and the Olympics it was used to take some of the strain off Riem. Twelve miles from Munich, isolated and surrounded by woods and a six-and-a-half-foot-high fence topped with electrified wire, the airport was perfect for the operation, thought the officials.[2]

The crisis committee decided the terrorists and hostages would be flown in two helicopters to Fürstenfeldbruck, where they would be told a jet was waiting to fly them out of the country. The German police would then launch a massive rescue operation and kill or capture all of the terrorists.

A senior police officer was ordered to find a plane that could fly the terrorists out of Fürstenfeldbruck. Five police marksmen

immediately left the Olympic Village and flew to the airfield to prepare an assault.

As the officials developed the rescue plan, Zvi Zamir and Victor
Cohen, the senior Israeli intelligence officials, arrived in Munich
quietly on a commercial flight from Israel and were shuttled to the
Village to meet Genscher and Franz-Josef Strauss, the Bavarian prime
minister.[3] Zamir, an expert on counterterrorism, immediately offered
his help. But the Germans ignored him.

Zamir had developed Israel's standard response for hostage situations: keep the bargaining going for as long as possible so the psychological pressure on the terrorists eventually wears them down. Yet
he was treated as a mere observer by the Germans. "I said that the
longer we negotiate, the better it is because . . . we shall tire them
and the idea is to tire them," said Zamir. The Germans refused to
hear what he had to say. "They said, 'No, there is a plan. If we don't
carry out the plan, they threatened us that if we delay, then every
hour they will kill one of the Olympic team.'"

Victor Cohen had similar problems, although he was the im-
ported expert negotiator. "Nobody talked to me," he said.[4]

Both men believe that the Germans, particularly the Bavarians,
did not want the two Israelis around. Zamir recalls: "The Bavarian
officials were extremely hostile to us throughout, literally refusing to
talk to us. Genscher and our ambassador in Bonn, the late Eliashiv
Ben Horin, had to intervene again and again."[5]

Eventually, Zamir was briefed on the German plan. "The basic
elements were that the Israeli group would be flying with the terrorists in two helicopters to [Fürstenfeldbruck], which is not far away
from Munich."[6] The Israeli and German officials would follow in another helicopter.

At the airport, Zamir was told, squads of German officers were
already preparing to launch a rescue assault. "They told us that the
plan was agreed upon by the terrorists. Once they arrived at the airport, then two of their team, including . . . the head of the group,
would walk to the . . . plane," confident it was ready to fly them to an
Arab country of their choice.

Zamir approved of the plan. The Olympic Village looked like a series of beehives to him, and he recognized it would be hard to launch an assault on the terrorists while they were still in Connollystrasse. Taking them all to an open site where elite troops could then attack seemed like an "excellent idea."

The Israeli began to have doubts only when he realized that Genscher and other officials from Bonn seemed to have no influence over the Munich and Bavarian authorities. Zamir was discovering the reality of the German federal system: federal officials were impotent outside their own domain.

"In all the operation, they didn't say, they didn't intervene, not even [to] say one word," stated Zamir bitterly. "They were sitting where they were told to sit and were standing where they were told to stand."

Several of the Germans were also becoming uneasy about the operation: "I certainly was fearful of the outcome," said Walther Tröger, "because, having spent so many hours with the terrorists, I knew exactly that they were absolutely desperate, that they were really tough guys and they would not give in without defend[ing] themselves, and any defense from the terrorists would be to the detriment of the hostages."[7]

Hans-Dietrich Genscher was also skeptical. He did not like the rescue plan because it endangered the German helicopter crews, and he wanted more time to negotiate with the terrorists.[8] But the Bavarian authorities had already made up their minds. "I think they [Merck and Schreiber] were convinced that they could do the job," said Ulrich Wegener. There was tension between Genscher and the Bavarian officials, according to Wegener. "Of course there was — there was a certain conflict," he said, adding that Genscher tried to give advice and said the proposed assault should be reconsidered. "They were not in agreement."[9]

Zvi Zamir and even several German officials allege that during this time the Bavarians were coming under intense pressure from the Olympic organizers to resolve the situation. To this day the political machinations of the Olympic organizers remain the subject of dispute and controversy.[10] However, a speedy resolution of the crisis was the clear priority for IOC president Avery Brundage, a stubborn, stoical man who fought blindly to maintain the mythical "Olympian spirit." At 7:00 P.M. the IOC executive board began meeting in Munich for brainstorming sessions on how to react to the crisis. A memorial service for the two Israelis already killed was planned for the next morning, and the committee decided that — whatever happened to those Israelis still being held hostage — the Games would continue.[11]

From the beginning of his tenure as president of the IOC in 1952, Avery Brundage had sought to protect his treasured Olympic Games from political pressure.[12] There was no way he was going to allow the hostage crisis to interrupt the Munich Games,[13] a fact that Manfred Schreiber seems to confirm.

"The organizers of the Games naturally wanted the Games to resume as soon as possible, which meant that the situation had to be resolved in one way or another," revealed Schreiber, in an extraordinary acceptance of the IOC's power and influence. "The organizers have extremely specific wishes: they want peace and quiet, they want the event to take place unhindered, they want the event to continue without any delays. Our own aim, however, was to resolve the hostage situation in a gradual, moderate, carefully considered way and achieve a positive result. We were in no hurry at all. On the contrary. This didn't lead to any conflict, but it is undeniable that there are differing objectives when something like this happens."[14]

At 6:35 P.M., Genscher, Schreiber, Merck, and Tröger all walked down Connollystrasse once more to discuss with Issa how the terrorists and their hostages would be leaving Germany. The Germans told Issa they had arranged for two helicopters to fly the terrorists and hostages from the Village to a local airfield, where a plane would be waiting to take them on to Cairo. Issa and another terrorist would then be allowed to walk over to a waiting jet to make sure they were happy with the transport.

But Issa was not convinced. Why couldn't a bus take them directly to the airport, he demanded. Schreiber and Merck, who were both afraid the terrorists might stop the bus and take more civilian hostages, told him the traffic congestion in Munich was appalling, and thousands of Germans were roaming around outside the Village baying for Palestinian blood. The safety of the terrorists could not be guaranteed, they said. They also wanted more time to organize the flight. Issa was unconvinced.

"Listen!" said Hans-Dietrich Genscher furiously. "You can kill all of us right here, but that won't alter matters any; we need two hours to make ready for your flight."[15]

Issa hesitated, then agreed. The new deadline was to be 9:00 P.M. Negotiations over the precise details of the transfer continued at 6:48 P.M. and 6:58 P.M., but the German officials knew he would not tolerate another extension.

"Our aim was to drag out the proceedings for as long as possible, to wear down the perpetrators, and to establish at what point we might have the opportunity to liberate the hostages," claims Manfred Schreiber.[16] But his ploy failed.

Instead of wearing down their defenses, the continual delays and lies just made Issa ever more suspicious.[17] By 6:30 P.M. he was "nervous and worried" that he was being cheated, according to Annaliese Graes, and by 7:00 P.M., as he chatted quietly with Graes outside 31 Connollystrasse, he had grown even more fatalistic. He appeared outside the Israeli building holding a submachine gun, the first time Graes had seen him carrying anything but a hand grenade all day.

The Black September commander told Graes he felt threatened. He would shoot all of the Israelis if he had to, he said, and then he would take German hostages. In an apparent display of bravado, he even told her there were several carloads of "his people" waiting outside the Olympic Village ready to join the fray. Issa eyed the surrounding German officers warily. "I bet you 20 deutschmarks there will be an attack on us and I will lose my life."

By 7:20 P.M. helicopters were ready and waiting to transport the terrorists and hostages from the Olympic Village to Fürstenfeldbruck. Parked in a wide field behind the G-1 administrative building were two dark-green Bell UH-1D helicopters, or "Iroquois," dependable workhorses used to shuttle more than a dozen American GIs at a time around Vietnam.

Magdi Gohary, the Egyptian intermediary who had tried so hard to resolve the crisis, watched from the windows of the crisis management center in the Village as the ground was prepared for the choppers to land. Hans-Dietrich Genscher ran outside and tried to move a Volkswagen Beetle "to increase the space for the helicopters," said Gohary.[18]

The crisis committee was using the choppers like taxis. At 7:30 P.M., as thousands of tourists and locals watched intently from vantage points behind police cordons, Bruno Merck and Manfred Schreiber ran towards one of the Iroquois and took off in the direction of Fürstenfeldbruck. They wanted to see the airfield for themselves and check the preparations Georg Wolf, Schreiber's deputy, was making for the assault and rescue.

The flight took just ten minutes, and when Schreiber and Merck arrived they were quickly shown around the base and gave their approval to the rescue plan. By 8:37 P.M. they were back at the Olympic Village, engrossed in more discussions with the rest of the committee about the best method of attacking the terrorists. As they chatted a new plan began to emerge. Issa had been told his entourage would be flown by helicopter to Fürstenfeldbruck, but it might be possible to persuade him that to reach the two helicopters his men and the hostages must walk 180 yards through the warren of parking tunnels underneath the Olympic Village.

The underground would be perfect for an ambush, decided the members of the crisis committee. The five German snipers waiting at Fürstenfeldbruck could be brought back to hide in the shadows underneath Connollystrasse. When the fedayeen emerged with their hostages they could be annihilated with no risk of harming any German civilians. All of the Israelis were unlikely to survive, admitted the officials, but at least the Germans would have tried to save them.

Although they had reservations about the plan, Schreiber and Merck ordered the five snipers to be flown back to the Olympic Village, and a chopper took off immediately to fetch the team from the airfield. All that remained was to convince Issa to walk to the helicopters for the shuttle trip to Fürstenfeldbruck.

At 8:50 P.M., Genscher, Merck, Schreiber, and Tröger strolled down Connollystrasse to the Israeli building for a chat with Issa. They told him they had found four German aircrew who would volunteer to fly the helicopters to Fürstenfeldbruck, but they had to have his word that he would not harm them or take them hostage. Issa solemnly promised to respect their neutrality. He also promised that he and another terrorist would leave the helicopters when they arrived at Fürstenfeldbruck and check the waiting jet. He was in a generous mood. "I would like to thank you and your government very sincerely for doing everything in your power," he told Genscher courteously.[19]

But when the Germans suggested to Issa that the terrorists and hostages should walk to the choppers waiting 180 yards away in the Olympic Village, he was less than receptive. "[Issa] said that this might be feasible, but that he had to check it out first," said Schreiber.[20] The Germans thought he would accept immediately — they still considered the Palestinians complete amateurs.

Issa said he would walk the route to the helicopters and told the other terrorists to begin shooting the Israeli hostages if he had not returned in six minutes. With Schreiber, Tröger, and several other German officials, he walked down the stairs within No. 31, the same route Gad Tsabari had taken more than sixteen hours earlier to escape, and out below into the underground parking lot.

As the group started walking, German police officers stationed in the shadows tried to slink into the darkness, but Issa was no fool. "Gunmen of the German police were lying in the side streets of that underground street of the Olympic Village and when we approached they were crawling away," said Tröger.[21]

Issa may have seen one of the officers, or he may not. He certainly realized the Germans could turn the tunnel into a shooting gallery. He walked the full length, then turned to the waiting German officials and told them their suggestion was rejected: he wanted a bus to take the group to the helicopters.[22] The Germans wearily agreed. It was the end of their attempts to free the Israelis within the Olympic Village.

"Looking back, I can't say what the outcome would have been," said Schreiber. "The attack in the underground parking lot seemed extraordinarily risky in terms of casualties on our side. Had we proceeded, someone might well have said to us: 'Are you out of your minds, instigating a mass shootout down there?'"

The new demand for a bus gave officials a little more time to make preparations at Fürstenfeldbruck airfield, according to Schreiber. Hundreds of German officers were turning it into the perfect site for a rescue attempt, or so Zvi Zamir and Victor Cohen were told.[23]

"Dr. Wolf, my deputy, flew on ahead to Fürstenfeldbruck and made preparations for the operations there," Schreiber recalled. The Germans also sent reinforcements to the four other airfields within 20 miles of Munich, "because we couldn't be sure that the perpetrators wouldn't use force in order to make the pilot divert to another airfield during the helicopter trip," according to the Munich police chief.[24]

It was half an hour after Issa's abortive walk through the underground before the Germans parked a white sixteen-seater minibus outside the basement-level door to the Israeli building, ready to shuttle the hostages and terrorists through the dark parking lot. But again Issa was not happy. He told the Germans the minibus was too small.

When the Germans found a larger bus they realized it needed a driver with a special license; even at this crucial stage of the crisis the Bavarians insisted on doing everything by the book. Officials began hunting for a willing volunteer.

All this extra time was supposed to be used by the police officers at Fürstenfeldbruck airfield to prepare their assault. But the Palestinians were also preparing. They knew they would be at their most vulnerable during the period of transfer from bus to helicopter, and from the helicopter to the plane. "We knew of the possibility of an ambush," said Jamal Al-Gashey. "That was a possibility that had been worked into the original plan. The person who gave us our instructions told us to allow for the time it would take to get from the Olympic Village to Munich airport. He said that if they took us by bus, it would take an hour or slightly more, and that if we went by helicopter, it would take half an hour. He said that when going to the plane, we should take care, since it was a big airport with a lot of flights and planes. We also had instructions as to how to take the hostages to the plane, to search them first and then lead them out in small groups."[25]

Just before 10:00 P.M., a larger, dark-green bus with license plate 19–3583 turned into the Olympic Village, accidentally ran over some shrubs, and then finally parked underground outside the basement door to the Israeli building, the driver patiently awaiting his passengers.

At 10:03 P.M., one of the terrorists darted out of the door of the house with a gun in his hand and scanned the area. The blindfolded Israelis were then pushed out of the front door and loaded onto the bus, the nervous terrorists waving their gun barrels at the shadows, fearing a trap. "The hostages are removed in groups of three, closely followed by armed men who come down the stairs," notes the Stasi record. "One masked guard secures the third floor with a machine gun at the ready."[26]

As the bus pulled away heading for the Olympic Village plaza, the Munich police prepared to enter the house. At 10:10 P.M. a squad of armed officers crept towards the house, their guns trained on the blue front door, and pushed it open with their feet. Two floors above them officers vaulted over a balcony to enter the third floor. The officers were confronted by carnage. In the room where the hostages had been held, food and feces littered the floor and the white walls were splattered with blood. Yossef Romano was dead on the floor.

As the police were picking their way through the debris the bus carrying the rest of the hostages came to a halt at the Village plaza near the two helicopters. A frisson swept through the thousands of spectators just outside the exclusion zone guarded by the Munich police. For most of the day the crisis had been out of sight on Connollystrasse. Now the principal players in this lurid drama were on a stage in front of the crowd, visible to the world. Camera flashes sparkled as people immortalized the scene. Some onlookers jeered and pushed their bodies against the police barricades, but most just watched, appalled, as history was spun before their eyes.

Issa took no notice of the spectators. He left the coach, sauntered over to the helicopters and began checking them for traps with a powerful flashlight. "He even climbed onto the roof of the helicopter to see if there were snipers," said Magdi Gohary, who was watching from the G-1 administration building.[27] Apparently satisfied, Issa motioned to his colleagues to begin the transfer.

"It was a very bad and moving moment when the chained Israeli hostages left the bus towards the helicopters," said Gohary. Thousands of onlookers saw the Israelis being moved: Gutfreund, Halfin, Springer, Spitzer, Friedman, Shapira, Berger, Shorr, and Mark Slavin.

Poor Mark Slavin: the Russian-born Jew had only arrived in Israel four months before the Games. He had taken up wrestling to avoid being beaten by anti-Semitic bullies in his home city of Minsk and discovered he was a natural. In February 1971 he won the Soviet junior Greco-Roman wrestling championship. Slavin was a great hope for the entire Israeli team and was due to have made his debut at the Olympic Games at 9:30 P.M. on that very evening, in the Greco-Roman tournament at the Ringerhalle of Munich's Exposition Park. Instead the teenager was being pushed at gunpoint through the Olympic Village.

"After the Holocaust . . . Jews once again walking tied on German land," recalled Zvi Zamir sadly. "It was something I'll never forget in my life, but I thought, Well, if this is what we have to do in order to release the team, then everything is justified."[28]

Esther Roth was watching with the rest of the surviving Israeli delegation. "The terrorists stood there with rifles. They looked as if they felt like heroes dominating the world."[29] As camera flashes erupted, Roth and the Israeli team were angry ("It's our people we are talking about! It's not a movie!" she said). Gad Tsabari was standing nearby. "I've missed my flight," he said with dark irony.[30]

Hans-Dietrich Genscher was also watching, standing next to Zvi Zamir. "One, two, three, four . . ." he counted. Finally the Germans would know for sure exactly how many terrorists were ranged against them. Genscher gasped as he counted eight terrorists. All day the Germans had thought there were only five Palestinians in 31 Connollystrasse.

There were only five snipers waiting at Fürstenfeldbruck airfield.

"Honestly I wasn't very worried with this information because if there is a good plan to rescue the team then whether they are eight or nine does [not] make a lot of difference," said Zvi Zamir.[31] "It gave me a feeling that the operation is prepared down to very small details."[32] But it was too late to change the plan.

Under the full glare of dozens of television cameras and zoom lenses, Issa darted around waving his pistol, and the hostages and terrorists were divided between the two helicopters. Into the first helicopter, crewed by Pilot Reinhard Praus and Engineer Klaus Bechler, went Berger, Friedman, Halfin, and Springer, followed by Tony and three of the other terrorists.

With a screaming whine the helicopter's rotors began to turn. Issa ran to the second chopper piloted by Ganner Ebel and pushed in Shapira, Spitzer, Slavin, Shorr, and Gutfreund. Jamal Al-Gashey, his Uncle Adnan, and another terrorist were to act as their guards.

The world watched live on television as the aircraft rose slowly into the air, and by 10:21 P.M. both choppers had thundered off over the Olympic Village, their red flight lights twinkling in the sky.

"I remember thinking at the time this was going to be resolved," said Peter Jennings "It seemed like a denouement was coming but . . . I know at the time that I thought it was going to be resolved politically."[33]

International Olympic officials seemed to care little whether the crisis was resolved peacefully or not. The important thing was that the terrorists and hostages had been shovelled out of the Olympic Village, and the Games could now continue. Esther Roth was even asked if she would be prepared to run the very next day. "They approached me and told me, 'You will run,'" said Roth.[34] She was an emotional wreck, but a doctor gave her two sleeping tablets and she fell asleep.[35]

As she collapsed into bed the helicopters flew towards the air-field. On the outskirts of Munich they passed over a road to Fürsten-feldbruck that feeds into one of Germany's main autobahns. By the side of the road was a signpost reading: "To Dachau and Fürstenfeld-bruck."

Fürstenfeldbruck

As the terrorists and their hostages flew the twelve miles to Für-stenfeldbruck airfield, Genscher, Merck, Schreiber, Strauss, Zvi Zamir, and Victor Cohen clambered into the third helicopter and left the Olympic Village. The Bavarians obviously wanted to keep prying eyes away from the forthcoming rescue attempt. Both Zamir and Cohen had difficulty finding a seat in the helicopter. "I can tell you they did not want any foreign eyes to see this 'rescue activity,'" said Zamir.[1]

The German plan was for the two helicopters carrying the hostages and terrorists to fly slowly towards Fürstenfeldbruck, thus allowing the officials in the third helicopter to race ahead, land first, and take control of the rescue operation.[2] But the terrorists knew the most dangerous part of their mission was beginning. If the Germans were going to try to rescue the Israelis, they would have to launch an attack at the airfield. Jamal Al-Gashey was given strict instructions before the Palestinians left Connollystrasse: "There was an order from the leadership not to get involved in any military action and to resort to fighting in one instance only, if we were attacked, and then to defend ourselves vigorously and not die cheaply."[3]

As soon as the choppers were in the air the terrorists began to suspect something was wrong. It had all been too easy. "As we were

flying we began to get the feeling that a trap was waiting for us," said
Al-Gashey, adding ominously, "So we began to prepare ourselves."[4]

The Germans were also preparing. The helicopters were due to
land by the main airbase building in the center of Fürstenfeldbruck,
around which German officers were selecting firing positions for the
rescue operation. They had plenty of options. The main building at
Fürstenfeldbruck comprised three blocks: the control tower, with a
broad panoramic view of the airfield; a low, two-story, flat-roofed office block facing north in the direction where the helicopters were
due to land; and a small two-story fire station, with two large doors
opening into a garage, and a level above where firemen could change.
In front of the buildings the Germans had parked a blue and white
Boeing 727 jet, borrowed from Lufthansa, with its engines idling.
The helicopter pilots had been told to land in the area near the tower
lit with basic spotlights.[5]

The Germans had agreed with Issa before leaving the Olympic
Village that after landing he and another guerrilla would climb out of
each helicopter and walk across a broad sweep of tarmac to the 727
to check if it was suitable. Simultaneously, the two German officers
crewing each helicopter were supposed to be released by the terrorists and allowed to walk to safety.

The police claim they had decided the two Palestinians would
be allowed to get halfway back to the choppers after checking the
plane, and then snipers would open fire, cutting them down in front
of their colleagues. Other snipers would then pick off the other terrorists visible from outside the helicopters. The plan hinged on the
ability of the German snipers to down the terrorists within a few seconds of firing the first shots. And yet there were just five snipers
ready to face eight terrorists at Fürstenfeldbruck airfield. Not ten,
twenty, or even fifty, but five.

Snipers 3, 4, and 5 — Munich police officers — were supposed
to lie flat on the roof of the middle building, their guns pointing
down on the terrorists. Sniper 2, a member of the Bavarian riot
police, was told to position himself outside, behind and to the side
of where the helicopters were due to land, hidden behind the "signal garden," a low wall just a foot high. Sniper 1, another riot police-

man, was told to hide behind a truck parked between the plane and
Sniper 2.[6]

Sniper 1 was more experienced than his colleagues, and he insisted on being accompanied by another policeman armed with a
submachine gun.[7] Together they made their way out onto the field.

The snipers still thought they would be tackling only five terrorists. Even after Manfred Schreiber and his senior officials in the
Olympic Village had discovered that there were actually eight terrorists during the transfer from bus to the two helicopters — and not
five as had been thought all day — nobody warned the officers at
Fürstenfeldbruck.

Sniper 2 had been at Fürstenfeldbruck for several hours before
the terrorists left the Olympic Village and had actually been flown
back to the Village with his colleagues when the police began considering attacking the Palestinians in the underground parking lot.
When that was cancelled, the snipers were flown back to Fürstenfeldbruck with Georg Wolf, and told to return to the same positions
they had found earlier in the afternoon. "I had still not heard anything [to suggest] that there [would] be more than five terrorists . . ."
said Sniper 2.[8]

With the final resolution approaching, Sniper 2's orders were
simple: Manfred Schreiber told him that if shooting started, "everyone would have to continue shooting until it was certain that the terrorists were no longer capable of fighting. I understood that to mean
that the security, the safety of the hostages, was more important than
the life of the terrorists."[9]

But the five snipers were just one element of the plan to stop
the terrorists. What the Germans actually planned, it now emerges,
was for two of the expected five terrorists to leave the choppers
when they landed and check the Boeing jet. The five snipers would
then kill the remaining "three" terrorists, while police officers hidden on the Boeing jet would capture or kill the first two terrorists.

"We were supposed to act as a fake crew," confirmed Heinz
Hohensinn, the young superintendent detective with the Munich
Sonderfahndung (Special Search Group).[10] Earlier in the evening
Hohensinn had been one of the officers supposed to lead Operation

Sunshine in the Olympic Village. After it was aborted he and sixteen other heavily armed officers were then flown to Fürstenfeldbruck and asked to hide in the Boeing jet and attack the terrorists if they managed to reach the plane. Among the other sixteen was Friedrich Liebold, a twenty-four-year-old police officer. "I was chosen to volunteer for the crew," he said sardonically.[11]

The officers had serious reservations about the plan from the beginning. That number of personnel "appearing in such a rather small machine would have raised the suspicion of a trap for the terrorists, which would have made them throw their hand grenades," said Hohensinn.[12]

Rheinhold Reich, the police shift leader charged with securing the plane and preparing the assault on the terrorists, had similar reservations: "After arriving and viewing the Boeing 727, the officers began to be concerned about the fact that during a firefight with the terrorists the officers would have very, very slim chances of survival."[13]

Two of the "action commandos" in Reich's group were taken to be disguised as ground crew, while the rest were shown around the plane by a real Lufthansa crew who explained how to work the internal lights.

The commandos, who were actually police officers, were each given a pistol and seventeen bullets, and Reich asked for three submachine guns, which were given to his men with two magazines each.[14] The squad was dressed in the uniform of Lufthansa flight and cabin crew, but because of a shortfall several officers were forced to wear Lufthansa shirts with what were obviously standard police-issue trousers.

Although Reich and Hohensinn were already concerned about the dangers of their mission as they glanced around the 727, their fears increased dramatically when the team of officers began trying to find places to hide around the plane, which they discovered was fully loaded with nearly ten thousand gallons of fuel.[15]

Reich recalled: "It was clear to the officers in general that we were all in the highest of danger. The following arguments were brought forward: the officers disguised as pilots would be killed by their own fire; should it not be possible to immediately eliminate the hostage takers, the plane seats would not offer any kind of cover from any kind of bullets; a hand grenade which could be thrown by the terrorists into the rear of the plane — the part of the plane where the officers would have had to take their positions — would have meant that all officers would have been killed, or at least maimed; also the outer skin of the plane offered no protection against shots coming from the outside."[16]

By the time the officers had decided their position was untenable, the terrorists were just a couple of minutes away from the airfield. "We were all of the opinion that our mission in the machine was far too dangerous . . . and would be without effect," said Friedrich Liebold, a member of the fake Lufthansa crew.[17]

The German rescue operation suddenly degenerated into an obscene farce. According to Reich, "I thereupon cast a vote and after all the officers had voted for leaving the plane, we all left." Hohensinn agreed: "It was nothing more than a suicide mission which was cancelled unanimously."[18]

Reich ran to find Georg Wolf, the deputy commander of the Munich police, and told him what had happened. Wolf was aghast; a central element of the rescue plan had collapsed. "What am I to do now?" Wolf bellowed in desperation at his subordinates.[19] The choppers carrying the terrorists were coming in to land. Wolf was looking into an abyss, but there was nothing he could do. It was too late to invent a backup plan. There was no time to send a new team into the plane. The terrorists now had to be stopped before reaching the jet, whatever the consequences.

The helicopter carrying the German and Israeli officials had raced towards Fürstenfeldbruck, followed at a short distance by the two helicopters carrying the hostages and terrorists. The officials landed at approximately 10:30 P.M. Zvi Zamir, whose expert advice on counter-terrorism was repeatedly ignored by the German authorities, was immediately troubled by what he saw: "When we got to

Fürstenfeldbruck, it was very dark. I couldn't believe it. We would have had the field flooded with lights. I thought they might have had more snipers or armored cars hiding in the shadows. But they didn't. The Germans were useless. Useless, all the way."[20]

Zamir and Cohen sprinted into the main airfield building with Genscher and Franz-Josef Strauss and ran up the stairs to an office on the second floor, from where they could see the airfield. Schreiber ran to the top of the building to find Wolf, but, astonishingly, none of the arriving German officials thought to tell Wolf there were eight terrorists.

Within a few moments the helicopters carrying the hostages were above Fürstenfeldbruck and began circling the airfield. The Israeli officials tensed as they watched the choppers dropping slowly to the ground. They landed directly in front of the main building, around 100 yards from where Zamir and Cohen were standing with Genscher and Strauss.

Issa, Jamal and Adnan Al-Gashey, and another terrorist arrived in the "western" helicopter, along with five hostages: Gutfreund, Shorr, Slavin, Spitzer, and Shapira. At 10:40 P.M., all four fedayeen climbed warily out of the chopper onto the tarmac, their guns raised. Out of sight in the main building policemen peeked at the Palestinians, their fingers also on triggers.

Tony and three more terrorists then landed in the "eastern" helicopter with the other four hostages: Friedman, Halfin, Berger, and Springer. Tony and another fedayeen stepped onto the tarmac and surveyed the scene.

"We were watching from the second floor," said Zvi Zamir, but "we couldn't see them, [because] there was no light. I mean it was a very simple thing which the Germans could have prepared . . . if they want to do a [rescue] operation in the helicopters you should have lights!"

It had been dark at Fürstenfeldbruck since 7:45 P.M., and pitch-black since 8:36 P.M.[21] One set of floodlights was used to illuminate the Lufthansa jet, which the snipers had been given strict instructions not to shoot at because it was laden with fuel, and two more were used to light the helicopters. They were patently inadequate for a sniping operation but made the terrorists instantly suspicious.[22]

"We felt that there was probably some form of deception going on," said Jamal Al-Gashey. "Firstly, the trip took more than half an hour, then we found the airport completely closed, and we couldn't see many planes, as we had been told to expect."[23] The flight from the Olympic Village had taken so long the terrorists had screamed at the pilots to speed up. By the time they arrived at Fürstenfeldbruck Issa and his men were ready for a trap. On the ground they could see the 727 parked by the main buildings, but they also realized there could be scores of snipers hiding and waiting for them behind the searchlights.

As Issa and Tony assessed the scene, Schreiber and Wolf were desperately marshalling their men. Anton Fliegerbauer, a thirty-two-year-old Der Münchner Polizeiobermeister (City of Munich Police brigadier) in charge of a small squad of officers, was ordered to back up the snipers with his submachine gun. He ran downstairs to the ground floor of the control tower and positioned himself near a window facing the helicopters.

The five German snipers, meanwhile, were trying to draw a bead on their targets. They immediately found they had problems. The snipers should have been positioned so they could see into the interior of the choppers and attack the terrorists. Instead it was the German pilots who were directly in their firing line.[24]

Sniper 2 was particularly concerned about his positioning on the airfield. He had been told the choppers would land slightly to the west, and not fifty yards away, "directly in front of my nose," as he put it. "If I had known that they were going to be landing where they actually did land, I would have searched . . . for a different position for myself."[25]

The sniper was directly in the line of fire of his three colleagues on the control tower. He quickly realized that if a firefight erupted he could be killed by a stray bullet fired by another German officer.

The police had also not expected the helicopters to land so close to the Boeing, nor had they anticipated that even with the airport's floodlights, the helicopter's huge rotor blades would cast long, confusing shadows, making target selection difficult close to the craft.

As the rotor blades slowed to a stop Issa and Tony gingerly

began to walk the 160 yards between the helicopters and the Boeing 727 to inspect the plane supposed to take them to freedom. The German helicopter crews also stepped onto the tarmac. The terrorists had guaranteed the four German flyers would not be harmed or held hostage, and the Germans had been told to walk calmly away, keeping their white helmets on all the time.[26]

But as the four Germans began to walk slowly away the terrorists made it clear they were not going anywhere. "No words were exchanged," said pilot Ganner Ebel, "they just raised their guns."[27] The watching German officials were livid; now the terrorists had thirteen hostages.

Behind the choppers Sniper 2 tried to glance over the low wall to see what was happening but was worried the terrorists would spot him and be alerted to the trap.[28]

The time for action was now just moments away. Although the plane's engines were running, the police officers posing as the dummy crew had already left, and Issa and Tony were walking towards an empty 727. As soon as they were inside the Boeing they would suspect there was a trap.

"I am sure this will blow the whole affair!" said Ulrich Wegener to his boss, Hans-Dietrich Genscher.[29]

The official German version of events at Fürstenfeldbruck states that the officers who abandoned their positions on the 727 were merely acting as backup for the five snipers. However, the officers were absolutely crucial to the rescue, and the real German plan was for the men on the plane to capture Issa and Tony when they came to check the 727, at which point the five snipers would kill the remaining terrorists. Thus the men on the plane had been a vital component of a precarious and dangerous rescue plan. When they abandoned the plane the operation fell to pieces.

Issa and Tony clambered up the stairs into the plane and spent a few moments checking it for police officers and hidden booby-traps.[30] Issa guessed it was a trap. "They came back and were yelling," said Ulrich Wegener.[31] "They were running back to the helicopters."

Georg Wolf was lying on the roof above Wegener with two

snipers looking down on the helicopters, their guns trained on the terrorists guarding the German chopper crews. Further to one side another sniper had his gun trained on Issa and Tony as they trotted back to the helicopter. Wolf had no idea what Snipers 1 and 2 were doing because, astonishingly, none of the snipers was given a walkie-talkie. The other two had only been told that the snipers on the tower would open fire first, and they should pick their targets immediately and start shooting at will.[32]

Three terrorists were standing beside the western helicopter and another by the eastern chopper. Two terrorists were still inside the second helicopter, which had its sliding doors open.[33]

As Issa and Tony reached the middle of the tarmac apron on their way back to the choppers, shouting as they jogged, the other terrorists guarding the hostages were lifting their gun barrels, wary of a trap. At this point the sniper with his gun on the two Black September leaders had to move slightly to keep the terrorists in his sights. It was a fateful moment.

Wolf, an honorable man left in an appalling position by other officials, quietly gave the order to open fire. Immediately, two shots rang out from his two snipers, and the two terrorists guarding the helicopter pilots — Ahmed Chic Thaa and Afif Ahmed Hamid — fell to the ground, although only one was killed outright. The rescue operation had begun.

There was instant chaos. The four German members of the chopper crews began sprinting for safety in all directions. Issa and Tony began running back towards the helicopters, as the third sniper near Wolf opened fire on them. His first shot missed, ploughing into the tarmac near Issa, who steadied himself and then sprinted in a zigzag towards the helicopters. The sniper fired again, hitting Tony in the leg. He collapsed on the tarmac.

Jamal Al-Gashey and the other three terrorists immediately ducked into the black shadows underneath the choppers, rendering themselves invisible to the German snipers, and began returning fire with their Kalashnikovs. Battle commenced as the terrorists swept the airport buildings with bullets.

The firepower of the terrorists was awesome. They raked the

airfield with fire, pumping bullets at the main building, at the lights, at the 727, and at the fleeing chopper crews.

Bullets sliced through the room where Wegener was standing with Genscher, Zamir, and Cohen, shattering model aircraft on top of a cupboard. Genscher dived under a desk to avoid being hit.[34]

The terrorists were shooting wildly, but their bullets began hitting targets.[35] As the snipers had fired their first shots Anton Fliegerbauer, the young police brigadier at the base of the control tower, opened fire on Issa and Tony with his submachine gun. He had fired less than half the bullets in his magazine when a random shot from one of the fedayeen tore through a window in the control tower and hit him in the head. He died immediately.

Out on the airfield behind the choppers, Sniper 2 was still stuck in the line of fire, keeping shelter behind a low wall: "Immediately after the first shooting a hand grenade exploded near my position, only a few yards away from me."[36] The sniper glanced over the top of the wall and could see a man standing between the two helicopters "who was shooting . . . continuously in the direction of the tower." The sniper steeled himself as bullets whizzed around his head, then raised his gun. "I was just going to shoot at that man when I suddenly saw that a second person was running in a permanent zigzag towards my location and kept crossing my line of sight."

As automatic gunfire echoed around the airport the sniper aimed his gun at the man sprinting towards him and then realized it was not a terrorist but one of the helicopter pilots desperately trying to reach safety.[37] The pilot's life was saved because Sniper 2 had been warned the German flyers would be wearing white flight helmets. It was one of the few pieces of crucial information the authorities actually remembered to tell their gunmen. The pilot, Ganner Ebel, dived for cover by the wall, the sniper screamed across to him that he was there, and the two men sheltered together as the gunfight raged on.[38]

By now the German snipers on the tower were starting to return fire. Jamal Al-Gashey was hit in the hand and claims "my gun flew out of my hand."[39] It was probably a lucky shot. Ulrich Wegener said the Germans were firing wildly: "They were firing on everything . . . which was moving in front of the tower. They didn't see the targets, you know, they fired into the helicopters, and I only hoped that our people, and the Israelis, could get out of the helicopter. But they'd tied them together."[40]

Some of the German shots hit home. Another terrorist was shot in the chest. But Heinz Hohensinn agrees the operation was chaotic: "Nobody had an overview. There were shots and nobody knew where from and towards whom."[41] It was only at 10:50 P.M., well after battle had commenced, that one of the senior officers at the airfield decided armored support was needed, and several of the armored cars still waiting at the Olympic Village were finally ordered to race towards Fürstenfeldbruck.

Even Manfred Schreiber appears to believe the situation was out of control. He claims he had wanted the snipers to shoot Issa "in such a way that he would drop in front of his comrades."[42] Schreiber believed that having seen their leader killed in front of their eyes the rest of the terrorists would immediately surrender: "Unfortunately, [Issa] wasn't fatally wounded and so he didn't lie there on the ground as a psychological . . . monument, thus furthering our cause. Instead of lying there . . . he crawled to the helicopters." Issa eventually reached safety and began sweeping the airfield with machine-gun fire.

Schreiber admits that the German officials watching felt "paralyzed." "We had expected a kind of steady progression, beginning with my initial 'embracing' tactic [when he had considered taking Issa hostage early in the morning] and culminating in the exertion of psychological pressure on the airfield. We all felt paralyzed. The only person who exploded in rage against the perpetrators was the former Minister-President Strauss. He screamed at them and cursed them. The rest of us were incapable of doing even that."[43]

The litany of errors made by German officials at Fürstenfeldbruck is staggering. The five snipers at the airport, some of whom were approximately 100 yards away from their commander, were not issued walkie-talkies, an oversight of awesome proportions. In contrast, unarmed security guards at the Olympic Village had all been issued the devices.

Sniper 2 requested a walkie-talkie while he was still at the

Olympic Village and then repeated his demand on arriving at the airfield ("I was told none was available.").[44] Sniper 1 demanded a walkie-talkie at 6:00 P.M. while conducting a preliminary examination of the scene at Fürstenfeldbruck.[45] Ludicrously, the Bavarian authorities later decided there had not been enough time to obtain the walkie-talkies.[46]

Yet there were hundreds of walkie-talkies in the Olympic Village, and they were absolutely vital to ensure a coordinated assault by the snipers. Without them the rescue commander Georg Wolf was able to issue instructions only to the three snipers lying next to him.

The arming of the snipers with rifles with twenty-inch-long barrels must also be questioned. Some officials claim rifles should have been chosen with barrels at least twenty-seven inches long to ensure accuracy over the range the snipers were expected to shoot at Fürstenfeldbruck.

It is also alleged that several of the snipers' guns were not fitted with telescopic sights, although the order to obtain such weapons had been given as early as 5:40 A.M.,[47] and none of the officers had infrared sights. Not one of the snipers was issued a bulletproof vest or steel helmet (a bullet actually grazed Sniper 4 on the head), yet Schreiber and Wolf had demanded the vests and helmets as early as 8:45 A.M.[48] Bulletproof vests and helmets would have given the snipers a greater degree of self-confidence and may have encouraged them to expose themselves and secure better shots at the terrorists. German officials have never been able to explain these multiple failures.

There can be little excuse for the lack of equipment. The resources of the Munich police were vast: for example, there were twenty-four helicopters of the Bundesgrenzschutz (border patrol) and the Bavarian police at the disposal of the Munich crisis center. Yet the police were unable to provide their own snipers with adequate protection.

Tactical mistakes compounded these failures. Snipers 3, 4, and 5, who were on top of the control tower building, were not told where snipers 1 and 2 were positioned.[49] So Sniper 2 was placed in the firing line without his colleagues even being aware of his presence.

However, the most damning complaint against the Munich police and the Bavarian government relates to the number of snipers:
only five men were allocated the task of tackling a larger group of
heavily armed and committed Palestinian terrorists.

Some German officials have claimed there was "not enough
space" for additional snipers to hide themselves at the airfield. This is
palpable nonsense. The office complex at the Fürstenfeldbruck airbase consisted of three sections: the tower, measuring roughly thirteen yards on the northern front where the choppers landed, a
middle section of offices (forty-four yards), and the fire station (ten
yards).[50] Three marksmen were lying on the tower platform; below
them were three floors containing a total of fourteen windows facing
north towards where the helicopters landed. The middle section of
the building comprised two stories, a flat roof and sixteen windows,
plus two entrances to a cellar on each side. The fire station was
smaller, but it still had two large gates (each four yards wide) behind
which snipers could have hidden and a story above the main garage
with four windows facing the helicopters. Snipers should have been
spread around the complex (linked, of course, by walkie-talkies),
thus ensuring that they had a clear line of fire into the helicopters and
the terrorists guarding the hostages within.

It now appears that three well-trained snipers from the Munich
police were left behind at the Olympic Village, where two of them
thought they had been forgotten and asked to be released, and a third
was told he was no longer needed and drove home.

Another problem was the standard of police marksmanship
among Munich officers. Even before the debacle at Fürstenfeldbruck
it was known to be poor, and the authorities had allocated time for
extra training. Even Sniper 2 criticizes his lack of training for the
task: "I am not a sharpshooter. Unlike the officers of the city police
I was not asked whether I would participate in such an action or not.
I was just ordered. I thought it was certainly very, very bad that we
were practically cut off from the action leadership and that we had no
radio."[51]

The watching Israeli experts were astonished at the ineptitude of

the German rescue operation. "There was no rescue plan, no preparations, nothing whatsoever," said Zvi Zamir contemptuously. "There
[was] no light on the helicopters, there were no snipers, if they were
[snipers] I don't know where they were. I mean, it was just nothing."
Zamir had no doubt that a well-planned rescue operation at Fürstenfeldbruck by trained officers could have been successful: "I couldn't
think of a better place anywhere, because it was an open area." While
admitting "it doesn't mean that all the Israelis would have come
[through] unhurt," Zamir believed a majority would have survived.[52]

Zamir and Cohen, watching the first few minutes of battle unfolding
before them, were devastated by the events. They could not believe
the Germans were just taking potshots at the terrorists from a distance, as if they were shooting rats with air rifles. However, their expert advice had been ignored by the German authorities, and they
were unable to warn the government in Israel that events were not
going according to plan because of the battle. The Israelis knew that
without proper sniping equipment the only way of defeating the terrorists was to rush at them from all sides simultaneously. But they suspected that the Germans were not prepared to risk their lives, and
they were terrified the hostages would not survive the battle.

Desperately, Zamir asked Genscher and Strauss what was going
on: "They repeated the same phrases that I heard a few times: 'We
can't do anything,' 'This is not within our authority,' 'This is a Bavarian affair.'"[53]

But Zamir was not prepared to stand back and watch his countrymen die without trying to do something. With Cohen following,
he ran out of the room where the two men were watching the "rescue" to try to find someone in authority.

"What else? What are you going to do now?" screamed Zamir
at a police officer.

Outside there was deadlock. The Germans could not see the
terrorists under the helicopters, and they could not risk shooting too
close to the hostages inside. One of the senior German police officers
told the Israelis he was waiting for armored cars to arrive. The cars,

said the officer, would enable the German police to get closer to the action, and officials were cutting holes in the perimeter fence to allow them access to the airfield.

Zamir and Cohen decided time was being wasted and pleaded with the German officers to allow them to go onto the roof with a megaphone and negotiate with the terrorists in Arabic. "They refused at the beginning," said Zamir, "but then they said 'all right,'" but only if Cohen and Zamir spoke only in Arabic and other "stupid conditions which we agreed to."

A megaphone was found for the two Israelis, and as the terrorists fired sporadically from under the two helicopters, Zamir and Cohen ran up to the roof.

"Stop firing," hollered Cohen in Arabic at the terrorists. "The plane is ready for you, as you want. If you carry on you'll be hurt or killed. STOP FIRING!!"[54]

It was too late for negotiations. "Their reply was clear . . . They opened fire on the building, on the roof," said Zamir.[55] The two Israelis ducked for cover.

On the ground below, in the heart of the battle, two of the German helicopter crew were desperately trying to crawl to safety; another was playing dead, praying that he would not be hit by fire; and the other was pressing himself into the ground behind the low wall protecting Sniper 2. For the German officials watching it was a tragic sight; it was bad enough that Jewish foreigners were facing death, but several of their own men were under threat.

Yet there was nothing they could do. They had no adequate plan for saving the hostages or the German pilots and were unprepared to rush the terrorists from all sides. The deadlock could be resolved only by armored cars, and they were still on their way to the airfield. It turned out they were stuck in appalling traffic jams caused by the thousands of Munich sightseers trying to reach the airfield to see what was happening.

Ulrich Wegener was almost as distraught as the Israelis. He pleaded with one of the senior Munich police officers: "What are you going to do? You have to move your people there! Pull out the hostages! DO SOMETHING!"[56] But, recalled Wegener sadly, "They didn't do anything."

"I have no orders," a senior German police officer told him meekly.

"It was a really tragic story," Wegener said. "We could only look."

With the exception of the snipers, Georg Wolf had told the other police officers present at Fürstenfeldbruck not to open fire or intervene unless they were personally threatened.[57] So the standoff continued — the German snipers occasionally taking potshots at the terrorists, the Black September guerrillas raking the main building with bullets — for more than an hour.

At one point Sniper 2 glanced over the low wall again and through the darkness could make out a terrorist at the back of one of the helicopters occasionally moving. Despite the ferocious battle, he was close enough to hear the terrorists singing to themselves, apparently to keep their spirits high. But he did not open fire.[58]

The blunders continued. Even when a special "assault group" comprising heavily armed police officers finally arrived on the scene at 11:34 P.M., it landed by helicopter on the western side of the airfield . . . more than a mile from the battle zone. By the time they crossed the airfield and arrived at the control tower there was little they could do, and they were simply told to protect the senior officials and politicians in the control buildings.

At 11:55 P.M., well over an hour after the start of the battle, at least four armored cars finally arrived at Fürstenfeldbruck and began maneuvering into position at one minute after midnight. As the armored cars moved closer to the helicopters (Manfred Schreiber now claims he just wanted to leave them positioned near the terrorists "with the intention of . . . starving them out psychologically") the terrorists apparently thought they were about to be machine-gunned. "It all happened very fast," said Schreiber.[59]

Inside the helicopter parked on the eastern side of the apron, one of the terrorists began firing at point-blank range at the four hostages. Springer, Halfin, and Friedman died instantly, but some-how David Berger was only shot in the leg.

The terrorist then leapt out of the chopper, pulled a pin from one of his grenades, and tossed it back inside. Issa immediately reemerged from the shadows under the other helicopter and opened fire again on the airfield buildings. Officers inside dived for cover, but within seconds the snipers on the roof of the control tower returned fire on Issa and his comrade, killing them both almost simultaneously. It was too late.

As both terrorists fell to the tarmac, a huge explosion rocked the eastern helicopter. The grenade ignited the fuel tank and the heli-copter and captive Israelis burned.

As the flames licked across the tarmac, Adnan Al-Gashey slipped out from under the western chopper, climbed inside, and began machine-gunning the other five Israelis: Gutfreund, Shorr, Slavin, Spitzer, and Shapira.[60] Ulrich Wegener says he can still hear their screams.[61]

Zamir remembered sadly, "This was the end of the Israeli people in the helicopters."[62]

"I ran down from the tower where I'd been standing near the sharpshooters and ran downstairs to the tower exit," said Schreiber. "But by that point, the massive fireworks had already begun.[63]

The final moments of the battle were as chaotic as the first. Khalid Jawad, the soccer-mad Palestinian who had been sheltering under-neath the surviving helicopter, made a break for freedom, sprinting away from the airfield buildings towards Sniper 2, who was still hid-ing behind the low wall. The sniper raised his gun and fired several shots from a distance of five yards: "I shot this terrorist another three times while he was falling. In total I certainly fired seven shots."[64] Khalid collapsed on the ground just three or four yards from the sniper. "I could hear him moaning and gasping for air several times," said the German officer. Ganner Ebel, the German chopper pilot sheltering beside Sniper 2, heard Khalid "gurgling" as he died.[65]

Meanwhile one of the newly arrived armored cars was

trundling towards the helicopters. The commander had been ordered
to rescue the pilot of the western helicopter, but nobody had told
him Sniper 2 was positioned behind the low wall nearby. As the armored car moved forward its crew saw a man with a rifle around
forty yards away fire at Khalid Jawad. The entire operation was such
a shambles that the armored car opened fire on the armed man —
Sniper 2. Bullets zipped around the heads of the sniper and Ganner
Ebel. Then one bullet found its mark.

"The pilot screamed," said Sniper 2. "Almost at the same time I
felt that I was hit on my bottom." Ebel was hit in the lung and seriously wounded; Sniper 2 was shot in the buttocks. "It was not possible for me to call for help because I had no [means of making]
contact."[66]

The gunner of the armored car apparently realized he had shot
two of his own men (or perhaps he thought he had killed them both)
and he swivelled his gun away from the two injured Germans and
back towards the burning helicopter. Ganner Ebel tried to scream for
help, but it was thirty minutes before an ambulance arrived.[67]

Meanwhile a squad of unarmed airfield firemen, who had been
watching the battle from their station at the side of the main building, decided that if the German police were not going to do anything
to save the hostages, they would at least try. The base fire engine shot
out of the station and skidded to a halt a short distance from the
burning chopper. The firemen immediately began spraying the
chopper with a vast covering of foam, but at least four of the terrorists were still sheltering under the western chopper and opened fire
with their Kalashnikov rifles, driving them back.

As the terrorists shot at the firemen the German snipers on the
control tower began firing at their muzzle flashes. Another terrorist
died. Only then, remembers Zvi Zamir, at roughly 12:30 A.M. —
nearly two hours after the helicopters first landed — did the firing finally stop.[68]

The scene that confronted the two Israelis and the dozens of
German officials who ran towards the helicopters, desperately hoping
to find survivors, was sickening. Foam dissipated in the burning helicopter to reveal a scene of carnage. The top of the front half of the

burning chopper had been blown away by the force of the grenade explosion. Inside, several of the Israelis had been virtually fossilized by the intense heat.

Heinz Hohensinn was sent out to check whether there were any survivors among the hostages or terrorists. Cohen also ran towards the choppers. "I saw a lot of blood near the helicopter." "I looked into the helicopter, hoping that some of the hostages were alive, and I saw all of them. They were bound by rope and all of them were dead."[69] Police Chief Schreiber was also distraught. The scene, he says, plunged him into "a deep depression, which stays with you for the rest of your life . . . the rest of your life."[70]

In the chaos, police officers began counting the corpses and discovered that three of the terrorists were missing. "I didn't see the perpetrators escaping," said Schreiber, "it was the police officers who got closer who realized."[71]

The four armored cars raced off into the darkness to find the terrorists, followed by policemen with dogs. Two of the Palestinians were hiding in the foam surrounding the burnt chopper: one feigned death, another was quickly arrested racing away from the scene.

Hohensinn recalled: "A colleague . . . shouted to me that somebody had moved, so we came closer and turned the bodies."[72]

Three of the Palestinians, Jamal Al-Gashey, Adnan Al-Gashey (code name Denawi), and Mohammed Safady (code name Badran) survived and were taken back into a room on the ground floor of the main airfield building. "We arrested them and brought them in and undressed them," Hohensinn recounted. "They got undressed to their pants. One of them fell on his knees in front of us. He believed that the worst would happen to him — immediate execution."

According to Hohensinn, the terrorists were "terribly scared," but "all three of them actually were very happy to have survived. This was rather strange and unexpected for us . . . We always had thought of terrorists as suicidal, but these three were completely happy that they hadn't been seriously injured." One of the terrorists, Jamal Al-Gashey, had been shot through his hand, but the others were completely unscathed. Their clothes were taken away for forensic analysis. "We gave them training suits. They were very cold because it was evening, and also from the foam . . . Then they were taken away."

Outside, shell-shocked, Zvi Zamir and Victor Cohen wandered the tarmac, unable to believe what had happened.

Eventually helicopters arrived to ferry the federal and Bavarian officials back from the airfield to the crisis center at the Olympic Village. The scene was still chaotic. Victor Cohen recalled suddenly realizing he might be stranded at the airfield, a Jew, unable to speak any German, alone on a German military airfield near the bodies of his fallen countrymen.

As the blades of one helicopter began turning for a flight back to the city, Cohen ran toward it, thinking he would be stranded. Zamir was suffering the same indignity. "They wanted to fly to Munich and to leave us there, but Genscher and Strauss said, 'The Israeli general and his companion are here, we have to find where they are and to take them.'"[73]

There were more than 450 policemen at the airfield, with state police reinforced by officers from neighboring forces and even from the border police. It was the first time in German history all the different forces had cooperated.

The four members of the German helicopter crews all survived. Five of the terrorists died. One German officer was killed and several more were injured, at least two by "friendly fire." But not a single Israeli survived. The German "rescue" operation was a criminally shambolic failure.

Champagne Celebrations

From the moment the hostages and terrorists left the Olympic Village to fly to Fürstenfeldbruck, a media blackout was imposed on the closing stages of the tragedy. In the Village the siege was played out in front of the massed ranks of the world's media; it was global theater. Fürstenfeldbruck was the slaughterhouse, the dark end of the crisis, and no spectators were allowed.

For members of the Israeli delegation waiting back at the Olympic Village, and for dozens of relatives in the Middle East, Europe, and the United States, the most difficult period of the day began when the helicopters left the Village and disappeared into the night sky. The live television footage of Connollystrasse, which had turned the siege into one of the great media events of the century, suddenly ceased; nobody seemed to know what was going on.

Peter Jennings remembered the tension: "When the helicopters swept away into the night I left the building and I went back to ABC News headquarters, where we just basically waited. The entire broadcast had been devoted to this now. I mean, there was nothing else going on the air. So I just went back and waited. All I learned was that they had gone to Fürstenfeldbruck. And I learned what I thought were the details of a transfer to a jet that would take them out of the country."[1]

Most people in the Village — even officials involved in the negotiations — thought the crisis was being resolved peacefully. "Everybody was happy," said Magdi Gohary, the Egyptian negotiator, who felt confident the Black September guerrillas would leave Germany with their hostages, and the Israelis would then be released at their destination.

British television reporter Gerald Seymour left the Village before the terrorists and drove out to Fürstenfeldbruck with a camera crew. He left early, but was still stuck in a traffic jam created as hundreds of Munich sightseers drove to the base. "Hundreds and hundreds of cars. To see what? A plane leaving in the distance?" wondered Seymour.[2]

The Germans who arrived at the gates of the airfield and then spread out along the perimeter peering through the fence were in jovial mood. The world had come to their city for the Olympics, and now they were present to witness the departure of their most unwelcome visitors. "The problem was moving on; the Games were saved" was the prevailing thought among those present.[3] It was surreal. The German sightseers took their children, Thermos flasks, rugs to sit on; some even took collapsible chairs. And then as the helicopters carrying the Israeli hostages flew low overhead and landed hundreds of yards away in the center of the base, a frisson passed through the crowd.[4] Necks strained as those watching struggled to see over the fence and catch a glimpse of the distant action. They could not see Issa and Tony walking, half-running, back from the Lufthansa jet.

But then tracer bullets flashed through the sky. And the sightseers fell completely silent.[5]

Some German officials have claimed that the first burst of shots from the terrorists at Fürstenfeldbruck destroyed a crucial antenna on the control tower, preventing incoming and outgoing telephone calls. But reports of firing at the base slowly began to trickle out.

Hans-Jochen Vogel was among the officials waiting for news back at the Olympic Village. What, everyone wanted to know, was happening at the airfield?[6] He decided to call Fürstenfeldbruck to see what was going on. His first attempts failed — either the line went dead or nobody answered at the other end — but eventually Vogel managed to get through to a Munich police officer he had dealt with during preparations for the Games.

"What is going on at Fürstenfeldbruck?" Vogel shouted down the crackling line.

"It is difficult to talk!" the officer shouted back down the phone.

"Why?" queried Vogel.

"I'm sitting under a table, and there is shooting," said the man. "They are shooting. I can't give you any information."

Magdi Gohary was driven in a German army car from the Olympic Village to the local railway station as the terrorists were landing at Fürstenfeldbruck. He was going home, confident the crisis had been resolved without further loss of life. As he arrived at the railway station and went to buy his ticket the clerk had a small radio in the back of his office tuned to the local news. As Gohary stood in line he listened idly. Then the broadcast was interrupted with a newsflash: the first reports were coming in of shooting at Fürstenfeldbruck. Gohary paled.

Initial information from the scene was sketchy, but the first reports and broadcasts indicated there had been a sharp exchange of fire. Then rumors began spreading that some of the terrorists had been killed. But after the first reports the world was left without any reliable news as communication with Fürstenfeldbruck broke down. What was going on? Television reporters, journalists, officials, politicians and — of course — relatives, were all desperate for information: *What was happening at Fürstenfeldbruck?*

Then at 11:00 P.M., some twenty minutes after the two helicopters had landed at Fürstenfeldbruck and with a fierce battle raging across the tarmac, fate played its cruellest trick on the relatives of the Israeli athletes.

At the main gate of Fürstenfeldbruck airfield, where scores of journalists and German sightseers were gathering, out of sight and earshot of the center of the base, a male spectator or civilian — for reasons no one can now explain — walked out in front of the assembled media throng wearing an official Olympic hat.

"Everything is fine!" he yelled. "The hostages have been released!"[7]

In the frantic atmosphere outside the airfield, the rumor the Israelis had been freed spread like wildfire. The press, with its voracious
appetite for news of the hostages, took the spectator at his word, believing he was some sort of Olympic functionary.[8]

Bavarian police officers outside the gates, who were also cut off
from the events at the center of the base, heard the fake Olympic official's claim and reported the news back to their superiors. The rumors became fact as the officers passed them up their chain of
command. Journalists simultaneously passed the good news back to
their news desks.

In the space of thirty minutes history was prematurely written.
At 11:31 P.M., the Reuters news agency issued a dramatic stop-press
wire-report to the world: "ALL ISRAELI HOSTAGES HAVE
BEEN FREED."

After an extraordinarily tense daylong siege, the report was
siezed upon by the world media. It seemed to fit so perfectly into
their news schedules: the exhausted journalists could finish their bul-
letins for the evening on a positive note and get to sleep early enough
for another day of Olympic events. Everyone wanted to believe it
was all over.

As the first news reached Shmuel Lalkin, the head of the Israeli
delegation, he struggled to contain his joy. "We were so delighted
and joyful," he said.[9] All those who had escaped from the terrorists
were sitting together when they were told that the athletes had been
released. "This was a real joy. I mean, we all jumped and said, 'Okay!
They've been released!' We didn't know how, but they were released."

Soon the whole world knew. Vogel was standing with Chancellor Willy Brandt when a director from a German television station
arrived and suggested that Brandt might like to broadcast the news to
the German people. "The director of the second German television
system . . . said he [Brandt] should give the good news through his
channel to the public." But Brandt instinctively knew that all was not
right at Fürstenfeldbruck.

"No," he told the media executive, "I won't go on television without confirmation from my interior minister."[10]

As the good news spread through the Olympic Village, Brandt's officials were still trying to get through to the airfield to confirm the story. But by then everyone was repeating the report — it had to be true. Brandt and his officials compromised.[11] Conrad Ahlers, Brandt's urbane press secretary and the official spokesman for the German federal government, went on national and international television and announced the crisis had been resolved.[12] "I am very glad that as far as we can see now this police action was successful," he told interviewer Jim McKay on ABC television. "Of course," added the German, using a phrase that would later haunt him, "it's an unfortunate interruption of the Olympic Games, but if all that comes out as we hope it will come out . . . I think it will be forgotten after a few weeks."

The relief on Ahler's normally poker face was obvious. "For us Germans," he told the world, "it was a tragic situation that all this happened to Jewish people." Thank goodness it was all over, he said, "otherwise some of the old memories might have come back . . ."

Not everyone believed Ahlers. Walther Tröger, who had personally negotiated with the Palestinians, was one of the skeptics. He knew the Black September guerrillas would not surrender without a fight. "I don't believe it," he told his friends.[13]

Meanwhile, the rest of the world began celebrating the release of all the hostages. Later that morning the front page of the *Jerusalem Post* was dominated by the banner headline: "HOSTAGES IN MUNICH RELEASED — ALL SAFE AFTER GERMANS TRAP ARABS AT MILITARY AIRPORT."[14]

In the Four Seasons Hotel in the center of Munich the executive members of the IOC were told unequivocally that the rescue mission had been a complete success. Avery Brundage announced that the Games would definitely continue and went off to bed at 1:00 A.M. declaring himself "a relieved man."

In Israel Golda Meir drank a toast with her "Kitchen Cabinet" group of advisers and personally rang some of the relatives with the good news. Not everyone believed her. Miriam Gutfreund knew "something awful" had happened. Even as her children began celebrating, Rosa Springer also had her doubts: "The neighbors came over with flowers and champagne. They all said, 'It's so good that it's ended that way.' I said, 'If he's still alive he must call to inform me.' Because he knew that I worried. I asked them not to open the champagne or flowers. I said it was so nice of them. A pianist by the name of Kerner brought me the flowers he got in a concert. I promised them when he returns I'll throw a party."[15]

Her children were swept along by the celebrations. Alex Springer, the young son of Jacov, remembers their neighbor appearing with a bottle of champagne.[16] "We were very happy," said his sister Mayo. "We went to sleep thinking that all of them were rescued." However, "Mom was very skeptical . . . She was waiting for a sign of life to confirm this information."[17]

In Holland Ankie Spitzer also refused to believe the news.[18] One of the first to call her was the Israeli ambassador to The Hague.

"Ankie," he said, "I just heard the news. Congratulations! Everybody is saved and everything is okay!"

"Well, I heard it just the same as you heard," said Ankie, "but I don't believe it."

"It's on the radio, it's on television, why don't you believe it?" asked the ambassador.

"I will believe it," said Ankie, "the moment Andre calls me, because I know that even if he is wounded or if he is in bad shape the first thing he will do is get in touch with me, and the moment I hear his voice then I will believe you and then I will also be very, very overjoyed."

"Okay, Ankie," replied the ambassador wearily, "I'm going to sleep now, because it was such an awful day. The minute he calls wake me up, even if it is in the middle of the night, and then I would like the two of you to come out for dinner at the embassy and then we can laugh about this whole thing."

Despite the desperate belief of her parents and friends that the crisis had been resolved with no more Israeli loss of life, Ankie simply could not accept it. "So here I am, midnight, good news, people all over Holland were calling me, all my friends, my family, and I said,

'I just don't want to listen.' My father went and opened a bottle of champagne and I asked him to put the bottle away, and I said the minute Andre calls I will be drinking champagne and talking to everyone."

Then the agony began again. The minutes ticked by as Ankie waited for Andre to call. "It became one o'clock and no phone call from Andre," she said.

Ankie called the Olympic Village and spoke to Shmuel Lalkin. "Shmuel, what is happening?" she asked. "Where is Andre? Why aren't they calling?"

"Ankie, I don't know, we are here separately, those that survived, and the hostages are still over at the airport and we haven't seen them yet, but call in another half an hour," replied Lalkin.

Another dreadful thirty minutes passed until 1:30 A.M. On ABC television, and around the world, Jim McKay was telling viewers, "The latest word we get from the airport is that — quote 'All hell has broken loose out there,' that there is still shooting going on. There is a report of a burning helicopter. All seems to be confusion. Nothing is nailed down."

Ankie rang Lalkin again. "Now I have heard that some of them are wounded," the delegation leader told her. "Hang on a little bit longer."

At 2:00 A.M. Ankie again rang Lalkin for more news and was told that all of the Israelis had been wounded, and some of them were heavily wounded. "I called every half hour and every time the news got worse and worse," she said.

Meanwhile Jim McKay was warning the world that the reports were getting more desperate: "The first one we get now is that at least three Arabs are in hospitals and that a helicopter did burn. Still no word on what we really want, on the hostages . . ."

At 3:00 A.M. Ankie rang Shmuel and said: "Look, Shmuel Lalkin, if you know that something happened, then you tell me now, because I'm not Hercules. I have been waiting from seven o'clock in the morning and now it's three o'clock the next morning. I just want to know what happened to Andre!"

But even Lalkin had still not been told what had happened at the airfield. "Nobody knows here," he said apologetically and asked her to call back at 3:30 A.M.

The appalling truth was not revealed until just after 3:00 A.M., when Zvi Zamir and Victor Cohen finally arrived back in the Olympic Village and Zamir telephoned Golda Meir at home in Israel.[19]

"Golda . . . I've got bad news," he said slowly. "I've just come from the airport . . . Not one of the Israeli team is still alive."

Golda Meir could not believe what she was hearing. She started to protest: "The good news is on the radio, on the television . . ."

"Golda," interrupted Zamir, "I've seen them . . . We saw them in the helicopter . . . Nobody was alive."

Meir was devastated.

The bad news spread just as quickly as the earlier news of the hostages' release. Reuters released a correction at 3:17 A.M.:

"FLASH! ALL ISRAELI HOSTAGES SEIZED BY ARAB GUERRILLAS KILLED."

Jim McKay broke the news to much of the world. Looking pale and drawn, he turned directly to the camera and, as the latest news was fed to him through a tiny radio link in his ear, said: "I've just gotten the final word. When I was a kid my father used to say our greatest hopes and our worst fears are seldom realized," he paused. "Our worst fears have been realized tonight . . . They've now said that there were eleven hostages. Two were killed in their rooms yesterday morning. Nine were killed at the airport tonight . . . They're all gone," he added simply, in a phrase that echoes down the years. McKay was visibly weakened. "It's all over," he said. "What will happen to the Games of the XXth Olympiad? None of us knows . . . What will happen to the course of world history? . . . I have nothing else to say . . ."

The news sank in slowly. Relatives of the athletes and television viewers around the world had shared, to an extent, the same tragedy. Millions of people had spent the entire day watching the drama unfolding live on their television screen. They could not believe what they were seeing.

It was a terrible moment in television history. According to

Peter Jennings, "I was sitting with Jim [McKay] and Lou Cioffi, another ABC News correspondent, when the news came in that it had all gone to hell in a hand basket. It was like the air had left the room because I don't think any of us had given any time to thinking it was going to end like this."[20]

The news tore into relatives and the Israeli survivors. "I mean, this was a very hard situation for everybody," said Shmuel Lalkin.[21] "Whether you're a leader or you're an athlete, this was too much for us. Five minutes before, they were all released. Five minutes later, they were all dead."

Ankie Spitzer was one of those glued to the television. She had been supposed to call Shmuel Lalkin in Munich at 3:30 A.M. to find out what had happened to her beloved husband, "but I didn't have to call at 3:30, because ten minutes later on television came the announcement that all of the Israelis were killed, all of the hostages, not one was saved."[22]

Ankie rang the Olympic Village, desperately hoping the reports were incorrect. Her call was answered by Dov Atzmon, a journalist with *Yediot Aharonot* of Tel Aviv. Atzmon did not need to deliver a long speech. He struggled for the right words, knowing they would shatter her life.

"Ankie," he said simply, his voice crackling down the line, "I am with you."[23]

The young wife, a new widow, understood immediately. "Then the mourning broke out in my house, in my family, my brothers and my sisters."[24]

It was dawn by the time the news broke in Israel. "I was cold and couldn't sleep the whole night, although I didn't know exactly what had happened," said Rosa Springer. At first light she heard the doorbell and ran downstairs. It was two family friends — a member of the Israeli team and his father — who had been monitoring the international news all night. The athlete broke the dreadful news. "He told us that a mistake was made," said Rosa, "everybody was murdered, and among them was my husband."[25]

Her daughter Mayo remembers the sense of utter devastation: "I didn't know what to do with myself. From this great joy and relief that we felt, you're falling down to the lowest point. There is no lower to go."[26]

In Munich German officials were also devastated. Vogel remembers there was silence when the news came in. "It was terrible," he said.[27]

The sense of panic among German officials was palpable. Their blunders had been laid bare. The hostages had died because of German incompetence leading to a protracted firefight. The world then had been informed the hostages were all safe. The good news had then been retracted and replaced by the awful truth. Could anything else possibly have gone wrong?

At 3:00 A.M. German officials had sat down in front of two thousand journalists packed into the press center at the Olympic complex. Among those present were Bruno Merck, Manfred Schreiber, Hans-Dietrich Genscher, and Georg Wolf. With constant pauses for translations into English and French, Merck spent fifteen minutes laboriously detailing negotiations between the Germans and the terrorists.

It was all the fault of the Jews and the Arabs, according to the Germans. The terrorists and their nine Israeli hostages could have flown from Munich to Egypt if the Egyptian government had guaranteed the safe release of the Israelis immediately after their arrival. But Willy Brandt had failed to obtain a guarantee of their safety by telephone from the Egyptian prime minister, and the order had been given to attack the terrorists after they landed at Fürstenfeldbruck.

After Merck finished speaking, Schreiber took questions from the stunned audience. He claimed everyone involved in the operation knew "the chances of success were small," but he said Israel had been fully informed of the plans for an ambush at the airport and was aware that there was a high possibility of failure.

According to Schreiber, there was little the police could do. At first they had considered storming the building but rejected the idea as too risky. Then, he said, they had thought about isolating the terrorists from their prisoners in the underground parking lot while all were being escorted to the helicopters. That plan was also scrapped because the terrorists had demanded a bus for transportation to the airport. "So the last chance was to attempt to get at the Arabs at the airfield. That was the plan we went for."

Schreiber had flown to Fürstenfeldbruck in a third helicopter and said he was standing at the entrance of the main airport building when the first shots rang out. "In fact I was standing next to the policeman who was shot in the head, and was myself fired at. By then, I could not control the situation any more."

Captain Joseph Kistler, a Munich police spokesman, initially said the police did not fire the first shot that began the airfield bloodbath. Kistler claimed one of the terrorists was first to fire, shooting one of the helicopter pilots: "Somewhere between the helicopter and the plane the terrorist got nervous and shot the pilot." Only later did Schreiber admit that police at the airport had fired first, but then said the order was given by a senior police officer only when it became clear the terrorists had spotted police marksmen lying in wait.

Schreiber insisted: "The hostages could only have been saved if their captors had made mistakes. Our chances of freeing them were virtually nil. We had no influence on the Israeli government nor on the terrorists." Schreiber was adamant: the terrorists were fanatical, "no amateurs," and thus virtually unstoppable. "Some people say that police mistakes caused the death of the hostages. But it was the other way round. The hostages died because the terrorists made no mistakes."

However, the Fürstenfeldbruck massacre was not the first time Schreiber's leadership had been questioned. His force had been accused of being trigger-happy before, most notably in a notorious bank siege the previous August when a young female hostage was accidentally killed by police. "Criminals must realize that Munich is not a city which can be held to ransom," Schreiber had reportedly said then — prophetically as it turned out.

Other German forces also seemed trigger-happy. Three months before the Munich Olympics, Iain Macleod, a Scottish businessman, had been shot and killed in his apartment in Stuttgart by a plainclothes detective. Police wrongly believed Macleod was involved with the Baader–Meinhof terrorist gang and that his apartment was occupied by a violent group of anarchists. Macleod was alone and asleep when he was machine-gunned to death. A month later police in Duisburg killed a drunken moped rider when he ignored an order to stop at a roadblock and raise his hands. Around the same time three policemen were killed during a furious gun battle inside the apartment of a suspected armed robber.

Palestinian activists involved in the attack are all to ready to portray the German police as the aggressors. "We intended a bloodless operation," claimed Abu Daoud, one of the men behind the attack. "The plan was for international pressure to be brought to bear through five hundred million TV sets, so that the Israeli government could not get away with stubbornly pursuing its own agenda without giving any thought to other human issues . . . We really never intended the bloodshed. Our plan was for it to pass peacefully. We even planned for a safety valve, that in the event of everything being refused, we would move the hostages to another Arab country and release them there."[28]

The fedayeen "were to ask for the release of prisoners from prisons in the occupied zone, to wait a day or two maximum, and then, if there was any obstinacy from the Israeli side, to arrange with the German authorities for a plan to take them and the Israeli athletes to another country, specifically where was left open, but to choose an Arab state, Morocco, Algeria, Egypt, countries we could put pressure on for the release of our people. When they arrived there, they were to surrender their weapons, release the hostages, and give themselves up to the authorities of that country. Unfortunately, they were never given the opportunity to do this." Daoud describes the "rescue" operation at the airport as an ambush. The Palestinians, he says, "defended themselves and a gun battle ensued."

While it seems unlikely that the Palestinians would have let the Israelis go, since they could not afford another failed terrorist attack, the debate is rendered hypothetical by the shambolic German "rescue" mission.

Even Willy Brandt later seemed to admit that it was a complete fiasco: "My disappointment at the time was intense, first because the Olympics on which we had expended so much loving care would not go down in history as a happy occasion — indeed, I was afraid that our international reputation would be blighted for many years — and secondly because our counter measures had proved so abortive. Some critics referred, not without reason, to their 'down-right amateurism.'"[29]

With all the Israeli hostages killed, the torment of the captured athletes was replaced by the anguish of the survivors and relatives. The German authorities asked Shmuel Lalkin, as head of the Israeli delegation, to fly to Fürstenfeldbruck and identify the bodies of the athletes. Dawn had not broken when Lalkin and a doctor were flown by helicopter along the same route the hostages had taken a few hours earlier. "We saw it all," said Lalkin. "It was a hard . . . picture. Very hard. This was . . . really horrifying."[30]

In Holland, meanwhile, Ankie Spitzer was desperately trying to arrange a flight to Munich.[31] It was the only thing on her mind. In the early hours of the morning she rang the Israeli ambassador to The Hague at home.

"Did Andre call?" said the ambassador sleepily. "I told you that he would call."

"No," said Ankie sadly, "he did not call. You slept but everybody is killed. Will you please send a car for me, because I have to get to the airport, and arrange a flight for me . . . I have to go back to Munich."

In the Olympic Village many athletes went straight to bed after hearing the first reports that the hostages had been released. It had been an exhausting day. For others though, sleep was impossible. "We stayed up all night," said Gad Tsabari. "We couldn't sleep even one minute."[32]

Esther Roth had been sedated the night before, when the pain of knowing that Amitzur Shapira was being held at gunpoint became unbearable. She awoke in a daze early in the morning. "People were entering my room, but nobody dared to tell me what happened. They all knew and I could tell from their expressions . . . that something had happened. People looked down. They didn't know how to tell me the horrible news."[33]

Few of the relatives, survivors, and senior officials can remember exactly what they did in the hours immediately after hearing news of the massacre. Most were shell-shocked — their suffering magnified by the initial belief that the hostages had been released.

The murders of Moshe Weinberg and Yossef Romano at the outset of the Palestinian assault were supposed to be commemorated at a 10:00 A.M. memorial service in the Olympic Stadium. As dawn broke over the Village, officials announced that the other nine Israelis and Anton Fliegerbauer, the German police officer murdered at Fürstenfeldbruck, would also be remembered.

Ankie Spitzer arrived just in time for the service. She was met at the airport and then taken to the Olympic Stadium. There were just a few minutes before the service was due to start, and Ankie had to run through the Village towards the stadium. As she did she glanced from left to right and could see athletes limbering up and training for their events. "I said, 'This is surreal!' I'm running through the Olympic Village and people are training and I'm running to a memorial service of eleven athletes who were just murdered. How are they still doing sports? I could not understand it."[34]

The crowd at the memorial service in the Olympic Stadium that morning was devastated by the events of the previous thirty hours. Several heads of state were among the seventy thousand present, and the American athlete Jesse Owens and Sou Kitel of South Korea, both heroes of the 1936 Olympics, wept openly to the strains of the second movement of Beethoven's *Eroica*. The Olympic spirit had been shattered.

Eleven seats were left empty in memory of the dead. The surviving Israelis, including Gad Tsabari, still wearing a pair of flip-flops he had been given by the German police the previous morning, found the memorial service nearly unbearable. "Everybody was crying," recalled Shmuel Lalkin. "It was very hard to be there."[35]

As head of the Israeli delegation, Lalkin was called upon to deliver a speech to the assembled thousands and the millions watching on television. "I said that on behalf of the Israeli sports authorities, the athletes, coaches, and the Israeli government . . . we will come back to the Olympic Games, although we lost eleven of our best athletes, and coaches, in Munich."

Then Avery Brundage, addressed those present and those watching on television: "Every civilized person recoils in horror at the barbarous criminal intrusion of terrorists into peaceful Olympic precincts. We mourn our Israeli friends . . . victims of this brutal assault. The Olympic flag and the flags of all the world fly at half mast. Sadly, in this imperfect world, the greater and the more important the Olympic Games become, the more they are open to commercial, political, and now criminal pressure."

And then Brundage lost any remaining vestige of sensitivity: "The Games of the XXth Olympiad have been subject to two savage attacks. We lost the Rhodesian battle against naked political blackmail. We have only the strength of a great ideal. I am sure that the public will agree that we cannot allow a handful of terrorists to destroy this nucleus of international cooperation and goodwill we have in the Olympic movement." With a defiant flourish, Brundage famously added: "The Games must go on, and we must continue our efforts to keep them clean, pure, and honest and try to extend the sportsmanship of the athletic field into other areas. We declare today a day of mourning and will continue all the events one day later than originally scheduled."

The elderly American had been unable to resist making a dig at African Olympic representatives with his reference to "naked political blackmail" regarding their attempts to keep the racist Rhodesian state out of the Games. He also upset the millions mourning the dead Israeli athletes by equating the Fürstenfeldbruck massacre with what had been simply a healthy debate over Rhodesian participation. Even those who agreed with Brundage's comments on the importance of keeping the Games going were outraged and upset by his speech.[36] Lord Killanin, his successor, later wrote: "It was not what he said that was objectionable in itself, but the occasion on which he said it."[37]

Other dignitaries also failed to show the memorial service the respect it deserved. The Duke of Edinburgh, no stranger to controversy, was seen on television laughing and conversing with colleagues while wearing the red jacket of a senior IOC official. Arab teams boycotted the service, remaining in the Olympic Village, and officials from the Lebanese team told journalists, "We did not go to the stadium. We are confined to our quarters by our chief of mission." The response from the Saudi team was more outrageous: "What service? What shootings?"

Ankie Spitzer, Moshe Weinberg's mother (an elegant lady who lived close to Munich), and Carmel Eliash, a cousin of Weinberg who travelled to the Games as a tourist from Israel, were the only relatives of the murdered athletes present at the memorial service. Both women maintained extraordinary dignity behind dark glasses.

When the service ended the crowd dispersed, leaving behind a small group of mourners, high in the stands, surrounding the spot where Carmel Eliash was still sitting. It had all been too much for him. His body sagged slightly, his head was thrown back, and his mouth gaped open at the heavens. Carmel, a fit forty-year-old, had suffered a massive heart attack during Shmuel Lalkin's speech and died in his seat. The Munich tragedy had claimed another Jewish victim.

When the service was over Ankie went back to 31 Connollystrasse with the surviving athletes and waited while they went inside the building to collect their personal belongings.[38] Even in the first hours of her grief, Ankie wanted to know exactly what had happened.

"Okay, I'm here, so I would like to take Andre's personal belongings," she told German and Israeli officials.

"No, you're not going into his room because that's the room where they were all kept hostage, and that's where they shot Yossef Romano," she was told.

"I have to go and get his clothes and the things that he left behind," Ankie told the officials defiantly. She could not be stopped.

As she walked into the apartment and looked up she could see blood coagulating on the stairs. "I said, 'If the staircase looks like this, how is it going to look inside?'"

"Ankie, do not go up, do NOT go up," said officials.

But Ankie refused to listen. She desperately needed to see where her husband had been held hostage. Ankie followed the trail of blood on the stairs back to a pool that had soaked the floor in the room where Yossef Romano's corpse had been left during the day.

Ankie remembered: "I saw what happened with my own eyes. I saw what they did to these hostages. It looked terrible there. I never forget the chaos in that room." It was a scene of devastation, a room full of abandoned food cartons, blood, feçes, and a stench of death and terror. Bits of body tissue and brain were splattered across the wall, along with four huge holes were bullets had passed through Yossef Romano's body and gouged out chunks of plaster.

"The rubble, the blood, the incredible chaos — I can still see it in front of my eyes," said Ankie. "And I stood there and I said to my-self . . . if Andre sat here with his friend dying in front of his eyes, tied with his hands and his feet to the bed there, and to look around in this room, I said if this is where he spent his last twenty-one hours, somebody is going to pay for this."

As she stood amid the carnage, Ankie solemnly swore she would not rest until she had secured retribution. "I'm still looking for those people that have to pay the price. I'm still wanting them to pay the price for what they did then."

The Mourning Begins

*E*ven as the memorial service in the Olympic Stadium was ending, preparations were being made to airlift the remains of the eleven athletes back to their relatives in pinewood coffins. Jewish tradition dictates that the bodies should be covered in prayer shawls, but some of the bodies were so badly charred and mutilated this was a difficult task.

While David Berger's body was flown home to his family in the United States on a U.S. Air Force jet sent by President Nixon, the bodies of the other ten athletes were flown home to Israel in an El Al Boeing. The coffins arrived at Lod Airport, twelve miles southeast of Tel Aviv, at 11:45 A.M. on September 7, amid sweltering heat. All shops in the country were closed, work in government offices and ports stopped, and ships sounded their horns for hours.

Esther Roth, who travelled on the same plane as the corpses, remembers it was a "very difficult day for us."[1]

Tuvia Sokolovsky, the weightlifter who managed to escape from 31 Connollystrasse via a window as Black September arrived at the front door, travelled on the same flight. Almost immediately he had to confront feelings of "guilt" because he had survived the attack while others had died: "I came back to Israel on my own. I lost my best friends there. There were five of us and I was the only weightlifter who returned."[2]

Henry Herskowitz, the Israeli sharpshooter who had carried the national flag during the Olympic opening ceremony, suffered the same emotional torment: "It was horrible. We returned to Israel alive and well and the others returned in coffins." Herskowitz's wife ran to greet and kiss him. "I told her that I was well and asked her to go away. I felt so bad. I saw the rest of the families getting coffins and I felt guilty for being alive. I thought 'Why do I deserve to be alive while they are back in coffins?'"[3]

The athletes sobbed as they watched the coffins containing their colleagues being unloaded. Then it was time for the families to begin their grieving. For Ankie Spitzer, who had been virtually alone in her grief in Munich, it was the first time she had met other relatives of the dead. "Suddenly I saw the grief of all the families who were waiting for the coffins to come back." She stepped out of the plane to breathe Israeli air but felt such an outpouring of emotion that she went back inside. Some forty-five hundred people were at the airport waiting to receive the coffins. "I really had to get a hold of myself to get down the stairs of the plane and meet all the other families. That was hard; it was very, very hard to see the grief. As a person from Holland, I wasn't used to that . . . very outgoing type [of] grief. It was very difficult for me to connect to that because I was not raised that way . . . It was terrible."[4]

Still Ankie felt very much alone at the airport. After the memorial service in Munich she had phoned her parents' home in Holland to check that baby Anouk was well: "I phoned my parents' house and there was no answer. And I phoned my brother's house and my sister's house, and nobody was there. And then I phoned the hospital to ask if Anouk was all right and they said, 'She's not in the hospital any more.'" Ankie was incredulous.

"So where is she?" Ankie demanded to know.

"We have been given a number that you have to call," said the hospital official. "They will have the answer for you."

When Ankie called the number she was put through to the

Israeli embassy in The Hague. "They said we have decided to evacuate your whole family for an unknown period because your parents got threats, four threats that we also taped, probably from Germany, from a German-speaking person with an accent, asking where the baby was."

It was the stuff of Jewish nightmares. After all Ankie was going through, now someone calling from Germany was threatening the life of her baby daughter. Security officials at the Israeli embassy, fearing that Black September terrorists might try to kidnap Anouk and ransom her for the freedom of the three remaining Palestinians captured at Fürstenfeldbruck, had taken her away. It meant that when Ankie arrived in Israel with the coffin of her husband she had no immediate family support. Instead, other relatives offered support and comfort. Nobody was alone as the entire nation grieved.

But Ankie Spitzer's torment was prolonged. Israeli security officials decided to put the whole family under protection. "The same evening of the funeral I sat in a long meeting with all kinds of people who said to me, 'Maybe the threats are nothing, maybe it's very serious.'" The security officers did not want to take any chances. Anouk, they said, was "going to stay in Holland as long as we decide." Ankie was not even able to speak to her family in Holland in case terrorists traced the call. It would be three weeks before Anouk was flown to Israel to be reunited with her mother.

For Mayo Springer, the daughter of Jacov, one of the most painful moments of the day was seeing all the coffins standing in rows next to each other at the airport. She is still tormented by the knowledge she was never able to bid farewell to her father. "They all got there in coffins so it was impossible to approach and say 'Goodbye.' You couldn't even look at him and say 'The man is dead.'"[5] Her suffering was just beginning.

It was only when the bodies of the ten athletes were transported from Lod Airport for burial that many relatives finally began to understand that their loved ones would never be returning alive from Germany. Until then the tragedy had all seemed so unreal, so impossible.

As a line of army trucks left the airport bearing the coffins and parted to go to individual cemeteries across Israel, the country began to mourn. Mayo's mother, Rosa Springer, was in such a state of shock that she says she "didn't function," but the mass of mourners at the funeral — "so many people" — still seared itself into her mind: "I remember the screaming. So many people who knew him, especially the youth group from Jaffa, where he was the head of sports, and the parents of those youths. They were so sad." When the ceremonies were over she suffered a mental collapse. "For three weeks I could hardly function. I used to cry a lot, and I got a lot of injections."[6]

Ilana Romano entered a similar dreamlike state of shock: "I couldn't stand on my feet," she said. Ilana was helped to Yossef's funeral by a doctor who gave her doses of tranquillizers. "I felt very comfortable, and I used to close my eyes and say, 'Oh, it's only a dream. This is not real. How could they take Yossef away from me?'" It was the screams of other mourners that made her realize it was reality. "In those moments the pain was intolerable," she said.[7]

Pain and grief soon turned to fury. Within hours of burying their husbands Ankie Spitzer and Ilana Romano had roused themselves from their mourning and vowed to discover exactly what had happened in Fürstenfeldbruck. "I came back home during the funerals [and] I swore one thing . . . that I will put all my energy and efforts, every ambition will be delegated, to the horrible thing that happened in Munich," said Ilana Romano. "I'll make people remember it and I won't let them forget."

Ilana wanted to see her daughters and share the pain. Relatives tried to persuade her to relax and take things calmly. "No way," she told them.

She sat on the edge of her bed as her three young daughters, six-year-old Oshrat, four-year-old Rachel, and five-month-old Schlomit, were brought into the room. "There was no light in their eyes . . . and they were afraid to cry," she said.

"Do you know what's happened?" Ilana asked quietly.

"Daddy's died," said the girls.

"That's right," replied their mother. "Do you know how?"

The two older girls looked at each other. "We were told that he went 'BANG' in an airplane," they said.

"No, darlings, Daddy didn't die in an airplane. Daddy was murdered by terrorists in the Olympic Village. He and Friedman and Slavin and Halfin and Berger. Everybody."

The girls could not believe what they were hearing. Zeev Friedman had been "one of the family." Ilana and the girls had been expecting him to return home to Israel, comfort them, and explain what had happened to Yossef. "Zeev as well?" the children asked incredulously. Ilana hugged them close. Their devastating loss galvanized and angered her.

"I promise you," she told her three little girls, "that I will get up and I will take the role of a father, a mother and a friend and an investigator. I will investigate and I will never leave it for one second. I owe it to you, to Yossef, to his friends, to know the whole truth. Even if it's painful don't be afraid. Mommy is strong. Mommy is set on this mission." It was an unbreakable oath between a mother and her children.

They may have caused unimaginable grief to the Israeli families, but the five dead Black September fedayeen also had relatives across the Middle East who mourned their loss with equal passion.

The first reports of the attack broadcast in Palestinian refugee camps suggested five fedayeen had been "martyred," and another three were missing. Hajja Hamid, the mother of Afif Ahmed Hamid, was initially unaware that her son was involved in the operation.[8]

"The next day, the neighbors' son came over and said, 'Have you heard the news or seen a paper?'" recalled Hajja.

"I've got one, but I haven't read it," she replied. Hajja thought nothing more of what he said, but when she returned home she found her other son Mohammed lying with his arm over his face.

"What's wrong?" she asked him. "Get up and have some breakfast."

"I don't want any breakfast," said Mohammed.

"But you help me with the breakfast every day," said Hajja in surprise.

Mohammed passed her the newspaper. A large photograph of her son, lying dead by the helicopters at Fürstenfeldbruck, stared out at her from the page.

The family of Khalid Jawad, the eighteen-year-old who was shot in the face by Sniper 2, also discovered his fate after finding his photograph in a local newspaper. "Someone brought a paper and there was a picture of him with a bullet in his face, and they were saying, 'Isn't that Khalid?'" said his brother Mahmoud Mohammad Jawad. "I can't describe the feeling."[9]

But amid the mourning that erupted across Chatila and other Palestinian refugee camps, some of the relatives admit they also felt pride. They viewed the fedayeen as soldiers fighting a battle against the state that had stolen their land. "I was proud," revealed Hajja Hamid, "not because Afif had gone to kill, but because he had tried to have the prisoners freed."[10]

The Arab world viewed the dead terrorists as martyrs. Their bodies were flown from Germany to Libya and buried as heroes. More than thirty thousand mourners followed a swollen procession from Tripoli's Martyrs' Square to Sidi Munaidess Cemetery.

Radio announcers on the *Voice of Palestine* called for solemn commemoration and said the guerrillas had sent a letter to the station, just before they launched their attack in Munich, containing all the money they had between them — $500 and 37 German marks — to be used in the service of the Palestinian revolution. "We are neither killers nor bandits," the *Voice of Palestine* quoted the Munich terrorists as saying in their last letter. "We are persecuted people who have no land and no homeland." The men knew that they might die during their assault on the Olympic Village but said they were willing "to give up our lives from the very first moment." There was not even a hint of remorse, and the statement continued: "We will the youth of the Arab nation to search for death so that life is given to them, their countries, and their people. Each drop of blood spilled from you and from us will be oil to kindle this nation with flames of victory and liberation."

There remains some question over who wrote this, the last testament of the Munich terrorists. Israelis suggest it was manufactured after the massacre was broadcast around the world in a desperate attempt to win public support. Many viewed it as a warped cry for attention, and it was followed by more proclamations supposed to have been issued by the Munich fedayeen before they launched their attack in the Olympic Village. "It would do no harm to the youth of the world to learn of our plight only in a few hours," they are supposed to have said. "We are not against any people, but why should our place here [in Munich] be taken by the flag of the occupiers? Why should the whole world be having fun and entertainment while we suffer with all ears deaf to us?"

The commanders of the attack returned to the Middle East after the operation. Ali Hassan Salameh left his forward command post in East Berlin, where he stayed with the connivance and support of the East German regime, and returned to a hero's welcome in Beirut. According to Israeli intelligence sources, Yasser Arafat greeted Salameh personally and congratulated him on the success of the mission.[11] "You are my son," the PLO leader proclaimed in front of a small crowd of senior Fatah and PLO officials. "I love you as my son."[12] It was a huge boost for Salameh and immediately identified him as Arafat's chosen successor as leader of the entire Palestinian liberation movement.

Many Germans also mourned the dead of Fürstenfeldbruck, and churches across the country held vigils for the Israelis and prayed for their souls. Brundage, however, seemed more concerned with mourning the delay caused to his precious Olympic Games.

A massive argument erupted in Munich over a decision by the Olympic organizers to continue the Games. Many officials wanted them cancelled. Willi Daume, for example, the head of the German National Olympic Committee and the de facto head of German amateur athletics, was devastated by the Israeli deaths.

Daume "felt that his child, the Olympic Games, was killed and he was not willing to go on," said Walther Tröger. Despite Daume's sorrow, Avery Brundage and Tröger convinced him "that we could not yield to such oppression," and Daume agreed to let the Games continue.[13]

Intense pressure was applied to other Bavarian politicians by the IOC to keep the Games going. According to Ulrich Wegener, "The IOC in their meeting after the incidents forced the Bavarian government to go on with the Games, no question about this. I think there was the feeling behind it that this impression of the dead Israeli athletes should not be the last picture that the people had to see from the Olympic Games."[14]

Many athletes were sickened by the decision to go on. The entire Philippines athletics team left Munich, as did six members of the Dutch team. Sprinter Wilma van Gool said they were leaving in protest at the "obscene" decision to continue. Dutch wrestler Barend Koops said he would not go on because he was a friend of one of the dead Israelis. Thirteen Norwegian athletes, almost a quarter of their nation's Munich squad, said they would not continue "when eleven of our sports colleagues have been murdered."

Opinion among other teams was split, and the Games continued, officially resuming with a handball match between Romania and Hungary. Even then the match was nearly abandoned because of a bomb threat thirty minutes before the start. Police cordoned off the hall and searched spectators before allowing it to proceed after a delay of ten minutes.

Those involved have differing opinions. "Personally I think the Games should have continued, otherwise you give in to the terrorists," said Shmuel Lalkin.[15] Roone Arledge, head of ABC Sports, concurred: "I think most people agreed that the Games shouldn't be called off, but it did seem like it was kind of brushed off very quickly and business as usual."[16]

Even Abu Iyad, one of the terrorists who ordered the attack, was surprised by the world's indifference: "We were obliged to note, with considerable sadness, that a large segment of world opinion was far more concerned about the twenty-four-hour interruption in the grand spectacle of the Olympic Games than it was about the dramatic plight endured by the Palestinian people for the past twenty-four years or the atrocious end of the commandos and their hostages."[17]

However, two American marathon runners, Kenny Moore and Frank Shorter, had no doubt they should continue with their gruelling event. They had sat on their fifth-floor balcony grinding fennel seeds into their palms in anger and anguish at the terrorist attack on their fellow athletes. "We have to not let this detract from our performance," Shorter said to Moore, "because that's what they want."[18]

Although the Munich Olympics continued, most of the world cared little. Controversy dogged the Games until they closed. In the 400-meter race Vince Matthews and Wayne Collett, two black American athletes who took first and second place, made their own quiet protest about racism in the United States by refusing to stand to attention on the awards podium. One yawned, the other fiddled with his medal. Some sections of the crowd booed and whistled at them as they left the stadium, and when Avery Brundage furiously demanded that the IOC executive board condemn the men and expel them from the Olympic Village, the board quickly agreed.

The embarrassments were not only political. In the final stages of the marathon a long-haired young man emerged from the stadium tunnel ahead of the pack to appreciative roars from the crowd. He looked remarkably fresh-faced for a long-distance runner, and bounced down the track towards the finish line. Suspicions were only raised as he approached the line and officials realized his number, "72," did not appear on their list of competitors. The joker was a twenty-two-year-old Munich sports student who had apparently wanted to remind the world that the Games were supposed to be light-hearted. Behind him the American Frank Shorter emerged from the tunnel to cross the line as the real winner and take the gold medal. Kenny Moore came in fourth and treated the race as a personal memorial to the dead Israelis.

"I can't speak for Frank," said Moore, "but I know I ran the 1972 Olympic marathon expressly measuring my own suffering against that of my fellow Olympians. Every time I would get a stitch in my side, or a cramp running up a hamstring, I would ask myself if this passing ache were comparable to what they felt in that phosphorous conflagration. That settled, I would run on, chastened."[19]

In the ongoing battle between the Americans and Soviets for

sporting supremacy, Shorter's medal was a much-needed gold for the U.S. team. For not only had the attack on the Israeli delegation been interpreted by many as an attack on the concept of Western democracy, but communist athletes excelled in all events. By the time the Games finished the Soviet Union had accrued fifty gold medals, far ahead of any other competing nation (the U.S. won thirty-three), a symbolic figure that Soviet leaders claimed was a celebration of the fiftieth anniversary of the formation of the Soviet Union in 1922.

After two weeks of fine weather it was perhaps appropriate that the wounded Munich Games limped to their close on a cold, dark night. Athletes from the nations present at the Olympics, a fraction of those who had marched in confidently more than two weeks before, ambled into the main stadium in relative formality for the closing ceremonies but then fell out of line and began milling aimlessly about. As drunken Germans and tourists began pushing their way down towards the field, apparently wanting to have a party with the athletes, loudspeakers brought everyone to order by playing the German national anthem, and Avery Brundage finally rose above the crowd like a monarch to pronounce the Games closed.

"Goodbye, Avery Brandage [sic]," read the scoreboard in the Olympic Stadium as the Games came to a close. It was an ironic ending to an Olympics dogged by tragedy. Brundage climbed into the back of his metallic blue Mercedes 600, slid its small curtains across the windows to block out the world, and disappeared into quiet retirement.

As the Games were closed in Munich the mourning continued in Israel. Golda Meir had been unable to attend the funerals of the athletes because of the death of her beloved sister Sheina. Instead she was represented by Moshe Dayan, the indomitable defense minister, and dozens of other politicians and officials. Dayan stood with his hands on his hips, smoldering with rage, and the world braced itself for inevitable Israeli reprisals.

For Israelis the tragedy was a horrific reminder of the past. Once again Jews had walked stoically to their doom under the watchful eyes of armed Germans. And yet again Germans and the world had stood by and failed to save them.[20] The Arabs were coming for the Jews just as Germans had done decades before. The context of the killings meant that the repercussions would extend further and deeper than Israel's immediate loss of eleven sons.

Arabs knew that Israeli fury would be awesome. In Syria, army units were put on a heightened state of alert and the armored regiment stationed just outside Damascus moved to defensive positions around the city, to protect it first from Israeli air attacks, and from a possible Israeli invasion or airborne landings.

The Israeli press was certainly adamant on the subject of national vengeance. "The time has come for a major stocktaking, settling the one and only account we have with the guerrillas and the dispatchers," read an editorial comment in *Ma'ariv*, the nation's top-selling newspaper. "We shall hit them at home. We shall settle our account with them and their dispatchers, with those who sheltered them in Munich, assisted them in infiltrating their Olympic Village and bringing their weapons there."

Some commentators even went so far as to postulate that war might erupt in the Middle East. "The hands of Israel will know what to do," said Yosef Burg, the Israeli minister of the interior. "We will smite them wherever they may be," reiterated Golda Meir in an address to the Knesset.

Her forces did just that. Before the Munich attack there had been an unspoken agreement between the Palestinian and Israeli leaders that overt acts of terrorism would be eschewed. Munich changed everything. It was seen as an attack of such barbarity that Jews around the world were threatened. Israel vowed its response would be swift. The world did not have long to wait.

On September 8, Israel struck back. In the largest operation of its kind since the 1967 war, the Israeli air force launched simultaneous strikes on at least ten PLO bases inside Syrian and Lebanese borders. War planes bombed seven guerrilla camps in Syria and three in Lebanon; a short dogfight between Israeli and Syrian fighters ended with the downing of three Syrian jets. The main rail line out of

Beirut was cut, and targets were also attacked near the Mediterranean port of Latakia. Israeli anger was ferocious. Many innocent people were killed, among them women and children.

There were few complaints from the Western world. Few outside the Middle East seemed to care about the dozens of children killed by Israeli bombs as they played on the edge of one of the refugee camps. The Israeli public, still numb with shock at the events in Munich, barely registered the carnage caused in the name of their dead athletes. But Israeli revenge did not end with these aerial attacks.

On September 16, in Israel's largest-ever military strike into the region, three Israeli armored columns crossed the border into southern Lebanon, passed through more than ten villages in a show of force, and attacked and destroyed at least 130 houses suspected of housing PLO militants. Bridges were destroyed and artillery pounded suspected guerrilla positions until the Israelis eventually withdrew, leaving a trail of devastation in their wake.[21] Still Israeli anger was not sated.

Many Israelis felt the Munich attack was of such unparalleled brutality that it warranted an unprecedented response. Zvi Zamir was prominent among senior Israelis who called for a focused response to the Palestinian terrorist threat. In meetings with Golda Meir he gave a highly emotive and passionate description of the events in Munich and Fürstenfeldbruck and reduced several other Israeli politicians to tears with his account of manacled Jews again walking to their doom. General Aharon Yariv, the brilliant head of Aman, the intelligence branch of the Israeli Defense Forces, also told Meir that she had to respond dramatically to this new Palestinian threat.

Yariv had few doubts about the correct form of retaliation: "My carefully considered advice, checked with other chiefs of the security services, was to go for the leaders of the Black September . . . eliminate the leaders of Black September, as much as possible, or as many as possible."[22]

Meir was utterly devastated by the Munich attack. "She took it very personally," said Yariv.[23] The Aman head seemed to have the solution, a way of exacting revenge, of turning the tables on the terrorists. His idea, discussed with Meir within days of the Munich massacre, was to make the terrorists the targets.

Zamir agreed that Israel should take the war back to the terrorists and go after the leaders of Black September, not just the men who pulled triggers, but the officials who told them where and when to attack. As Meir wavered over such a hawkish (and internationally illegal) response, most Israelis had few qualms. Several Israeli politicians were heard quoting the ancient "Olympic Truce" to justify launching attacks on Black September:

> Olympia is a sacred place.
> Anyone who dares to enter it
> by force of arms commits an
> offense against the gods.
> Equally guilty is he who has
> it in his power to avenge a
> misdeed and fails to do so.

"I remember people coming to me and saying, 'I volunteer to fight Black September,'" said Yariv several years later. But Golda Meir was unhappy with the proposals. "As a woman she was not very exhilarated by the idea, but I felt very strongly about it, very strongly indeed. In the end, I succeeded in convincing her. She relented."[24]

Israel had been known to kill its enemies prior to the Munich massacre, striking them down ruthlessly with knives, bullets, and bombs. Israeli agents had sent letter bombs to former Nazi scientists working for the Egyptian government and prominent Palestinians campaigning against the Israeli state. But most Israeli killings had been launched against specific individuals for specific acts. Munich, however, changed everything. After the Olympic attack Meir authorized her intelligence agents to launch a secret war against Palestinian leaders.

On October 24, 1972, the first of a flood of Israeli letter bombs began appearing on the desks of Palestinian leaders around the Middle East. In Libya Mustafa Awadh Abu Zeid suffered severe facial injuries when a parcel exploded in his face, while Abu Khalil, a senior Fatah official in Algiers, was seriously injured by a similar device.

21 A view along Connollystrasse, the pedestrianized street in the Olympic Village housing the Israeli delegation at number 31.

22 A long-range photograph taken of "Issa," the commander of the Black September attackers. During negotiations he would take the pin out of a grenade and pass it to another terrorist to ensure his safety while speaking to German officials.

23 The negotiations begin: outside 31 Connollystrasse terrorist leader Issa (far right) begins dictating terms to Munich police chief Manfred Schreiber (far left), German Interior Minister Hans-Dietrich Genscher (second from left), and Village Mayor Walther Tröger (middle, with back to camera).

24 Senior German officials walk back down Connollystrasse after further negotiations with the terrorists: Walther Tröger (second from left), Hans-Dietrich Genscher (middle), Manfred Schreiber (second from right), and Bavarian Interior Minister Bruno Merk (far right).

25 Hans-Dietrich Genscher, Issa, and Walther Tröger walk along a road underneath the Israeli delegation building during the evening of the siege while checking a possible route the terrorists might take to reach helicopters intended to take them to a local airport.

26 & 27 After leaving the Olympic Village the nine surviving hostages and eight terrorists were flown in two helicopters to Fürstenfeldbruck airfield outside Munich. After a German "rescue plan" collapsed when officers abandoned their positions, a firefight ensued that ended with the deaths of all the hostages.

28 The scene at Fürstenfeldbruck airfield at dawn after the battle. German officials form a ring around the two helicopters.

29 Khalid Jawad, the young Black September terrorist, lies dead on the ground at Fürstenfeldbruck airfield. He was shot in the face by a German sniper.

30 Anton Fliegerbauer, a 32-year-old Munich police brigadier in charge of a small squad of officers at Fürstenfeldbruck airfield. He was killed by a shot to the head at the start of the battle.

31 Zvi Zamir, the head of Israeli intelligence, the Mossad, in 1972. He was present during the battle at Fürstenfeldbruck airfield and in the months following was instrumental in establishing the covert revenge team that tracked down and killed most of the terrorists involved in the attack.

32 During the Israeli revenge operation,
soldiers masquerading as tourists
entered Beirut and murdered three
senior members of the PLO in an
attack code-named "Spring of Youth."
In the photograph above, the central
figures relax together. Background, left
to right: General Aharon Yariv, commander of the Israeli revenge missions;
Haim Bar-Lev, former Israeli chief of
staff; David "Dado" Elazar, chief of
staff during "Spring of Youth." Fore-
ground, middle: Ehud Barak, commander of the elite Israeli Sayeret
Matkal and later Israeli prime minister;
and (right) Muki Betser, a platoon
commander in the Sayeret Matkal.

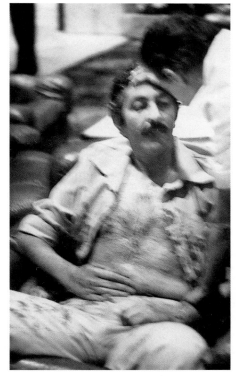

33 Abu Daoud, one of the founders of the
Black September faction within the
PLO and a mastermind of the 1972
Munich Olympics massacre, after
being shot five times at close range by
an unknown gunman in the coffee
shop of the Victoria Intercontinental
Hotel in Warsaw, Poland, on August
2, 1981.

34 The widow of Adnan Al-Gashey, one of the three Black September survivors of the Munich attack, in a photograph taken recently in Beirut, where she still lives. Her husband was killed by Israeli secret agents after the Munich attack as part of Operation Wrath of God.

35 The brother and parents of the Black September terrorist Afif Hamid, who was killed at Fürstenfeldbruck airfield. They still mourn his loss, but hope for reconciliation between the Palestinians and Israelis.

36 Anouk Spitzer-Rekhess leaves sunflowers on the grave of her father Andre.

Officials and officers elsewhere in Algeria, Egypt, Libya, and Lebanon were also targeted.[25]

That was to be just the beginning. "Hawks" and "doves" in the Israeli government were still debating whether the scope of the revenge attacks should be widened when events in Europe encouraged Meir's government to declare all-out war against Black September and Palestinian leaders believed to be connected with Munich.

On the morning of Sunday, October 29, a Lufthansa Boeing 727 on its way from Damascus, Syria, to Frankfurt, Germany, was hijacked by two Palestinian terrorists as it left Beirut airport, one of its stopovers. They demanded to be flown to Munich, and after a refuelling stop in Cyprus, Captain Walter Claussen flew the jet into German airspace by noon. The terrorists immediately demanded that the three Black September terrorists who survived the carnage at Fürstenfeldbruck were to be released immediately. Alternatively, said the terrorists, they would blow up the plane. Black September had not allowed its men to languish for long.

Without even informing the Israeli government about what had happened, the Germans capitulated and told the hijackers that the three men would be at Riem airport within an hour and a half. The terrorists were invited to land at the airport and wait for their men, but instead they diverted the 727 to Zagreb in Yugoslavia, where it began circling with diminishing fuel levels.

According to Chancellor Willy Brandt: "The passengers and crew were threatened with annihilation unless we released the three Palestinian survivors of the Fürstenfeldbruck massacre. Like the Bavarian government, I then saw no alternative but to yield to this ultimatum and avoid further senseless bloodshed."[26]

Jamal Al-Gashey, Adnan Al-Gashey, and Mohammed Safady had been arrested immediately after the gun battle at Fürstenfeldbruck. They had feared summary execution, but the Germans treated them with a dignity reserved for dangerous foreigners.

"They treated my hand and then began extensive questioning," recalled Jamal Al-Gashey. "I was not subjected to physical pressure, by which I mean torture, but I was put under enormous psychological pressure. The questions were all about the operation, our organization, its leadership, how we had entered Germany and who had helped us, whether we had been helped by any Germans . . . things relating to the operation and organization."[27] Al-Gashey and his two comrades had all hoped their friends would try to force their release.

As soon as the two hijackers had issued their demands, the three terrorists were hustled out of their individual prisons in preparation for a fast plane ride to Zagreb. The terrorists had to be there before the 727 ran out of fuel at around 5:30 P.M.

Heinz Hohensinn, the young Munich police officer involved in the siege at 31 Connollystrasse, was again involved in the operation, but this time, ironically, to arrange not the capture of the terrorists but their release: "They were brought from Straubing, Landsberg, and Stadelheim to the sports field of the riot police and from there I was supposed to take over the convoy to Munich-Riem airport. And because there was not much time left, because the hijacked plane already sent emergency signals due to lack of fuel, we took the helicopter to Riem and there a Lufthansa plane was waiting . . ."[28]

As Hohensinn flew in a helicopter with one of the terrorists, he was astounded when the Palestinian told him that he had seen him before: "I didn't know what he meant, I didn't immediately think of the Olympics." The terrorist explained he had seen Hohensinn on television, in a training suit preparing to assault the Israeli building during Operation Sunshine, the aborted attempt to free the athletes. The terrorist, said Hohensinn, "was very peaceful" when he said he had seen the German before. "It was not meant to be a confrontation or anything nasty. They actually were happy to have survived and to be flown home. And they knew they would be welcomed as heroes at home."

Shortly before they left, Hohensinn "sneaked in" to a holding room at Riem to say "a sort of goodbye": "I saw them sitting with a huge food packet, eating and in a great mood. One still had his hand bandaged [Jamal Al-Gashey] but they were pretty much in good health . . . future heroes. Then they were in the air and the hijacked plane finally could land."

Initially the terrorists were unsure of their destination. "We thought they were taking us to a different prison," said Jamal Al-Gashey. "When we were on the plane, they told us they were transferring us to another country where we would be handed over to our organization. That was when I knew we were being released, on board the plane."[29]

When the three terrorists, escorted by a senior official from Lufthansa and several Munich police officers, arrived in the skies above Zagreb, they discussed terms of the exchange with the two terrorists on the 727, which was by then dangerously close to running out of fuel. The two hijackers promised to release their hostages as soon as they were given custody of the three Black September guerrillas. But when both sides had landed and an exchange had taken place, the two hijackers announced that all of their original hostages would be accompanying them to Libya.

There was nothing the Germans could do, except make certain that when the plane landed in Tripoli after 9:00 P.M. that night, the German ambassador would be on hand to guarantee the speedy release of the hostages. It was all highly embarrassing for the German government, and Lufthansa, the national airline, especially when mass celebrations erupted across the Middle East in concert with the three Munich survivors' return to Arab soil.

And yet the entire hijacking was allegedly set up between Black September and the German government. The Palestinians had warned the government in Bonn that they would launch a wave of bombings and hijackings against Lufthansa unless the three Munich survivors were released. The "hijacking," according to German, Palestinian, and Israeli sources, was a compromise agreed to by senior figures in the German government.

Jamal Al-Gashey only discovered details of the setup after he arrived home: "As I found out later, an agreement had been made with the German government for our release after the hijacking of a Lufthansa plane."[30]

"Yes, I think it's probably true," said Ulrich Wegener. "The German government thought they could negotiate with the terrorist[s] and could convince them that they would give them money and something else to get rid of them . . . But of course it was the wrong way, no question, because when one case is solved in this way other cases will come."[31]

There are several strange aspects of the hijacking that support the allegation. The Lufthansa Boeing had left Damascus with seven crew members but without a single passenger. In Beirut it picked up just thirteen passengers — a surprisingly low figure (and that included the two hijackers), and then continued on to Germany.

Those officials prepared to speak on the record about this incident state that it fits the pattern of the German government's pragmatic approach to terrorism in the 1970s. It was a time when Germany made secret agreements with Palestinian and other international terrorist groups in a desperate bid to keep them away from German borders. "In such situations . . . Willy Brandt, as I remember very well, always makes this gesture," said Hans-Jochen Vogel, who then raised his outstretched arms, palms facing upwards, and shrugged his shoulders dramatically several times.

It was also not the first time Lufthansa had allegedly been involved in a deal with terrorists. In February 1972 Palestinian terrorists had hijacked a Lufthansa jet to Aden; Lufthansa reportedly paid the PLO a ransom of at least $5 million.[32]

Regardless of whether the release of the three Munich fedayeen was a "put-up job," in the words of one Israeli official, there was astonishment and fury in Tel Aviv when news came through of their release. Golda Meir said she "was literally physically sickened."[33] Perhaps some indication of the isolation felt by Meir and her government can be seen in her later thoughts on the release of the three terrorists. "I think that there is not one single terrorist held in prison anywhere in the world. Everyone else gives in. We're the only ones who do not," she said in disgust.[34]

For Meir, the release of the terrorists was the final straw.[35] Officials had already pleaded with her to authorize the establishment of an undercover unit to track down and assassinate those blamed for the Munich massacre. Any doubts she might have had about responding violently were quashed by the release of Al-Gashey and his two friends.

Meir called General Aharon Yariv and Zvi Zamir to her office,

the Red House, located in the heavily guarded Army General Headquarters. She spoke at length to both men about the endless suffering
of the Jewish people throughout history. She spoke of the Holocaust,
of the anti-Semites attacking Jews even after the death of Hitler. And
then she spoke of Munich, of eleven bright-eyed Israelis who had
battled their demons to compete against the world on German soil.[36]
They had gone to prove to the world that the Nazis had not beaten
the Jews. Still, they had died.

The old woman was speaking quietly. She had been witness to
so much Jewish suffering. Then she sighed, lifted her head to look
Yariv and Zamir in the eye, and said in a strong, clear voice: "Send
forth the boys."[37]

Operation Wrath of God

The small group of senior Israeli politicians and officials in charge of the assassination campaign against the terrorists involved in the Munich massacre was given the code name "Committee X."[1] It was a suitably dramatic title for a select cabal unknown even to other senior figures in the Israeli establishment.

General Aharon Yariv, one of the original proponents of the campaign, was appointed to the new post of "Prime Minister's Adviser on Counterterrorism," with a role as general overseer of the campaign. His instructions, agreed to by Meir, were to "put the fear of God" into the Palestinians. Those targeted for assassination were not just to be killed, they were to be hit dramatically. It was not enough simply to shoot them all down in the street; the Israeli agents had to use a degree of imagination in the assassinations to sow fear within Palestinian ranks.

Yariv was a strange choice for the role of avenger. A cerebral and mild man, born in Moscow in 1920, he emigrated to Palestine in 1935 when the "Jewish homeland" was still under British mandate.[2] In 1941 he joined the British army, rose to the rank of captain, and then joined militant Zionist groups in 1946. By 1957 he was the Israeli military attaché in Washington, rising to become the director of military intelligence in 1964. He proved to be an intelligence genius, and Meir had absolute faith in his abilities.

The plan Committee X devised was for Israeli secret agents, principally from Mossad, to conduct the killings using "all kinds of means." According to Yariv: "It could be by booby-trapping, could be by shooting, could be by blowing up a car. All these well-known methods."[3]

The revenge operation was to be clinical and international in scope. Agents of Mossad were to kill the terrorists "wherever we could find them, and wherever our people could do this damn job," Yariv has confirmed.

Few modern democratic states have dared to establish licensed assassination squads to eliminate their enemies, far fewer with the full agreement of the country's leader, but Yariv believes that after Munich the Israeli government had no alternative: "We had to make them stop, and there was no other way . . . We are not very proud about it. But it was a question of sheer necessity. We went back to the old biblical rule of an eye for an eye."

With the assault in Munich, the Palestinians had changed the rules of the conflict and the Israelis would adapt with speed. Yariv explained: "I approach these problems not from a moral point of view but, hard as it may sound, from a cost-benefit point of view. If I'm very hard-headed, I can say, what is the political benefit in killing this person? Will it bring us nearer to peace? Will it bring us nearer to an understanding with the Palestinians or not? In most cases I don't think it will. But in the case of Black September we had no other choice and it worked. Is it morally acceptable? One can debate that question. Is it politically vital? It was."

The campaign launched against the Palestinians has since become known as Operation Wrath of God, although few of those intimately involved seem to have regularly used such an emotive title. Initial responsibility for the campaign was delegated to Mossad and a small team of elite agents led by "Mike," the senior agent in charge of the operations department.

"Mike" was a forty-six-year-old veteran agent, a man who had

worked in the shadows for several decades. Trained as a radio opera-
tor, he was based in Rome after World War II, helping to smuggle
Jews back to Palestine. He was recruited into Shin Bet in 1950 after
leaving the army, and by the 1960s had moved on to Mossad, where
he rose steadily up the ranks within the operations department, taking command around 1970.

After receiving the initial order to establish the assassination
squad, "Mike" spent several weeks in reconnaissance, travelling around
Europe and the Middle East using various false passports, including
one which identified him as a French businessman called Edouard
Stanislas Laskier. He assembled a small team of Israeli agents and
moved them to safe houses in Paris, from where the operation would
be run, with the help of officials at the Israeli embassy.

Operation Wrath of God was an extraordinary campaign char-
acterized by planning, false identities, exotic weaponry, and guile.
While the truth remains obfuscated by secrecy, some details of the
unit assembled by "Mike" have become known. The hit team for a particular operation consisted of fifteen people divided into five squads:
"Aleph," two trained killers; "Bet," two guards who would shadow
the Alephs; "Heth," two agents who would establish a cover for the
rest of the team by renting hotel rooms, apartments, cars, and so on;
"Ayin," comprising between six and eight agents who formed the
backbone of the operation, shadowing targets and establishing an escape route for the Aleph and Bet squads; and "Qoph," two agents specializing in communications.[4]

Mossad's initial task, however, was to assemble a list of the terrorists behind Black September, and those Palestinians who offered
direct support and help for its terrorist attacks. Israeli intelligence
units across Europe and the Middle East began an intensive study of
those behind the Munich attack.

Full details of the list Mossad compiled have never been revealed.
Although Victor Ostrovsky, a former Mossad "katsa" (case agent),
claims "Meir signed death warrants for about thirty-five known Black
September terrorists,"[5] other intelligence sources claim the true figure
was closer to twenty. As soon as a target was identified, Israeli agents
conducted extensive surveillance of the individual to establish his

movements and the likely success of a "hit," while a senior member of the Israeli squad then contacted Committee X to seek permission for a kill.

Topping the Wrath of God list were some of the most senior figures within the PLO, including Abu Iyad, the leader of Black September, and Ali Hassan Salameh, the glamorous young guerrilla fighter being groomed by Yasser Arafat as a possible successor and leader of the Palestinian movement.

Salameh was far removed from the traditional Western image of a Palestinian terrorist born amid squalor in a refugee camp and raised on memories and a diet of hatred. The wealthy son of businessman Sheikh Hassan Salameh (a legendary figure in the early years of the Palestinian battle against the Zionists),[6] Salameh knew from an early age that he was destined to follow in his father's footsteps. "The influence of my father has posed personal problems for me," he said once. "I grew up in a family that considered 'struggle' a matter of heritage, which should be carried on by generation after generation . . . Even as a child, I had to follow a certain pattern of behavior . . . I was made constantly conscious of the fact that I was the son of Hassan Salameh and had to live up to that."[7]

As the mantle of family leadership fell to the younger Salameh, he moved from secondary school in Bir-Zeit on the West Bank to Cairo, and then on to West Germany, where he studied engineering.

At his mother's behest he married in Cairo in 1963, but Salameh continued to date stunningly attractive women, study karate, wear designer clothes, and drive fast sports cars. Not for him life in a tent in the Gaza Strip. Salameh became a glamorous playboy with a villa in Geneva and keys to a string of homes in the south of France. He became a living legend.

Despite this lifestyle, however, Salameh remained utterly committed to the cause of Palestinian liberation. While he was certainly different from the rest of the gray men who ran the PLO — for years Arafat's taste for luxury extended no further than a spoonful of honey in his tea — he was needed precisely because of his charisma and leadership skills. Arafat trusted him so implicitly that, after rising through the ranks of Fatah, Salameh was promoted to take over Force

17, Yasser Arafat's praetorian guard (so called because "17" was the unit's extension at the PLO's Beirut headquarters telephone exchange).

The Israelis saw Salameh not only as a terrorist threat but as a Palestinian leader with the ability to lead a broader-based movement against the Zionist state. They gave him the code name "Red Prince," and his assassination was to become an obsession for several senior Israeli agents. But in the early weeks of Operation Wrath of God the Israelis realized that Ali Hassan Salameh was a target that would have to wait for vengeance. He was too well protected, flitting with several bodyguards between heavily fortified homes. Instead, even before the Lufthansa "hijacking" encouraged them to increase their attack, Mossad chose as their first target an unprotected Palestinian intellectual living in Europe.

Wael Zwaiter was a slender Palestinian who had lived in Rome for sixteen years and was working as a clerk at the Libyan embassy. His official role was translator, and one of his major achievements had been translating the classic *A Thousand and One Nights* from Arabic into Italian. There is little concrete evidence of his involvement in terrorism, although since 1972 Israeli officials have claimed privately that Zwaiter was involved in Black September and played a pivotal role in the plot in August 1972 to blow an El Al Boeing 707 out of the sky with a bomb concealed in a tape recorder.[8]

To this day, many Palestinians claim that Zwaiter, originally from Nablus on the West Bank, was not involved in the Munich attack. "I challenge the Israeli government, or any of its departments, to prove that Wael Zwaiter, the philosopher who carries books and not guns, had anything to do with the Munich operation," said Abu Daoud, a leader of Black September. "Zwaiter had contacts in all the Italian political parties. He was . . . a philosopher, not an armed freedom fighter. They killed him because they wanted to kill off any kind of positive image of the Palestinian cause in Europe."[9]

The Israelis claim that Zwaiter was involved in organizing and running Black September attacks that originated in the Italian capital, and he was certainly heard justifying the Munich attack and even suggesting that the Israelis had deliberately allowed their athletes to be killed to gain a political advantage and an excuse to crack down on the Palestinian movement.[10] The claims may have been his death sentence. He was also, it later emerged, a cousin of Yasser Arafat.[11]

On the evening of October 16, 1972, Zwaiter visited his old friend Janet von Braun, a fifty-year-old Australian living in Rome. After a chat and dinner, Zwaiter ambled home to his apartment in a building on the Piazza Annibaliano in the north of the city. He bought some fig wine and groceries from a late-night store and stopped at the Trieste Bar near his apartment to make a couple of phone calls. Zwaiter finally entered his building just after 10:30 P.M., searching for a 10-lira coin for the elevator up to his small apartment. Two male Israeli agents had dimmed the lights in the entrance hall.

As he approached the elevator the Israeli agents drew small, modified Beretta .22-caliber pistols, the favored weapon of Israeli secret agents, and emerged from the shadows. They pumped twelve bullets into his body at close range, and Zwaiter died in a pool of blood in the entrance hall.

The two killers ran outside and dived into the back of a green Fiat 125, rented by Canadian tourist "Anthony Hutton," which had been waiting by the curb with two other agents, a couple who had pretended to be kissing passionately as Zwaiter passed them by.[12] The Fiat accelerated away from the scene, narrowly avoiding a collision with another vehicle, and was then dumped just a few hundred meters away on Via Bressanone. The killers transferred to another waiting car that took them to a safe house in the city. They were never caught.

The assassination squad moved quickly from Rome to Paris, as the Israelis turned their attention to Dr. Mahmoud Hamshari, the PLO's middle-aged, balding senior representative in France, a man whom Mossad have since claimed was the head of Black September in that country.[13]

Hamshari lived quietly without bodyguards in an elegant apartment at 175 rue d'Alésia, with his French wife Marie-Claude and their daughter Amina. He appears to have tightened his security slightly after Zwaiter's death, but he was still a "soft target" the Israelis could easily have killed in the street. Hamshari, however, was selected for a more dramatic death than Zwaiter, one that would frighten his comrades — or terrorize the terrorists, as the Israelis saw it. Killing Hamshari required the Israeli hit team to devise an intricate plan.

The agents spent at least a week conducting intense surveillance of Hamshari and carefully noted that his wife would take the couple's daughter to nursery school early every morning, and then return to the apartment later. It offered the Israelis a "window" of time for a surgical strike when their target was alone, thus avoiding other casualties.

In early December 1972, an Israeli agent, posing as an Italian journalist interested in the Palestinian struggle, arranged to meet Hamshari in a café near his apartment. As the two men sipped coffee and discussed Middle Eastern politics, two more Israeli agents quietly examined the lock on Hamshari's front door.

A few days later the "Italian journalist" arranged another meeting with Hamshari outside his apartment. As they met and talked again, at least two members of the hit team, explosives experts flown in especially from Israel, entered Hamshari's apartment and planted a small explosive device under a table by his telephone.

Israeli surveillance of the apartment continued, and the next day, Friday, December 8, just after Marie-Claude and the couple's daughter had left to make the short journey to Amina's school, the "Italian journalist" rang Hamshari at his home.

"Is that you, Mr. Hamshari?" asked the Israeli agent in Arabic when the Palestinian answered the phone.

"Yes, I am Mahmoud Hamshari," came the response.

The Israeli signalled to other colleagues on the hit team and they detonated the bomb. A split second before it exploded, Hamshari must have moved away from the table, because although he was fatally wounded, he was conscious long enough to tell astonished Parisian detectives what had happened. He heard a high-pitched whine just before the bomb exploded. The Israelis had transmitted a detonating signal down the telephone line, and forensic technicians later established that a sophisticated detonator had been installed in the bomb under the table using the same principle as "scrambler" telephones. Hamshari died in the hospital several weeks later.

Rumors that the Israelis were pursuing an assassination vendetta against Black September now started to circulate throughout the Middle East, but many activists still seem to have kept to their normal routines.

Assassinations were not the only tactic used by the Wrath of God team to terrorize the men and women they identified as terrorists. Mossad also started to run obituaries in Arabic newspapers, eulogizing Palestinians who were still in the prime of health. Warnings were backed up by telephone calls.

In Europe dozens of junior PLO, Fatah, and even Black September operatives were also told by Israeli agents to disassociate themselves from the armed struggle or face certain death. Agents would ring up a Palestinian, ask for them in Arabic by their full name, then confirm the names of the person's wife, children, and place of work. When it was clear to the Palestinian that the caller was well acquainted with most aspects of his life, the Mossad agent would warn him or her against any further involvement with the PLO or its various armed units.

Anyone brave — or naive — enough to put the handset down and still feel secure was often jolted out of his complacency by a brick being thrown through their window, or a battering on the front door. It was hardly a violent response to terrorism, but the Israelis were still trying to make it clear that — if they wanted to — they could wipe out anyone, anywhere.

By January 1973, Golda Meir's hit squad had moved from Paris to Nicosia on the Mediterranean island of Cyprus. Conveniently situated just a short hop from Israel, Lebanon, and Egypt, Cyprus had been the scene of many Cold War dramas.

The Cypriot target was Hussein Abad Al Chir (a.k.a. Hussein Bashir, a.k.a. Abd el Hir), a thirty-six-year-old senior Fatah official and, according to the Israelis, the head of Black September on the island. But this was not the only reason why Al Chir was targeted:

what angered and troubled the Israelis was Al Chir's close links with the Soviet KGB.

By the early 1970s the PLO was receiving help and support from Moscow in the shape of weapons (such as quantities of powerful AK-47 assault rifles) and training in bases behind the Iron Curtain. Al Chir was responsible for selecting or screening the Palestinians who would receive training. He is also believed to have been forging links with senior Soviet intelligence officers and with a KGB colonel who covered part of the Middle East from the Soviet embassy in Cyprus.

For the Israelis Al Chir's contacts with the KGB represented an entirely new threat, and one that could have led to their foreign agents being targeted by Palestinian hit men. The Munich massacre was just the excuse Mossad needed to justify killing Al Chir.

Al Chir had been in Nicosia only a short time when an Israeli surveillance team quietly began watching his movements. He followed few regular patterns, but his day always started and finished in his room at the Olympic Hotel on Nicosia's President Makarios Avenue. Al Chir had stayed in the hotel, which was popular with his comrades, several times previously. His loyalty may have cost him his life, for the Mossad decided he would die in his room.

In mid-January 1973, senior members of the Israeli hit team, including one agent using a British passport in the name of "Jonathan Ingleby," arrived on the island and booked themselves into the Olympic Hotel under a variety of false names. Exact details of their operation are still unclear, but it is believed they broke into Al Chir's hotel room while he was out during the day and planted a small charge of high explosive under his bed.

On the night of January 24, Al Chir returned to the hotel and trudged upstairs alone to his room. Minutes passed as he undressed and prepared for sleep. When the room light went out and Al Chir had settled into bed, a member of the Israeli hit team watching outside pressed the button on a detonator and an explosion destroyed Al Chir's body, wrecked his room, and blew the door off its hinges.

The executions continued. At the beginning of April 1973 Mossad returned to Paris to track Dr. Basil Al-Kubaissi, a professor of

law at Beirut's American University who is thought to have moon-
lighted as a senior official within the Palestinian guerrilla movement.[14] Kubaissi is alleged to have been a quartermaster for Black
September operations in Europe, arranging the supply and transfer of
weapons and explosives. He is also believed to have been involved in
an attempt to assassinate Golda Meir during a visit she made to the
United States. A massive car bomb was parked outside the El Al terminal at JFK Airport, but it was defused before her flight arrived.

On the night of April 6, the professor enjoyed a delicious meal
at the expensive Café de la Paix and was walking back to his hotel
near the Madeleine Church when two young Israeli agents who had
been tailing him came up beside him, produced their standard .22
pistols, and shot him about a dozen times.

Black September did not take these attacks lying down. Its operatives
soon began to respond in kind. In late April 1973 a killer called Za-
haria Abu Saleh was dispatched to Rome with orders to avenge the
latest Arab deaths. He followed Vittorio Olivares, an Italian employee
of El Al whom Black September suspected was an Israeli agent,
around Rome and then shot him in the stomach with a silenced pistol amid crowds of shoppers outside a department store.

Ali Hassan Salameh, the Red Prince, also ordered further "spectacular" terrorist attacks on Israeli targets during this period, which
would perpetuate the cycle of violence. One of the more unusual, if
only because of its geographical location, was an assault on the Israeli
embassy in Bangkok on December 28, 1972.

Four Black September guerrillas launched the attack just after
Rehavam Amir, the Israeli ambassador, had left the building to attend
the investiture of Crown Prince Vajiralongkorn, heir to the Thai
throne. Disguised as diplomats in elegant suits, two of the Black September unit slipped past guards to link up with two more armed gunmen. Together the unit took six diplomats, including two women,
hostage. They may have missed capturing Rehavam Amir, but they
did take Simon Avimor, the Israeli ambassador to Cambodia, who
was unlucky enough to be visiting Thailand at the time.

A familiar pattern of negotiations ensued. The hostages were herded into an upstairs room and threatened with death. The terrorists threw a letter containing their demands out of a window. They wanted the immediate release of the murderous Japanese terrorist Kozo Okamoto from his Israeli jail, along with thirty-five Palestinian and pro-Palestinian terrorists. The Israelis warned the Thai authorities they had absolutely no intention of capitulating to the demands, and the world prepared for more slaughter.

After protracted negotiations and with the help of Mustapha el Assawy, the Egyptian ambassador to Thailand, the Thai authorities managed to persuade the Black September guerrillas to leave the embassy and travel by bus to the airport, where they said a plane was waiting to take the group to the destination of their choice. It was all frighteningly similar to the debacle at Munich.

Perhaps it was precisely because the terrorists feared a repeat of the situation at Munich that they initially refused the suggested transfer. However, Ambassador el Assawy was constantly on hand to offer reassurance and promises of safe conduct, and the terrorists kept to their word. They left for the airport with their bound hostages, whom they then released to the Thai police. The guerrillas then left on a Thai Airways flight bound for Cairo. As a final display of trust, Ambassador el Assawy bravely travelled with Black September to ensure their safe passage.

Moderate Israeli politicians celebrated what they claimed was a diplomatic triumph: proof that terrorism could be defeated without recourse to bullets and bombs. Not surprisingly, the senior officials of Black September saw the conclusion of the Bangkok crisis differently. Ali Hassan Salameh was furious because the terrorists had effectively surrendered and emerged with nothing. Some reports suggest that Salameh ordered the murder of the four terrorists because of their perceived failure. Certainly he was desperate to launch another "spectacular" against Israel, and his opportunity was to come with an attack in Europe that he had been planning for several weeks.

In her quest for full international recognition of the state of Israel, Golda Meir had for many years wanted to visit the Pope in the Vatican. In the autumn of 1972 the two sides finally agreed on details. Meir would spend a day with the Pope on January 15, 1973, after spending two days in Paris at an international socialist conference, and before two days of meetings with President Felix Houphouët-Boigny of the Ivory Coast.

Somehow, perhaps through contacts in Israel, or through agents in the Vatican, the Palestinian leadership learned details of Meir's planned trip, and decided it was too good an opportunity to miss. A senior Palestinian leader contacted Salameh, who was in East Germany with the Stasi, and sent him a personal message: "Let's get the one who is spilling our blood all over Europe."[15]

Salameh swiftly began planning a daring attack on the Israeli leader. He moved quietly around Europe on a series of passports and jetted into Rome personally to oversee an assassination attempt.

After travelling the route Meir was likely to take from the airport to the Vatican, Salameh appears to have decided the best method of killing her would be to attack her plane with a ground-to-air missile as it landed at Rome's chaotic Fiumicino Airport. The PLO already had several shoulder-launched Soviet-made Strella missiles (code-named "Grail" by NATO) at bases in Yugoslavia. All Salameh needed to do was smuggle them across the Adriatic and into Italy for the attack.[16]

The Red Prince arranged for a small yacht to collect several boxes loaded with the devastating missiles from the ancient walled city of Dubrovnik and smuggle them into Italy. The missiles were unloaded near Bari in late December 1972, driven into Rome in a large van, and hidden in a Black September safe house. Salameh was ready to launch his attack on the Israeli leader.[17]

But even as the Red Prince was arranging this, a junior Mossad contact in the PLO was warning his Israeli handlers that he was being asked to take part in an attack on an unspecified Israeli target. At first the Israelis thought it might have been the December 28 assault on the Israeli embassy in Bangkok, but several senior European Mossad agents were not convinced. They became even more concerned in the second week of January when transcripts from bugs on the phone of a high-class prostitute in Brussels known to harbor PLO officials revealed calls from someone — thought to be Salameh — to a number in Rome.

"Clear the apartment and take all fourteen cakes," the man had said.[18]

The Israelis, suspicious of the message, quickly traced the call in Rome and broke into the apartment. There was nothing there except a torn piece of paper showing the end of a Strella missile and a few words in Russian explaining how it should be used.[19] Golda Meir was due in Rome in less than seventy-two hours, and her security officials began to panic.

The Italian police were warned of the possible assassination attempt, and they and the Israelis, working both separately and together, began searching the area around the airport for the terrorists. The exact sequence of events that followed remains confused, but just a few hours before Meir was due to arrive, a Mossad official seems to have found one of two Black September hit teams in a field to the north of the airport. They shot at him, he ran off, the Italian police arrived, and amid all the confusion another Mossad team managed to capture one of the terrorists and whisked him away for a swift interrogation.

There was little time for subtlety: by the time the terrorist was captured Golda Meir was due to arrive in less than one hour. The Mossad agents violently assaulted the terrorist, battering him until he first confessed details of the plan to kill Meir, and then admitted there was another Black September hit team in the area. Just as the Mossad agents were radioing Meir's plane and desperately pleading with their determined and fatalistic prime minister to turn back, another Mossad agent driving around the perimeter of the airport spotted something suspicious about a mobile café-van parked by the side of the road.

Victor Ostrovsky, the former Mossad case agent who spent several years in the service, has accessed secret files on the assassination plot. He claims the agent "had already driven by [the van] twice, but on the third time, it struck him: there were three stacks poking out of the roof, but only one was smoking."[20] The terrorists had apparently drilled holes in the roof and the missiles were actually jutting out of the top. "Without wasting a second, the Mossad agent did a sharp U–turn and drove his car directly into the cart, turning it over and pinning the two terrorists beneath it," added Ostrovsky.[21] As police sirens wailed in the distance the Mossad agent checked to see that the area was secured and there was no chance of the Black September terrorists escaping the Italian police. Then he disappeared.

Ali Hassan Salameh failed in his bid to murder Golda Meir, but his men did not halt their attacks. Quite the opposite. His network of agents had been tracking the movements and activities of a cerebral Israeli spy called Baruch Cohen, and within two weeks of the failed attempt on Meir's life, Black September was ready to strike again.

Cohen, a native Arabic speaker, had worked as the military governor of the large town of Nablus after the 1967 war and had been the commander of a team that nearly captured Yasser Arafat.[22] He joined Mossad in 1970 and was sent to Europe to build a network of Palestinian informants among young students, but he may have been fatally compromised by the extraordinary appearance of his photograph in an official Israeli army publication commemorating the 1967 war (the heavy hand of the Israeli censor normally prevented such disasters).

Cohen was far removed from the stereotype of a jet–setting spy, but he was still exceptionally good at his job. "Brochi wasn't a tough guy," said his widow, Nurit. "On the contrary he was short and very far from the image of a champagne spy. He didn't know how to dance. He couldn't drink. He was shy, very closed. But he knew how to listen. If he'd picked a different profession, he could have been a psychologist. It was a pleasure to talk to him. He'd say a word here, a word there, and the other person would open up. He exuded trustworthiness."[23]

However, while working in Spain, trying to recruit young Arabs, Cohen was deceived. According to Abu Iyad: "What he didn't know was that several of the students he had recruited belonged to Black September and pretended to cooperate with him at the request of the organization. When he began to have serious doubts about the loyalty of those who failed to carry out the tasks assigned to them on various pretexts, it was decided to execute him. His elimination became urgent when, in early January, shortly after Mahmoud Hamshari's assassination in Paris, Cohen announced that he was leaving Spain to take up other duties."[24]

On January 23, 1973, Cohen met a twenty-five-year-old Palestinian medical student he was cultivating as a contact at a busy café on Madrid's busy Grand Via. The two were having a quiet chat when the young Palestinian reached into his pocket, apparently for some documents, and pulled out a gun. Even as Cohen dived away from the table the Palestinian shot him four times at close range. This was the first time an Israeli agent had been murdered by terrorists, and it sent shock waves through the country's intelligence community.

The Palestinians had nearly succeeded in killing Golda Meir, and now they had managed to kill a Mossad agent. Interrogations of captured Palestinians, intercepted telephone conversations, intelligence from foreign governments, and Mossad's own research continually produced the same shortlist of names of those responsible for the attacks. Ali Hassan Salameh's name featured at the top of the list. His death was becoming an imperative for the Wrath of God team.

Operation Spring of Youth

*W*hile Israeli secret agents hunted and killed junior Palestinian officials across Europe, they were also compiling details on three men connected to the Munich massacre, who appeared to be living beyond the reach even of Mossad. Safely ensconced in fortified houses in Beirut, the three senior Palestinians, Abu Youssef (number three in Fatah behind Yasser Arafat and Abu Iyad), Kamel Adwan (PLO chief of operations), and Kamal Nasser (the urbane official spokesman of the PLO), were thought to be untouchable.

The Israeli government was determined that they should suffer the same fate as their junior colleagues. No senior Palestinian was to escape retribution. The Wrath of God team was given instructions that no matter how complicated the hit, the three were to be targeted for assassination.

The operation to kill them was to become legendary within the Israeli intelligence community. Instead of using Mossad agents, as for previous assassinations, the leaders of the Wrath of God team turned instead to the soldiers of Sayeret Matkal ("The Unit"), the elite Israeli equivalent of the British Special Air Services or American Delta Force.

In February 1973, the commander of this squad, Ehud Barak (who became Israeli prime minister in 1999), returned to his base from a meeting at the kirya, the Israeli military compound in Tel Aviv. He assembled Sayeret Matkal's senior officers around the brown Formica-topped table in his office.[1] As the hardened soldiers gathered around expectantly, Barak removed three grainy photographs from a folder lying on his desk.

"Abu Youssef, Kamel Adwan, Kamal Nasser," he said, slapping each of the photographs down on the desk. The soldiers recognized the names and faces. All three were intimately involved with Black September, said Barak, who then revealed where Adwan and Nasser were living: on the second and third floors of a building on the corner of a side street at the end of Rue Verdun, just off the Hamra, Beirut's main shopping center. Abu Youssef was living in a flat on the sixth floor of a building just across the street. Sayeret Matkal had been given the task of assassinating them, said Barak. A murmur ran through the men.

Israeli intelligence agents had obtained detailed architectural plans of the buildings, and the Sayeret Matkal soldiers immediately began considering the various methods they could use to launch an attack. Helicopters were ruled out, because there would be no element of surprise. Instead of an overt assault, the soldiers decided to enter Beirut disguised as tourists.

There was a sense of jubilation among the officers present at the meeting. Finally they would have a chance to deliver a body blow to the terrorists. "We knew that the government had decided to hit and kill each and every person or commander who had something to do with the events at Munich," said Muki Betser, then a Sayeret Matkal platoon commander. "I remember the feeling every [Israeli] citizen had, especially soldiers. We felt that there is a need to conduct a total war against each and every terror organization which was threatening us."[2]

Betser grew up in the village of Nahalal, in the Jezreel Valley, in modern Israel's first cooperative farming settlement, which had been founded by his grandparents. He had joined the Israeli Defense Forces in 1964 and was a proud and stout soldier, one of the elite placed on standby during the Munich crisis. He welcomed the chance to exact revenge for the massacre in Germany.[3]

An Israeli military computer selected the code name "Operation Spring of Youth" (also "Springtime of Youth") for the proposed Beirut attack, and the first preparations were soon under way. Wigs and dresses were found for several soldiers who were to disguise themselves as female tourists, while the rest of the unit began buying an array of holiday clothing. Security was imperative; an intelligence officer even warned the owner of a men's clothing shop on Tel Aviv's Allenby Street to keep quiet about a spate of bulky tough guys buying oversized jackets (which the soldiers would wear to conceal a small arsenal of weaponry).[4]

Betser and the rest of The Unit then spent weeks training every night at a construction site in north Tel Aviv, practicing the skills they would require in Beirut: rapid house entry, shooting from moving vehicles, role-playing. They even practiced walking down the road, with two disguised soldiers pretending to be a happy husband and wife.

Of the four-men teams assigned to each of the three targets, the squad led by Muki Betser had the hardest task. Their mission was to fight their way into the sixth-floor apartment of Abu Youssef, a senior guerrilla with numerous bodyguards. Betser now describes the mission as an "honor."[5]

Entering Beirut and assassinating Palestinian leaders was an operation with major international and regional political repercussions. The Israeli leadership knew it would lead to condemnation around the world, vilification in the United Nations, possibly even economic sanctions, as well as Palestinian retaliation. However, while the operation was still in the planning stage, Israeli concerns were allayed by a murderous Black September operation in the Sudan.

On the evening of March 1, 1973, a small Black September unit attacked the Saudi Arabian embassy in Khartoum as the Saudi ambassador hosted a party for George Moore, the deputy chief of the American mission, who was returning to the U.S. The Saudi embassy was a curious choice as a target, but the attack was designed to enable Black September to put pressure on Israel through a third party — their stalwart American allies — and warn the Saudis against cancelling a tax imposed on Palestinian workers in the kingdom that was fed into PLO coffers.

The terrorists must have been driven by what they saw as a disappointing finale to Black September's Bangkok mission, and the mass killing by Israel of 106 passengers on a Libyan airliner downed on February 21.[6] The attack was designed to demonstrate to the world that the Palestinians had not lost their resolve and remained committed to the revolutionary cause. But it did not immediately go as planned.

Most of the guests at the ambassador's reception escaped through the garden as the terrorists arrived at the front. By the time the Sudanese police arrived the Palestinians were holding just five hostages: Cleo Noel (the American ambassador), George Moore, Guy Eid (the Belgian chargé d'affaires), and the Saudi and Jordanian chargés d'affaires. They demanded that dozens of German, Palestinian, and specifically Black September terrorists be released from prisons in Europe and Israel.

Just as Golda Meir had refused to be blackmailed by the terrorists at Munich, so U.S. President Richard Nixon refused to be blackmailed in Khartoum. But when Egypt's President Sadat tried to intercede and resolve the crisis peacefully, the Black September commandos shot and killed the two Americans and the one Belgian hostage.

The terrorists later surrendered to the Sudanese, who raided the PLO offices in Khartoum and discovered that Fawaz Yassin, the PLO leader in the city, had been intimately involved in the attack, which had been supported financially by Colonel Gaddafi of Libya. There was fury in Washington at the killings, and the Americans agreed to turn a blind eye to the Israeli plans for an incursion into Beirut by Ehud Barak, Muki Betser, and their men.

On April 6, 1973, an advance party of Israeli secret agents arrived in Beirut to prepare for the military assault by The Unit. Posing as foreign tourists, and carrying expertly forged foreign passports, the agents checked into two upscale hotels and hired six cars (a Renault, three white Buicks, a Plymouth sedan, and a station wagon) from a local car rental company.

The attack was planned to take place at night, so the Israelis needed to convince hotel staff there was nothing strange about them travelling around Beirut in the wee hours of the morning. One of the Israelis, travelling with British documents and claiming to be English, told staff at his hotel that his hobby was night fishing. For the first few days of his stay in the city he would disappear after midnight and then return hours later with a contented smile and an impressive catch of fish.

As the Israeli agents plotted how to move The Unit around Beirut at high speed, and rehearsed the routes they would take in their rented cars, Ehud Barak's team was making their final preparations in Israel.

On April 9, the squad left the country from a naval pier at the port of Haifa. According to Muki Betser, David "Dado" Elazar, the Israeli chief of staff, and Eli Ze'ira, the military intelligence commander, were both there to bid them farewell. Dado had some final instructions for the team.

"We've got to kill those bastards," Betser quotes Dado as telling the men.

Betser raised his hand to query the instruction. Until that point he claims the team had been training to capture the three men — albeit using force — and return them to Israel to stand trial for their crimes.

"Did you say 'kill'?" Betser asked.

Dado glanced at Ze'ira and then looked back at his soldiers. "Yes. Kill them," he said.[7]

It took an Israeli speedboat seven hours to reach the waters off Beirut, where The Unit clambered down into Zodiac inflatables crewed by frogmen for a transfer to Beirut's Dove Beach.[8] The Israeli agent posing as an English night fisher guided the boats into land.

Under cover of darkness three cars with Mossad drivers were waiting for the sixteen heavily disguised elite Israeli troops, who landed at 1:30 A.M. on April 10. Muki Betser jumped into the first car, accompanied by Ehud Barak, Yonni Netanyahu (brother of the future Israeli prime minister, Binyamin Netanyahu),[9] and two soldiers, Lonny Rafaeli and Zvika Livneh.[10]

As the three cars drove the twelve miles into the heart of Beirut at a sedate pace, Betser glanced at Barak, his commander. The future prime minister of Israel was disguised as a woman, with a black wig and makeup, and hand grenades instead of breasts nestled in his bra.

"I wore a pair of trousers because the skirts in fashion then were a little short and narrow," Barak has said, recalling the mission. "I also had a very stylish bag, big enough for plenty of explosives."[11] Lonny was disguised as a blonde.

The cars parked near the Rue Verdun and Barak and Betser led the team towards their targets, with Barak's arm slipping around Betser's waist as they walked. Their disguises were apparently so convincing that, even when the "couple" brushed against two armed Lebanese policemen walking along the pavement, the officers did not give them a second glance.

Within a few minutes The Unit had reached the three apartment blocks and split into three groups to attack each one. Barak, navy liaison officer Dov Ber, and another soldier waited in the street while Betser led his four-man team through glass doors into the building housing Abu Youssef's apartment.

"We had grenades and rifles under our clothes and without being noticed we entered the apartments," recalled Betser.[12]

The men raced up the stairs, taking two or three steps with each bound, and drawing their guns as they ran. For maximum firepower Betser was wielding an Uzi submachine gun in one thick hand and a Beretta in the other.

At the sixth floor the men paused on either side of Youssef's front door, while Zvika bent down and placed an explosive charge on the frame. Betser clicked his radio three times to alert Barak in the street below that his team was in position.

Moments later the other two Sayeret Matkal teams clicked their radios to indicate to Barak they were also ready to attack. In the corridor outside Youssef's place, Betser waited expectantly for a five-click reply from Barak to start the operation: "Finally, the clicks began. I counted them off with my fingers, one, two, three, four, five. With the fifth click my open palm turned into a fist, and I pointed at Zvika."[13]

Zvika jumped up and detonated an explosion that blew the door open. Betser and his team raced inside, with the leader following a predetermined route and breaking left into the apartment's main corridor and on through Youssef's office. "The force had a picture and we knew exactly who the man was and what he did," said Betser.[14]

With Zvika behind him, Betser turned to see Youssef briefly appear at the door of the master bedroom. Even as Youssef slammed the door in a bid to escape, the chatter of machine-gun fire pierced the night. Bullets from Betser's and Zvika's Uzis tore through the door and wall. Then with a hefty kick Betser smashed down the remains of the bedroom door and found Youssef lying dead on the floor. At some point in the melee Abu Youssef's wife was also shot dead, as were three of his bodyguards.

In the apartment building across the road the other two Israeli teams also found their targets. Kamal Nasser managed to hide under his desk and squeeze off a single bullet, hitting an Israeli called Aharon in the leg, before he was killed by a burst of fire from Aharon's comrades.[15]

As The Unit burst into Kamel Adwan's flat their target leapt away from his wife Maha towards a Kalashnikov. He was riddled with bullets. Tragically, as the team left Adwan's flat another door opened on the landing and one of the Israeli commandos fired instinctively, fatally wounding a seventy-year-old Italian woman awakened by the commotion.

The Israelis had been hoping to find Abu Iyad and Ali Hassan Salameh, who they thought might be staying in one of the three flats that night, but the leaders of Black September were asleep in bed elsewhere in the city.

"My home was about 55 yards from the late Abu Youssef's home," Salameh said later. "The Israeli assassins didn't come to my home for a very simple reason: it was guarded by fourteen men."[16]

Outside in the street more shooting indicated that the Israelis were under attack. Betser led his team back out of the apartment and ran down the stairs to join the fight. As he emerged onto the street he was witness to an extraordinary sight.

One of the Israeli team, in drag with a blonde wig, was blazing away with an Uzi submachine gun at a Lebanese police Land-Rover that had been racing towards the scene. Another Land-Rover carrying four more policemen appeared on the road, only for bursts of Israeli fire to kill or wound all of the men.

The three Israeli getaway cars skidded to a halt near Barak, just as another police Jeep appeared. Betser pulled a grenade from under his jacket and lobbed it at the policemen. It bounced off the tarpaulin roof and exploded in the street. "Four gendarmes tumbled out of the jeep, either wounded or dead," said Betser.[17]

Meanwhile, a Mossad official was telephoning a senior Lebanese police officer. Posing as another local official, he told him that Palestinian guerrillas were fighting among themselves near Rue Verdun. Anxious that his men should not be injured in a gunfight between heavily armed Palestinians, the police chief apparently called off other police reinforcements who were on their way to the area.[18]

The Israelis clambered into their getaway cars and raced back to the beach, and Israeli fighters monitored their escape from on high, as helicopters dropped spiked "crows' feet" to disable the tires of any pursuers. To prevent the Lebanese government from taking military action against the helicopters, Mossad officials impersonating Lebanese army officers rang the Beirut police chief and told him they were launching helicopters to locate the source of the fighting. The Lebanese coastguard was then contacted by Mossad agents pretending to be the police and told the same thing.[19]

After spending a nervous half mile stuck behind several unsuspecting Lebanese armored personnel carriers on routine patrol, the Israelis arrived back at Dove Beach, where they parked their cars neatly in a line and were greeted by naval commandos who shuttled them back to the missile boat waiting offshore. From the moment Ehud Barak, Muki Betser, and The Unit had landed on the beach to the moment they left again, the operation had taken precisely half an hour.

Israeli forces struck elsewhere in Beirut that night, largely to cause diversions from the three main assassinations. The advance party of Mossad agents had hired six cars. Three were used to transport Ehud

Barak's team, while the other three took paratroopers led by the tenacious fighter Amnon Shahak to the Sabra refugee camp.[20] There they blew up the six-story headquarters of Naif Hawatmeh's Popular Democratic Front for the Liberation of Palestine and fought a vicious battle with PDFLP guerrillas.[21] More Israelis attacked "weapons manufacturing facilities" and PLO fuel dumps.[22]

Nevertheless, it was the attacks around the Rue Verdun that received most media attention. The strike was greeted with incredulity around the world, and while Lebanese newspapers wondered at the identity of the "two beautiful she-devils, a blonde and a brunette, who fought off the police and army like dervishes with machine guns,"[23] Western newspapers reported the killings with some degree of admiration. All agreed that the attack was conducted with typical Israeli flair and military ingenuity.

Muki Betser, has no doubts about the legitimacy of the operation.[24] The Munich massacre, he says, was "a traumatic event, it is part of our collective memory. [For] those who were alive at that time, those who read about it, it is a trauma that will be remembered for many years. And there was a feeling of anger and a deep need to punish the organizations and, once and for all, to get rid of the so-called fighting of terrorists against civilians.

"This operation, 'Spring of Youth,' was aimed to punish those who planned and committed this crime — the murder of the athletes in Munich. The operation was a source of honor and pride to Israelis. I think that every nation that respects itself should know how to punish those who harm them. I think that hitting their leaders made them, instead of planning operations, defend themselves."

Certainly, Israel's desire for revenge seemed to be sated. Golda Meir was delighted: "We killed the murderers who were planning to murder again," she told the Knesset.[25]

The raid certainly fulfilled one of the avowed aims of the wider Wrath of God operation: that of forcing the Palestinian guerrillas onto the defensive, using terrorist tactics against their leadership. Within days of the Beirut attack dozens more guards were attached to Palestinian leaders, the families of the leaders were flown to new homes in Egypt, and the most prominent Palestinians were told to change their addresses at least once a month — and to keep details secret.

The Israeli incursion into Beirut was not the end of the assassination missions. On April 11, just hours after the Beirut attack, the Israelis moved to Athens to kill their eighth victim. Zaiad Muchasi had replaced Hussein Abad Al Chir as the head of Black September in Cyprus and was in the Greek capital for a meeting. He did not last long. Wrath of God agents placed a bomb in his hotel room and blew him to pieces as he undressed before going to bed.

Victims nine and ten were two junior Black September terrorists. Abdel Hamid Shibi and Abdel Hadi Nakaa were blown up in their Mercedes in Rome as they prepared to attack an Israeli target.[26] Both were seriously injured. But the Israelis were still after bigger fish.

As Barak and his men were preparing for their daring raid into Lebanon, the men and women entrusted with killing those involved in the Munich massacre moved back to Paris and began surveillance of another target. This was the new head of Black September in France, Mohammed Boudia, a forty-one-year-old Algerian intellectual whose sexual exploits caused such titillation in Mossad that they nicknamed their prey "Bluebeard."

Boudia's involvement in terrorism seems clear. By the time the Israelis arrived in Paris to hunt him down, he was also being pursued by Italian police — they suspected him of attacking a refinery in Trieste on August 5, 1972, with forty-four pounds of explosives. The attack was a spectacular success, burning more than 250,000 tons of crude oil at a cost of $2.5 billion.[27]

Boudia had also been named as a terrorist leader by Evelyne Barges, a committed young terrorist who had been arrested by the Israelis while on a Black September mission in Tel Aviv. Barges, an attractive twenty-five-year-old blonde with more than a passing resemblance to Brigitte Bardot, had been sent with an elderly French couple and Nadia and Marlene Bardali, the daughters of a rich Moroccan merchant, to launch a campaign of bombings against tourist hotels during the Easter holiday season.

The group had entered Israel as walking bombs. Their coat linings were impregnated with chemicals which, when combined with other substances smuggled into Israel by Barges, made a potent type of napalm. The three women were also carrying powdered and liquid explosives hidden in their underwear, shoes, lipstick, and even Tampax. After they had been stopped and questioned at the airport by Israeli security officials the two sisters revealed details of the plot, and Boudia was named as the brains behind the planned attacks. Mossad were soon on his trail.

Boudia was then working as a director of the Théâtre de l'Ouest Parisien, but he was a tough man to follow. A master of disguise, he constantly changed identities (and even dressed as a woman) to throw off pursuing French government agents assigned to monitor his movements. His skill at cultivating a team of impressionable young female supporters who could be used to provide cover, sex, and security, was watched with admiration and later copied by Ilich Ramirez Sanchez, better known as "Carlos the Jackal."

Tracking Boudia took dozens of Israeli agents, and on the night of June 27, 1973, they watched as he left his blue Renault 16 on the Rue des Fossés St. Bernard, outside the home of one of his many girlfriends. The Israeli team knew that he always made a few perfunctory checks around the outside of his car for explosive devices, so instead they broke into the car and slipped a pressure-activated "land mine," packed with heavy nuts and bolts, under the driver's seat.

The following morning Boudia emerged, conducted his cursory checks and settled into his driving seat. His left foot was still on the ground outside when the "mine" under his seat detonated. The nuts and bolts rocketed upwards through his body, leaving gaping exit wounds and tearing out through his shirt. Police investigators found shards of Boudia's flesh all over the car parked in front.

Israeli officials wanted the families of the dead athletes to know they were pursuing the Black September killers. As Wrath of God teams roamed Europe and the Middle East hunting down those Mossad deemed responsible for the Munich massacre, a Mossad agent would contact Ankie Spitzer and other widows after each kill to tell them the dead of Fürstenfeldbruck were being avenged.

Relatives of the athletes had ambivalent feelings about the operations. "I knew about it," confirmed Ankie. "They would call me and they gave me the information: 'Listen to the news at ten o'clock this morning . . . This is another one for Andre . . .'"[28] Whereas some of the relatives privately admit they drew satisfaction from turning the tables on the terrorists, Ankie says it didn't give her any satisfaction. "It didn't fill me with joy to think, 'Oh, great, now they're revenging Andre,' because I never looked for that revenge. I don't live for revenge, I live for justice." All Ankie wanted, she said, was for the terrorists who killed her husband to pay the price in court for what they did.

Nurit Cohen, the widow of Baruch, the Mossad agent assassinated by Black September in Spain in January 1973, was similarly sickened by all the killing. The Wrath of God team was also assigned to investigate Cohen's murder and avenge his death. At least three Palestinian activists involved in planning and killing Baruch Cohen have since been assassinated by the Israelis,[29] but the executions were little comfort to his widow. Nurit has said, "Occasionally, service officers would come to visit me and ask, as if they were being casual, 'Did you see in the paper about that guy who was killed, or that one who was blown up?' What do you think, that it comforted me? It meant that another family had been hurt, another woman left alone, a few more children who lost their father."[30]

By the time Boudia was killed in Paris, it had become obvious to the three surviving Palestinian militants involved in the Munich operation that they were being hunted. But Jamal Al-Gashey, who was then barely out of his teens, now claims he was not afraid of being killed. "I wasn't afraid of anything," he says defiantly. Al-Gashey was flown to Libya after the Munich operation and released. He later married his sweetheart and started a family. But freedom was a cage, for Al-Gashey spent decades living in hiding.

His main fear during this time, he says, was protecting his new family from Israeli fury: "I was just afraid in case my wife had to live her life with no husband and my children with no father. I didn't want them to live like that. So we tried as hard as possible to live a normal life . . . going out, having holidays, spending time in the fresh air."[31]

The two other survivors of the Munich attack, Adnan Al-Gashey (who had machine-gunned the Israeli hostages in one of the helicopters at Fürstenfeldbruck) and Mohammed Safady, also faced the threat of Israeli vengeance. "I started to get scared after our first child was born that I might lose him, because I was very much in love with him," said the wife of Adnan Al-Gashey. "He never shared this fear. On the contrary, he just carried on his life as normal. The fear was on my part after the operation."[32] Adnan and his wife hid in Lebanon and moved from one secure house to another at night to avoid Israeli hit squads.

However, according to his wife, "Life just went on." Adnan had a fatalistic approach to the Israeli threat. "He said that Israel was going to have to get its revenge. It couldn't let them off. But he just carried on life as normal. I was surrounded by a feeling that Israel would separate us, because Golda Meir had promised that the Israeli athletes would be avenged with the deaths of those who had not been killed in Germany."

Nobody can hide forever. Several years after the Munich massacre, Adnan Al-Gashey travelled to one of the Gulf States looking for work. "He went abroad to work to earn money for the family, since our needs were growing. It was proof that he wasn't scared." Adnan had a cousin in the country whom Mossad had kept tabs on. As soon as Adnan arrived he made contact with his cousin and a Wrath of God team was alerted. Adnan Al-Gashey was quietly executed by the Israeli hit team.

"At first it was very hard," said his widow. "After a while, I started to see him more as a hero of the Munich operation, someone the Israelis were unable to leave alone. I lived a tragedy as they say, just as anyone who has lost her husband in an operation or a battle, but I brought up the children, who I still had, thank God."

Mohammed Safady was also hunted by the Mossad and assassinated, apparently because of connections he kept with his family in Lebanon.[33]

But Adnan and Mohammed were just foot soldiers in the Munich operation. The Israelis were desperate to find the commanders, the men behind the fedayeen: Abu Daoud, Abu Iyad, and Ali Hassan Salameh, the Red Prince.

Salameh could never be a fugitive shadow, hiding from his Israeli pursuers. He was a public figure who taunted the Wrath of God team by ordering more attacks on Israeli targets. Salameh was so angered by the killing of Mohammed Boudia in Paris that two days later he ordered a young Palestinian student in the U.S. to launch a one-man revenge operation.

The target chosen for the student was Colonel Yosef Alon, the deputy Israeli military attaché in Washington, who was responsible for supervising the transfer of fighters to the Israeli air force. Alon had just returned home from a party with his wife Deborah when the young Palestinian hit man confronted him and shot him five times as he stood on his lawn.

This action bore all of Salameh's hallmarks, and the Israeli government decided that turning their Wrath of God hit team on the senior Palestinian was a top priority. But it was not only for his involvement in Alon's death, the Munich operation, and a dozen other attacks that the Israelis wanted Salameh dead; they knew he was rising through the ranks of the Palestinian leadership.

Salameh was not just a glamorous Palestinian terrorist, he was a potential future leader of the PLO, and he was also managing something no other Palestinian guerrilla had ever achieved: he had established a beneficial relationship with the American CIA. For all these reasons Ali Hassan Salameh became Mossad's priority target.

The CIA had been talking to the PLO since 1969, when Robert Ames, their star Middle East analyst and the head of station in Beirut, made tentative links with Fatah, which he regarded as one of the more moderate factions within the PLO. By the time Salameh and

Ames began talking, the American was claiming that he had the full backing of President Nixon and omnipotent National Security Advisor Henry Kissinger, who were both said to want to open a new era of dialogue between the superpower and the stateless Palestinians.

Salameh, who became Yasser Arafat's personal representative at meetings with the Americans, was Ames's ticket to a senior position within the U.S. administration. While Salameh viewed the meetings as a route to eventual acceptance by the White House, Ames viewed the Palestinian as a potential recruit, or CIA "asset," from the beginning of their relationship. The CIA soon offered Salameh three million in cash to work for them, but Salameh was an idealist, appalled by the suggestion he would sell out to the Americans for something as tacky as money. He refused to speak to Ames for months afterwards.[34]

The relationship between Salameh and the CIA cooled after the Munich massacre, as the Americans were unsure of the depth of his involvement in Black September. Many U.S. agents were also genuinely shocked by the level of brutality shown by the Palestinian terrorists, whom they had previously thought of as educated freedom fighters. But things soon warmed up again.

The CIA's second attempt to recruit Salameh actually came after Munich, when Salameh was visited in Beirut by another senior CIA officer who gave him a blank check. "I saw somebody giving him a check without any amount written in, telling him, 'You write in the number you want,'" said Um Hassan, Salameh's first wife. "My husband was mad, very angry at the time, because it was very insulting to him. He threw the check back and left."[35]

It was inevitable that Salameh would be targeted by Israel, and he accepted the attention with stoicism: "It was natural that my name be singled out and a price put on my head . . . because . . . we sought to hit at Israeli interests and personalities . . . The enemy concentrated on specific names and personalities in order to portray us as terrorist gangs . . . That's why the enemy started to talk about deterring terrorism with terrorism and about assassinations . . . and I was one of the main targets . . . They are trying to make our assassination a legitimate act. That's why the concentration was on destroying my image: on portraying me as a playboy . . . a murderer, a bloodthirsty killer who cannot sleep without seeing blood. The intention, obviously was to pave the way for my liquidation."[36]

The Israelis were indeed preparing for an attempt on Salameh's life. Across Europe and the Middle East, the Wrath of God team began to hunt him down. Israeli agents rattled their contacts for several months until a tip-off came through in June 1973 that Salameh had flown to Paris from the Middle East (travelling via communist East Germany) for meetings with other Palestinian guerrillas. The tip even came with an address where Salameh was said to be staying: a quiet hotel on the Left Bank in Paris.

There are several versions of what happened next, but the most plausible account is that, just as two Mossad agents moved close to the hotel to begin surveillance of Salameh, their target slipped out of the hotel by a back entrance and disappeared.[37]

With Israeli agents hot on his trail, either Salameh began a masterful disinformation operation or the Israelis began following a trail of false leads. Some sources suggest that Salameh began spreading rumors that he had gone to live in Scandinavia, and Mossad began receiving reports from Geneva, Zurich, and Paris, all saying that Salameh had slipped out of their clutches and moved north.

Most of the agents in the Wrath of God team responsible for the earlier killings were exhausted by July 1973, and "Mike," the senior Israeli agent in charge of the assassination team, promptly began to assemble a new squad of agents in order to locate Salameh in Scandinavia and kill him.

At least fifteen Israeli agents were picked out for Salameh's assassination: "Mike" as team leader, two to carry out the killing, two to provide cover, two agents specializing in logistics, a communications expert, and seven more to fill in where required. "Mike" travelled under a French passport as Edouard Stanislas Laskier. His deputy "Abraham," who had worked for Mossad in the Israeli embassy in Paris, posed as Leslie Orbaum, a schoolteacher from the English city of Leeds.

"Mike" also brought in "Sylvia," a beautiful South African–born woman recruited by Mossad while working on a kibbutz. She had al-

ready crisscrossed the globe on missions for the Israelis, carrying a fake
Canadian passport and pretending to be a newspaper photographer
called Patricia Roxborough. Other agents involved included "Gustav
Pistauer," "Nora Heffner," "Raoul Cousin," "Jean-Luc Sévenier," and
a stunning auburn-haired female agent known as "Tamar."

"Marianne," a twenty-five-year-old blonde woman with joint
Swedish and Israeli nationality, was also recruited. "Marianne" grew
up in Scandinavia before emigrating to Israel and working as a data
processor for Israeli intelligence. She was supposed to help the team
of assassins pick their way around the region and smooth over any
problems the Israelis had in adapting to the unfamiliar North.

In his first major Mossad assignment, a thirty-six-year-old
Brazilian Jew called "Zwi" was recruited to help, and "Mike" also en-
listed "Michael," twenty-seven, as the communications specialist.

The killers retain a degree of anonymity, but one was tall,
blond, distinctly Scandinavian in appearance according to witnesses,
and travelled on a false British passport identifying him as Jonathan
Ingleby from Manchester.

On July 8, 1973, Mossad also approached "Dan," a thirty-six-
year-old Danish Jew working as a businessman in Herzliyya, to the
north of Tel Aviv, who had been living in Israel for little more than
two years, and asked if he would be prepared to act as an interpreter
for the unit. "Dan," glad to help his country, readily agreed.

The Dane arrived in Stockholm, Sweden, with two other Mossad agents on July 11 and rented a large apartment for six months,
which was to be used as a safe house for the operation. He also had
fifteen keys cut for the apartment and arranged delivery of six sets of
sheets and bedcovers.

At this point the Israelis were no closer to locating their target.
It was not until July 14 that "Mike" and his unit received a tip that
Salameh was living in Norway. He was about to receive a visit from a
courier called Kemal Benamane, who was supposed to be delivering
information or a package to the Red Prince. Mossad immediately
began hunting for the courier in the hope he would lead them to
their target, eventually tracing him to Oslo.

With what they thought was the initial link to Salameh uncovered, the rest of the Israeli team made preparations to leave for Scandinavia. Although the exact figure has never been confirmed, approximately fourteen agents are believed to have received a secret briefing in the VIP lounge at Tel Aviv's Ben Gurion Airport on the morning of July 18, 1973. Officials stressed the importance of their target. They could not afford to fail.

By the time the team arrived in Oslo on various scheduled flights, and under a variety of cover names and identities, Benamane had disappeared from Oslo and reappeared in the small town of Lillehammer, which nestles along the shore of Lake Mjøsa one hundred miles to the north. It was a strange destination for a man the Israelis suspected of delivering important information and documents to a senior member of the PLO. There could be only one conclusion: Benamane was in Lillehammer to meet Ali Hassan Salameh.

Ten members of the Israeli team hired cars, drove up to Lillehammer, and found Benamane staying at the small Hotel Skotte, a short walk from the railway station. Posing as tourists, two of the Israeli agents even managed to sit next to Benamane in the television lounge as he idly watched a sleep-inducing fishing drama in Swedish called *Fishery East in the Mountains.*

The next day, as the rest of the Israeli team began moving up to Lillehammer to join the first two agents, the advance unit lost track of Benamane, only to catch sight of him again talking intently to another Arab in the tiny Karoline Café near the Lillehammer town hall.

The Mossad agents could barely contain their excitement. Benamane was surely meeting with Ali Hassan Salameh. "Marianne" strolled inside to get a closer look, have a drink, and compare the man in the café with an out-of-focus photo of the Red Prince she was carrying in her pocket. She was not convinced that the Arab was Salameh, but one of her senior colleagues was certain. The fact that the Arab left the café and rode off on a bicycle did not apparently shake the agent's belief that the man was their target. Salameh was known as a wealthy international playboy, but the Israelis had also begun investing him with mythical powers of deception: he was, many believed, a master of disguise.

Benamane, his work apparently done, left Lillehammer on the 2:08 P.M. train and returned to Oslo, and the Israelis switched their attention to the Arab with the bicycle. When the man went for a swim in the local baths, "Marianne" jumped into the water and managed to get close enough to hear him talking in French with another man as he swam. This was the deciding factor for the Israelis. They knew the Red Prince was well educated and multilingual: the man *had* to be Salameh.

Half of the team immediately converged on the swimming baths, and when the Arab left after his swim they carefully tailed him back to his small flat at Rugdeveien 2A. The Israelis then began watching the residence continuously by sitting in hired cars out in the street, in plain view of the local residents.

Some members of the Israeli team apparently found it hard to believe that the Arab who left the Karoline Café on a bicycle was their target and continued surveillance of Benamane. However, he booked himself into the Stephen Hotel in Oslo, talked to the staff about how he was soon leaving for Geneva, and left for Switzerland the next day. Once Benamane had left the country, "Mike" and his team became convinced the bicycling Arab was their target. The entire team converged on Lillehammer.

The squad that would carry out the killing — "Jonathan Ingleby," "Rolf Baehr," and "Gérard-Emile Lafond" — arrived at around 2:00 P.M. on July 21 in a dark-green Mercedes and checked into Lillehammer's Oppland Tourist Hotel. An hour later Zvi Zamir, the head of Mossad, who had personally witnessed the deaths of the Israeli athletes at Munich, allegedly also arrived in the region to monitor the operation; he checked into the Esso Olrud Hotel south of Lillehammer with a bodyguard.[38] Israel would soon have its revenge on the man who planned the Munich attack.

But at the same time as the Israelis were preparing to launch their operation, another terrorist atrocity was unfolding elsewhere in Europe. The afternoon before the Israeli killers arrived in Lillehammer, a Japan Airlines Boeing 747 flight from Amsterdam to Tokyo with 123 passengers was hijacked by a mixed group of Japanese and Arab terrorists who announced they were changing the call sign of the plane to "Operation Mount Carmel."

There was panic in Israel when military commanders heard the news. For months Israeli intelligence had been hearing rumors that the Palestinians were plotting a massive suicide attack on the Jewish state. Terrorists had apparently persuaded an Arab pilot to deliberately crash a plane loaded with explosives into the heart of an Israeli city. Haifa was built at the base of Mount Carmel.

However, the leader of the hijacking accidentally killed herself with a hand grenade during the attack, and the other terrorists flew the plane to Dubai to wait for further instructions from their handlers.

So just as the hit team in Lillehammer was requesting further instructions from the Israeli government, officials in Tel Aviv were concentrating almost exclusively on the hijack. The lines between Lillehammer and Tel Aviv hummed briefly with news that Mossad had found Ali Hassan Salameh, and at 6:00 P.M. the Israeli government gave a green light for his assassination.

Working in shifts, the Israeli agents had kept up twenty-four-hour surveillance of Salameh at his home in Lillehammer. On the evening of July 21, 1973, they watched as he left his home with a young woman to go to a local cinema. It was showing the blockbuster *Where Eagles Dare,* a ludicrous Second World War thriller in which Richard Burton and Clint Eastwood take on the might of the German army only to discover traitors in their midst. When Salameh and his female friend left they were trailed by a team of Israeli agents. The couple caught a bus to their stop at Furubakken and then slowly began walking home, chatting and laughing together.

They were within sight of Rugdeveien 2A, walking slowly up the hill to their house, when a white Mazda jerked to a halt in front of them. With Rolf Baehr and Gérard-Emile Lafond covering them from inside the car, Jonathan Ingleby and the female agent Tamar leapt out, drew their guns in one fluid movement, and immediately began shooting.

They fired continuously, pumping lead shots into Salameh's body. He fell to the ground clutching his bloodied stomach, and Tamar shot him as he lay dying on the ground. One local described the fourteen bullets as sounding like popping "champagne corks."[39]

The screams of Salameh's friend echoed down the road as the Israelis jumped into their car. They drove away at high speed, and their victim died on the pavement.[40]

But the Israelis had not killed Ali Hassan Salameh, the Red Prince, the "mastermind" of the Munich massacre, wealthy scion of a legendary Palestinian family and close friend of Yasser Arafat. Instead they had killed Ahmed Bouchiki, a Moroccan waiter who had just been to the cinema with his pregnant wife Turil and was returning to his small home. It was one of the greatest disasters in the history of the Mossad.

11

The Red Prince

*T*he killing of Ahmed Bouchiki was the first in Lillehammer for forty years, and although the police who arrived at the scene realized it was a professional "hit," they initially suspected it was the result of a drugs feud. But the victim, said his neighbors, was certainly not involved in any form of criminality. He was well known locally and led an exemplary life.

Lillehammer was then a small provincial town of just twenty thousand people. The arrival of more than a dozen Israelis with swarthy Mediterranean complexions had not gone unnoticed, and Bouchiki's neighbors proved extremely helpful to the police in the first few hours of their investigations. Several strangers had been spotted outside Bouchiki's house in the days prior to the killing. Other locals said they had seen a mysterious group of foreigners roaming the town driving cars with out-of-town license plates. One of the neighbors even caught a glimpse of the white Mazda used by the killers as it raced from the scene.

It was a crucial breakthrough. As the Mossad agents were fleeing Lillehammer and returning to Oslo on their way out of the country, the Norwegian police had their first lead. "Mike" left Norway on a ferry and eventually returned to Israel,[1] but when "Dan" and "Marianne" tried to return their hired car to a rental company at Oslo airport, an observant rental agent named Asbjørn Slørdahl quietly alerted the police, and an officer arrived to arrest them.

The Norwegians, still unaware the killing had been conducted by one of the world's most "efficient" spy agencies, pressed ahead with their investigation. "Marianne" — on her first operation for Mossad — was flustered and scared, and she soon revealed details of their safe house, where "Sylvia" and "Abraham" were arrested. "Dan" was found to have written down the unlisted telephone number (14-15-80) for a man called "Zigal," who turned out to be Yigal Eyal, the head of security at the Israeli embassy.

The Norwegian police thought Zigal worked for El Al and raided his home, arresting "Michael" and "Zwi," who had taken refuge there. Zigal identified himself as a diplomat and ordered the police to leave, but by then the Norwegians had the scent of the trail in their nostrils. They left Zigal's apartment, but took "Michael" and "Zwi" along with them.

In contrast to their reputation as the world's finest intelligence operatives, the Israeli agents had fallen like flies. Within days of the killing the Norwegian police had six agents in custody. The Norwegian detectives soon heard rumors from Israel that the suspects were agents of the elite Mossad, and the affair became a full-blown diplomatic incident.

Even when in custody the Israeli agents proved embarrassingly willing to disclose details of their operation. "Dan," who suffered from extreme claustrophobia, proved most useful. As soon as his cell door slammed shut he was reduced to a nervous wreck and began revealing details of the attack in return for a transfer to a larger cell with a small window.[2]

Mossad's humiliation deepened when the Norwegians found a key on one of the suspects for a safe house in Paris. It was handed to the French police, who raided the flat and discovered keys to other safe houses in the French capital. They also found evidence that several of those involved in the Lillehammer killing had been involved in other Wrath of God revenge assassinations.

When news of the arrests reached Israel there was panic among senior government and intelligence officials. "Losing" agents was what Golda Meir had expressly warned against when Operation Wrath of God was conceived. Israeli agents were in Norwegian cells, and Mossad operations across much of Europe were threatened. Panic turned to fury when Norwegian newspapers revealed the true identity of their victim. Mossad, secret guardian of the Jewish people, previously so invincible in the eyes of the Israeli public, took a battering from which it took years to recover.

The Israeli government tried hard to cover up its scandalous involvement in the Lillehammer killing with a little help from the Norwegian intelligence services,[3] but the Norwegian police decided to try the captured agents for their involvement in murder. The court case that followed revealed the inexperience of some of the Israeli agents assigned to kill the Red Prince and exact revenge for the deaths of the eleven Israeli athletes in Munich.

Many of the more senior agents responsible for the initial, successful assassinations during the Wrath of God operation were exhausted after working continuously for months crisscrossing Europe and the Middle East, and their controllers gave them a rest. Thus, for the operation against Mossad's most important target, the group leader "Mike" was forced to rely on several amateur agents, who had little more than cursory experience of intelligence work.

"Dan," the claustrophobe, even gave his police interrogators the name of someone called "Miko" on a Mossad emergency line in Tel Aviv who would be able to confirm he was an agent working for the Israeli government. He thought it would somehow encourage his interrogators to release him. When the number was revealed in court it was pure theater. Journalists tumbled out of the courthouse to call Mossad, only to discover the emergency line — normally used to bring agents in from the cold — had been replaced by a prerecorded English voice, which curtly informed them the line had been disconnected.

Although the two killers and their commanders were never captured, on February 1, 1974, "Sylvia" and "Abraham" were sentenced to five and a half years, "Dan" to five, "Marianne" to two and a half, and "Zwi" (who was found guilty of spying) to a year in jail. "Michael" was acquitted.

"Sylvia," the world later discovered, spent her time in jail learning to play the guitar and studying psychology and Hebrew. When the Norwegian state prosecutor had an accident and was hospitalized, she sent him a get-well card and signed it "005, The Spy Who Came in from the Cold" (the number being the length of her sentence). "Sylvia" later married her Norwegian defense lawyer, Anneus Schodt, and settled in the country.[4]

With international outrage at the killing of innocent Ahmed Bouchiki mounting with every new revelation about Mossad's involvement, Golda Meir bowed to the pressure and told Mossad to suspend all operations connected with Operation Wrath of God. She also announced that an inquiry would be conducted into the Lillehammer debacle. "Mike," however, was eventually allowed to conduct the inquiry himself. The final report on the Lillehammer killing absolved all those involved of blame,[5] at which point several junior Mossad officers resigned in disgust, and others wrote strongly worded protest letters to the prime minister and the head of Mossad.

Despite this farce, and the obvious evidence of official Israeli responsibility, it would be years before anyone in the Israeli government considered apologizing to the pregnant Turil Bouchiki for the tragic loss of her husband, shot to death in front of her eyes as the couple walked home from an evening at the cinema.

Although Operation Wrath of God was suspended, Salameh remained a potent threat to Israel. Within two weeks of the Lillehammer incident, he was ready to avenge his three friends' murder in Beirut at the hands of Israeli Special Forces. A group calling itself "The Seventh Suicide Squad," which came under the broad leadership of Salameh and Black September, was given the task of avenging the Beirut deaths with an attack at Athens airport on travellers to Israel.

On August 5, 1973, Tallal Khaled Kaddourah and Shafik Hussein el Arida, Palestinians aged twenty-two and twenty-one, respectively, produced submachine guns and grenades in the departure lounge at Athens airport and began blazing away at what they thought were Jewish passengers leaving Greece for Israel. The two terrorists actually opened fire on passengers waiting to board a TWA flight to New York. There was carnage as they sprayed bullets indiscriminately.

"I saw two Arabs waiting with their suitcases for a security check," said Gerald Stern, a dentist from Pittsburgh. "An official asked them to open the cases and they took out submachine guns. I threw myself on the floor when the shooting started. All around me people were bleeding and screaming with pain. [The Arabs] barricaded themselves behind the bar and fired bursts from their guns. A man next to me had his chest ripped open by bullets. I looked up and saw an old man near the exit trying to run out. He was shot down. I saw someone else with a baby in his arms. He was all covered with blood."[6]

The departure lounge was a bloody mess, with the dying and the seriously wounded screaming for help. An Indian passenger and two Americans were killed outright, while Laura Haack, a sixteen-year-old American tourist, died later in the hospital. Another fifty-five passengers were wounded.

Although the two Palestinians were apparently supposed to martyr themselves in the attack, both preferred the idea of prison. They were caught, convicted, and then promptly released by the Greek government when terrorists hijacked a Greek ship in Karachi and used them as bargaining chips.

Athens was the last attack to be publicly linked to Black September, but the spiral of violence continued and many intelligence sources believe Black September was responsible for another attack in Paris precisely a month after the Athens murders, and exactly a year after the Munich Olympics attack.

Their aim was to secure the release from prison in Jordan of Abu Daoud, one of the leaders of the Munich attack and a senior official within Black September. In February 1973, Daoud had been caught conducting surveillance of government buildings in Amman, the Jordanian capital, in preparation for a major Black September attack organized by Abu Iyad.

Abu Iyad and Abu Daoud (who were both marked for death on

the Israeli Wrath of God list) had been determined to secure the release of Palestinian fighters languishing in Jordanian jails. In their plan, sixteen terrorists were supposed to occupy the Jordanian prime minister's office, take government ministers hostage, and bargain for the release of prisoners. But the plan did not unfold as expected.

Abu Daoud was stopped at random in his car by Bedouin police while cruising around Amman. The officers noted that his passport listed him as the father of six children; but the "wife" sitting in the front passenger seat next to Daoud was clearly a young girl. When the police asked him to accompany them back to their station for a quiet chat, Daoud's "wife" (Salwa Abu Khadrah, a fifteen-year-old activist from Haifa)[7] accidentally dropped his Czech-made pistol and some ammunition from beneath her clothes. "This complicated matters," admitted Daoud laconically. Both were immediately arrested.[8]

Daoud had been in prison for several months when, on September 5, 1973, five Arab terrorists forced their way into the elegant Saudi Arabian embassy in Paris, took thirteen hostages, and demanded his immediate release. However, while the world immediately assumed they wanted to secure the freedom of one of their Arab brothers, it now appears that the group — which gave itself the name "The Punishment Group" — actually wanted to capture and kill Daoud for disclosing many of Black September's secrets.

The terrorists were desperate, but they were not from quite the same murderous stock as the two Athens killers. The leader of the Paris assault, a man known only as "The Doctor," negotiated openly with the Kuwaiti ambassador, who led a group of Arab dignitaries trying to solve the crisis. Four of the female hostages were swapped for the Iraqi ambassador, who bravely offered to take their place, and the terrorists eventually left the embassy with five hostages. The French government allowed them to fly to Cairo, where they refuelled and then flew on to Kuwait and gave themselves up.

The failure of the mission was highly embarrassing for Ali Hassan Salameh and other hardline Palestinian leaders, who were trying to portray their fighters as brave and invincible. There was no benefit in claiming responsibility for the failed attack in the name of Black

September, and so the organization responsible for the Munich massacre officially disappeared after the attack in Athens.

The month of the Paris attack saw major developments in the Middle East. King Hussein, the diminutive Jordanian monarch still clinging to power despite the best efforts of Palestinians to dethrone or assassinate him, flew to Cairo for meetings with President Sadat of Egypt and President Assad of Syria. Until the meeting Hussein had been isolated within the Arab world because of his actions against the Palestinians three years previously (which had given birth to Black September). But Assad and Sadat welcomed him back into the fold, and the three began plotting a new military attack on Israel — an attack that the world would come to know as the Yom Kippur War.

When Hussein returned to Jordan, rehabilitated in the eyes of other Arab leaders, he threw open his jails and released more than one thousand political prisoners, including dozens of senior Palestinians. In an astonishing display of camaraderie, Hussein even went to the prison holding Abu Daoud, took tea with the man, and then personally arranged his release.[9]

The war Hussein, Sadat, and Assad planned in Cairo erupted on October 6, 1973. Syrian tanks struck deep in the Golan Heights and Egyptian troops swarmed across the Suez Canal on the holiest day in the Jewish calendar. Israeli men were interrupted midway through prayers and left synagogues to head for the front. The war that followed was short but devastating. If Egyptian commanders had not paused in their attacks, fearful of travelling outside the range of their rockets, Israel could have been destroyed.

But the Egyptians did not follow through with their attack, and the Israelis were able to reorganize and counterattack, with General Arik Sharon leading a desperate force back into Egypt and to within an hour of the outskirts of Cairo. As the dust settled during an internationally brokered ceasefire, Israeli leaders realized they had been pushed perilously close to the abyss. They could no longer be blasé about international support, and there could be no more blatant assassinations of those responsible for the Munich massacre. Instead there would have to be a pause in operations, and the final killings of those on the Wrath of God hit list would have to be conducted quietly in the future, with minimum chance of Israeli involvement being discovered.

Five years after the debacle in Lillehammer, senior Mossad agents decided it was time to resume the hunt for the Black September chiefs. The relatives of the athletes killed in Munich were still struggling to rebuild their lives, and the memory of the attack was still an open wound in the Israeli psyche. Government officials desperately wanted to avenge the dead.

When the list of those targeted for assassination was reconsidered, the Red Prince again came out on top. Ali Hassan Salameh was still the man that Israel feared. Salameh's contacts with the CIA and American government, broken after the CIA's embarrassing attempts to recruit the senior Palestinian were rejected, had been reestablished and were as warm as previously.

Salameh had apparently forgiven the Americans their diplomatic faux pas by the autumn of 1973. On November 3, 1973, as the official representative of Yasser Arafat, he met secretly with General Vernon Walters, deputy director of the CIA, in Morocco, and agreed on behalf of Fatah to participate in a Middle East peace process and suspend attacks on American citizens.

The extraordinary meeting shows the high regard in which Salameh was held by the Americans. It took place despite an agreement between Henry Kissinger and the Israelis that the U.S. would not talk to the PLO. But American trust in Salameh was repaid within weeks of the meeting when the Palestinian warned the CIA of a plot to kill Henry Kissinger in a missile attack on his plane as it landed in Beirut during a diplomatic trip around the Middle East. The CIA arranged for the plane to be diverted, and men from Salameh's Force 17 even guarded Kissinger while he was in Lebanon.

The CIA were delighted with the tip-off, which probably saved Kissinger's life, and Salameh and Arafat received their reward the following year, when Arafat addressed the United Nations in New York, and Salameh was entertained by the CIA at the Waldorf-Astoria. Salameh was so pleased by all the attention he was receiving from the

CIA, apparently believing it would open a direct line to the White House, that he promised the spooks he would ensure that not only Fatah but other PLO factions would avoid attacking American citizens.

Even when Salameh returned to the Middle East he continued to talk to and assist American intelligence, making him — despite his active involvement in international terrorism — one of the most important American contacts in the entire region.

Salameh again proved his worth to the U.S. after the Lebanese civil war began in 1975, when several hundred Americans needed to be evacuated out of danger. He provided scores of heavily armed guards from Force 17 for two convoys, one of which made its way from Beirut to a beach where people were taken to the U.S. Sixth Fleet offshore, and another that weaved through the Shouf mountains and on to Damascus, Syria. Other militia in the area were warned explicitly that attacking the convoys would invite the wrath of Fatah.

Henry Kissinger actually wrote to Arafat, thanking him for helping the Americans out of Beirut, although he was apparently careful not to add his name to the letter, or even that of Arafat.[10] Salameh was later thanked personally by the CIA when he twice visited agents at their headquarters in Langley, Virginia, at Arafat's behest, and briefed the attentive Americans on the state of the Palestinian movement and what was going on inside Yasser Arafat's head.

Relations between the U.S. and Salameh could hardly have been warmer. In June 1977 Salameh married Georgina Rizak, a former Miss Lebanon and Miss Universe (although he was already married and had two sons, Hassan and Ussama.)[11] The CIA paid for the couple to spend their honeymoon in Hawaii and fulfilled one of Salameh's lifelong ambitions by throwing in a trip to Disney World.

But Salameh's links to the Americans were not a security guarantee for someone at the top of Mossad's hit list. They had already killed one man in the erroneous belief he was the Red Prince, and Salameh could not possibly have thought they had given up on their mission. He knew he was still marked for death.

It was late 1978 when the Mossad hit team rekindled their interest in Yasser Arafat's young protégé. Years had passed — Golda Meir had been replaced in office by Menachem Begin, himself a former leader of the Irgun, a Jewish extremist organization[12] — but Mossad had kept a watch on Salameh and became concerned about his links with the CIA.

Eventually the connection became so obvious that Mossad apparently approached the CIA's station chief in Paris and warned him they were going to kill Salameh unless the CIA confirmed one way or another that he was "their man." This put the CIA in a difficult position. They could not say he was because the U.S. had told the Israelis it would not deal with the Palestinians. But if they did not support Salameh they stood a good chance of losing one of their finest contacts in the Middle East.

The conversation was relayed back to Robert Ames, who was then the national intelligence officer for the Middle East, and he told the CIA to tell the Israelis Salameh was not working for the U.S. Technically, it was the truth, but in denying the close relationship between the CIA and Ali Hassan Salameh, a death sentence was passed on another of the men behind the Munich massacre.

"Mike" was again given responsibility for the Red Prince's termination. "Mike" had remained a central figure in Israeli intelligence after Lillehammer and was quietly given one of Israel's highest awards for his pivotal role in the July 1976 Entebbe airport raid, when more than one hundred Jewish hostages being held by terrorists in Uganda were rescued in an astonishing international military operation. "Mike" apparently infiltrated the airport where the Israelis were being held by posing as an Italian businessman. He also persuaded contacts in the Kenyan government to arrange a refuelling stop for the Hercules plane used in the operation on the return leg to Israel, without which the mission would have been virtually impossible.[13]

Once again, "Mike" began recruiting a team of agents. This time Mossad could not afford a mistake. Only veteran undercover and covert operators were included in the mission.

By late 1978, Mossad surveillance experts had arrived in Beirut to begin monitoring Salameh and immediately discovered that his security precautions had grown lax in the five years since the Wrath of God team roamed Europe and the Middle East.

Years had passed after the Munich operation, he had married again, and he was growing careless; Salameh was no longer a virtually untouchable terrorist living out of bunkers and surrounded by armed fighters. He seems to have developed the fatalistic mentality he so readily criticized in others. "He told me that, once a decision for your assassination had been taken, it was only a question of when and where. You'd never know when it would take place," said Nidal, Ali Hassan's sister.[14]

Mossad agents began watching Salameh closely again during late 1978, following him from a distance during his visits to Beirut. Over at least six weeks they studied his movements and watched several patterns slowly emerge.

Salameh spent most afternoons with his pregnant wife Georgina, the beauty queen, in her apartment in the fashionable and wealthy area of Snoubra in West Beirut. He was also making regular visits to a local gym and a sauna. An early Israeli plan to blow him to pieces as he sweated in the sauna was vetoed because of potential high civilian casualties. Instead the Israelis chose to launch a less subtle attack on the Red Prince.

The Israeli operation began in November 1978, when a female Mossad agent, claiming to be an English bohemian called Erika Chambers, arrived in Beirut to begin working for a Palestinian charity with the peculiar name of "The House of Steadfastness of the Children of Telesata."[15]

The Israeli surveillance teams who had been monitoring Salameh for several weeks knew he often drove down a road called Beka Street on his way to and from Georgina's apartment and to the Fatah headquarters in the city. So on January 10, 1979, Erika Chambers paid 3,500 Lebanese pounds to rent an apartment on the eighth floor of the Anis Assaf Building overlooking Beka Street. A middle-aged eccentric, Chambers spent most of her time tending to unwanted cats, sitting in her window painting the streets below, and helping to control a vast surveillance operation against Salameh.

Other Israeli agents then began arriving in the city. According to Lebanese investigators, a Mossad agent using the name Ronald Kolberg, and travelling on a fake Canadian passport (no. 104277), arrived in Beirut a week after Chambers had rented the apartment. He rented a small room at the Royal Garden Hotel, rented a Simca car from the Lenna Car Hire Company, and started badgering local shopkeepers, offering to sell them a variety of Canadian kitchen utensils. Mossad certainly went to enormous lengths to ensure their agents had excellent covers; Kolberg eagerly distributed leaflets for his range of exciting products around Beirut.

Peter Schriver, the cover name for a third Israeli agent, arrived a day later on a forged British passport (no. 260866, dated October 15, 1972), and rented a Volkswagen car and a room at the Hotel Méditerranée. The three agents were almost certainly helped by other Mossad agents within the city, deep-cover operatives who may have been living there for several years.

By mid-January 1979, the Israelis were ready to launch their attack on the Red Prince. At dusk one evening two frogmen left an Israeli missile boat anchored off the coast of Beirut and slipped ashore at a deserted beach carrying a heavy package containing explosives and detonators.[16] Waiting for them nearby were two Israeli agents; on receiving a predetermined code from the frogmen's flashlight, they left the motor of their Volkswagen running and went to collect the pack.

As the two frogmen slipped back into the water and rowed their small boat quietly back to the missile boat, the other two agents returned to their safe house. They took eleven pounds of hexagene explosive, equivalent to roughly sixty-five pounds of dynamite, and hid it inside the hired VW, attached to a wireless transmitter.

Several days later, with "Mike" monitoring the operation from the missile boat off Beirut, the Volkswagen was carefully parked on Beka Street, and the agents settled down to wait for Salameh to appear.

At 3:45 P.M. on January 22, Salameh bade farewell to his wife and jumped into his battered Chevrolet station wagon to drive to his mother's house for a birthday party for his three-year-old niece. He was accompanied, as ever, by two heavily armed bodyguards and at least three more guards in a Land-Rover behind. A Mossad agent was almost certainly watching from nearby as the small convoy left, and he alerted the remaining members of the team that Salameh was on the move. From Erika Chambers's apartment another Mossad agent watched and waited for Salameh to appear.

Salameh's two-car convoy sped through the streets of Beirut, hooting other cars out of the way, and turned onto Beka Street. This time Mossad was making no mistakes. As the Chevrolet passed the Volkswagen the agent in Chambers's apartment detonated the bomb. The explosion could be heard several miles away.

The blast fatally wounded Salameh. He slumped out of the side of his car and collapsed.[17] He was rushed to the American University Hospital, but a sharp metal splinter was embedded in his brain, and he died on the operating table at 4:03 P.M. Eight other people also died in the explosion.[18]

"Mike" was watching Beirut through a telescope from the Israeli missile boat when the bomb exploded.[19] That night the Israeli frogmen returned to the same lonely beach near Beirut and collected two Mossad agents, a man and a woman. Safely back on board, the woman embraced "Mike" and said simply, "Mike, he's dead."

"Mike" had finally completed the mission Golda Meir had set him six years previously. The Munich athletes had been avenged.

More than one hundred thousand mourners went to Salameh's funeral at Beirut's Martyr's Cemetery. Yasser Arafat helped to carry his coffin, then comforted his godson Hassan Salameh, the Red Prince's thirteen-year-old son, at the graveside as his father was buried. Amid chaotic scenes Arafat bade a formal farewell, shouting above the throng at the graveside: "We will continue to march on the road toward Palestine. Goodbye, my hero."[20]

The loss of Salameh was a sore blow to the Palestinian liberation movement. But there were more names on the Israeli Wrath of God hit list, men who even by the late 1970s still occupied senior positions within the PLO. Near the top was Abu Daoud, the former teacher who had been so central to the planning of the Munich attack.

Despite the official suspension of the Wrath of God team after the Lillehammer fiasco, Mossad agents had continued trying to locate

Abu Daoud since his name first emerged during initial German police investigations into the Munich massacre. But Israeli efforts had been frustrated. He remained hidden in the shadows or out of their reach for years, finally emerging — in perhaps the most public way possible — in 1977.

After one of his friends was killed outside a Paris bookstore in early January 1977, Abu Daoud decided to travel to Paris for the funeral. He arranged a visa at the French embassy in Beirut, supplying a false Iraqi passport bearing the name Youssef Raji Hanna. Mossad learned of the application and notified German intelligence officials. They in turn eventually alerted their counterparts in the French Direction de la Surveillance du Territoire (DST), to Hanna's true identity.

By the time the warning came through, Daoud had already arrived in Paris as part of an official PLO delegation and was being wined, dined, and chauffeured around the city by the French government. French Foreign Office officials were understandably embarrassed when their own police arrested the Palestinian and threw him into a cell in the grim La Santé prison with a Belgian petty thief and a couple of hash-smokers for company.[21] Germany and Israel immediately submitted extradition papers.

It was a time of rejoicing for Ankie Spitzer, Ilana Romano, and scores of other relatives of the athletes killed at Munich. Finally, they thought, there would be a small display of courtroom justice. But their excitement was short-lived.

The French authorities had been bribing and blackmailing terrorist groups to persuade them to avoid France during their attacks, and Daoud's arrest by their officers threatened their delicate game. Before he had had time to introduce himself to his cellmates, Daoud was hustled into court. After a perfunctory hearing lasting just twenty minutes, the court decided he would have to be released immediately (on a string of technicalities). He was then hustled back out of the court, bundled into a fast car, and raced to Orly Airport. A first-class ticket to Algiers was thrust into his hand and he was shunted onto an Air Algérie flight. He received a hero's welcome upon landing in Algeria.

France chose to release Abu Daoud not only to protect itself from possible terrorist attacks but also because several Arab states threatened to withdraw deposits of cash totalling more than $15 billion — money from oil sales — that were stored in French banks.[22] The morning after Daoud's release, France also signed a deal with Egypt for the sale of two hundred Mirage jets.[23]

This apparent blackmail and bribery worked wonders, and Israeli demands for justice for the Munich athletes were ignored. Even the sight of eight of the athletes' children lined up outside the French embassy in Tel Aviv holding photographs of their dead fathers did not change the minds of the politicians in Paris.

When news of Daoud's release was broadcast on radio and television there were near-riots in Tel Aviv. Ironically, Ali Hassan Salameh had been in Paris at the same time as Daoud, travelling with his then girlfriend Georgina Rizak, but the Israelis did not know.[24] Their fury was directed at the French for releasing Abu Daoud, and the French embassy in Israel was pelted with rocks, tomatoes, and rotten eggs.[25] Eleven young French Jews holidaying in Israel burnt their French identity cards.[26] "Giscard [d'Estaing, the French president] is a bastard and a Nazi!" screamed the demonstrators.[27] Even U.S. President Jimmy Carter said he was "deeply disturbed."[28]

By then it was too late: Daoud was secure in the Middle East, taunting the Israelis by claiming he would be happy to go to Munich to prove his innocence. "I would go immediately. I would take the first plane," he said.[29]

Of course, Abu Daoud had absolutely no intention of returning to Munich. He had not expected the Germans and Israelis still to be pursuing him, more than four years after the massacre at Fürstenfeldbruck. After landing in Algeria he fled again, this time hiding behind the Iron Curtain with the help of anti-Semites in Eastern Bloc governments.

Abu Daoud began shuttling between the Middle East and communist states, where he found what he thought was absolute security from Israeli attack. His favorite destination was the Palast Hotel in East Berlin, where he stayed for long periods using an assumed name and occupying a luxurious two-room apartment on the eighth floor.

The $175-per-night bill was paid by the Stasi.[30] Even senior staff at the Palast were unaware of the real identity of their regular guest, although one chambermaid was shocked to discover he always slept with a large-caliber revolver under his pillow.

"We had known this 'Mr. Tarik' for years . . . But no one knew who this modest and utterly polite guest was," said Reinhard Hellmann, the Palast Hotel's protocol manager.[31] Daoud even discussed the problems of the Middle East with hotel staff. According to Hellman he made a "very cultivated" impression, but "said he was very unhappy about the discord within the PLO."

Daoud was clearly making useful contacts with the East German government. Colonel Rainer Wiegand, a former colonel in the Stasi who defected to the West in 1990, has related how disgusted he was by photographs of the Munich attack, and how appalled he was to discover Daoud was visiting East Germany in March 1979 as an honored guest of the regime.[32]

Wiegand discovered details of Daoud's trip two days before he was due to arrive in the country on March 19 and presumed he was entering without the knowledge of the East German government. Wiegand has since claimed that he gathered together a group of his officers and conducted a quick investigation into Daoud's case, finally concluding that he was a bona fide terrorist who should be arrested on arrival or denied entry to the country.

However, just as Wiegand was about to hand his report to a junior colleague for delivery to Colonel-General Bruno Beater, the first deputy to Stasi boss Erich Mielke, another senior Stasi official — Colonel Harry Dahl — rang him on the telephone. Dahl had heard through the Stasi grapevine that Wiegand was investigating Daoud and wanted to know what he intended to do.

"Daoud is planning to arrive at Schönefeld [Airport] the day after tomorrow," Wiegand said. "I think we should arrest him."

"You're not going to arrest anybody!" said Dahl angrily. "You keep your paws off! Abu Daoud is not coming to the DDR illegally but by invitation, and I have been personally charged by the minister to provide Daoud with around-the-clock protection."

Wiegand did as he was told but claims he went to Schönefeld

airport and watched Daoud arrive bearing a first-class ticket on a
flight from Damascus. He was apparently greeted by a delegation of
East German officials, then taken by limousine for meetings with
Communist Party officials and billetted in a suite at the Metropol, the
finest hotel in East Berlin. There can be no doubt the East Germans
knew exactly who they were dealing with.

A Stasi report due to be submitted to Erich Mielke, dated May
8, 1979, and classified "Top Secret," describes the Palestinian thus:
"Abu Daoud, a leading member of the Fatah and its intelligence
service. Responsible in the past for severe acts of terror, for example,
during the 1972 Summer Olympic Games in Munich. A key position
in coordinating worldwide activities. His appearance usually indicates
that large-scale activities are imminent."[33]

While Abu Daoud felt safe behind the Iron Curtain, his enemies
were prepared to go to any lengths to execute him. Late July 1981
found Abu Daoud staying at the upmarket Victoria Intercontinental
Hotel in Warsaw, Poland, travelling on an Iraqi passport under the
alias Tarik Shakir Mahdi. Despite his various attempts to evade pursuers, a small team of assassins had tracked him to the Polish capital.
They may even have simply waited for him to arrive in Warsaw,
where he was a frequent visitor, and then tracked him to the Victoria, his favorite hotel in the city.

On the evening of Saturday, August 1, 1981, Daoud was sitting
in the hotel's busy Café Canaletto, wearing a khaki safari suit and
sunglasses, waiting for a coffee and mineral water he had just ordered.
A young Israeli or Middle Eastern man in his early twenties walked
up to him, drew a pistol, and pumped five bullets into his body from
a distance of no more than two yards.

"The assassin shot one more time, but missed," said General Sla-
womir Petelicki, commander of the elite Polish counterterrorist Operational Manoeuvre Reaction Group. "The fifth bullet slightly
wounded a tourist from the Federal Republic of Germany."[34] As
other hotel guests dived for cover under their tables, the gunman
turned and raced out of the hotel to a waiting getaway car and driver.
Still conscious, Daoud somehow managed to stand and stagger after

the gunman into the hotel lobby before he collapsed into a lounge chair, blood pouring from his wounds.[35]

"Daoud survived," said General Petelicki, apparently impressed by his stamina. "He even managed to walk downstairs on his own to the hall by the front office. There he fell into an armchair."[36] The Arab was rushed to the Interior Ministry hospital, where Polish doctors removed one bullet from his neck and two each from his right side and intestines. Polish government agents spirited him away from the hospital the following day to begin several months of quiet recovery.

To this day there is official confusion over who was behind the assassination attempt. "There are two versions of this event: it was either settling internal accounts among Palestinian extremists, a kind of faction fight, or an operation staged by the Israeli intelligence service [Mossad]," said General Petelicki.

The modus operandi of the attacker is unlike that of normal Mossad hits attributed to the Wrath of God team, but many Palestinian leaders have no doubt the Israelis were responsible. "They were following our man and they hunted him here and chose the most convenient moment for them to shoot him," according to Fouad Mahmoud Yaseen, the PLO's spokesman in Warsaw.[37]

Daoud also believes Mossad tried to kill him. After receiving treatment he slipped back into the shadows, and grew used to a life on the run: "It was normal to be in danger. Everyone had to be careful and fear death, but I was not scared."[38]

Abu Daoud spent months, then years, hiding and successfully dodging Israeli pursuers. Other terrorists involved in plotting the Munich Olympics attack were not so fortunate, although the relatives of the Israeli athletes had to wait more than ten years for a final taste of vengeance.

Not every Black September terrorist was targeted by Mossad, however. Abu Iyad does not seem to have figured on the Israeli hit list, despite clear evidence of his involvement in the Munich operation. Whereas several Israeli agents became obsessed with killing Salameh, they did not pursue Abu Iyad with the same vigor. It is a curious contradiction, until one remembers that many of those killed in Operation Wrath of God were assassinated not only because of their involvement in Munich but also because they posed a future political threat to the state of Israel, through links with Western governments or intelligence services.

Salameh's murder was a priority because he was the point man for the budding secret relationship between the Americans and the Palestinians. "I will say that the pattern of people who got knocked off by Israel is suspicious," confirms Frank Anderson, a former CIA operations chief for the Middle East. "It says, 'He who is involved in diplomacy is troublesome for us.'"[39]

Even General Aharon Yariv, one of the leaders of the Israeli assassination campaign, has appeared to confirm that during Operation Wrath of God Israeli agents went after Palestinians not directly connected with Munich. Any senior Palestinian fighter was at risk, he said. Where "the man was clearly identified as being one of the leaders, either of the PLO or the Black September or Fatah, approval was given for an assassination operation."[40]

Strangely, however, Abu Iyad, the leader of Black September, was not murdered by the Israelis. Iyad was born in Jaffa, Palestine, in 1933, but when the state of Israel was declared in 1948 his family became refugees, eking out their existence in Gaza. He jointly founded Fatah with Yasser Arafat, Mohammed Yousef Najjir (assassinated by the Israeli hit squad led by Ehud Barak in Beirut in 1973), and Khalid Wazir (who was better known by his *nom de guerre,* Abu Jihad, and was assassinated in 1988).

After the 1973 Yom Kippur War, Abu Iyad moderated his political position and accepted it would be impossible to wipe the Zionist state off the map through armed struggle alone. As he moved into middle age, a corpulent, chain-smoking senior official in the PLO, he became something of a pragmatist, even arguing that dialogue with Israel was the price that would have to be paid for a Palestinian state in Gaza and the West Bank.[41] The Israelis had little to gain by killing him, so he was safe from the Wrath of God hit team. Instead, ironically, it was left to other Palestinians to avenge the eleven Israeli athletes.

On January 14, 1991, Iyad had gathered two of his most trusted colleagues — Fakhri al Umari (Iyad's head of security, closely involved in the Munich massacre) and Hael Abdel-Hamid, a senior PLO official — for a discussion on Iraqi leader Saddam Hussein and the crisis in the Persian Gulf.

At 11:00 P.M., Hamza Abu Zaid, a thirty-year-old bodyguard working for the PLO, entered the room in the villa in northern Tunis where the men were sitting to deliver a message to Iyad. As he turned to leave, Zaid paused at the doorway, whirled around, raised his submachine gun, and let loose a stream of bullets. All three men died instantly. Zaid, a supporter of the rival Palestinian Abu Nidal Organization, took hostages in a bid to escape but was caught and eventually sentenced to death for his attack.[42]

The Israelis might have had no hand in Abu Iyad's murder, but there were other assassinations and attempted murders during the late 1970s and 1980s that Middle East commentators and intelligence experts have attributed to the Wrath of God team. Israeli involvement in the attacks, however, has never been positively established.

One example is an attack on Zuhair Mohesen, the PLO's forty-three-year-old military operations chief, in Cannes on July 26, 1979. He had spent an evening at a local casino and was returning to his rented opulent fourth-floor apartment on the wealthy La Croisette Promenade at 1:00 A.M. when he was shot in the head by one of two men standing on the stairs near his front door.[43]

The assault left Mohesen in a coma, and responsibility has since been attributed to the Israelis, other renegade Palestinians, and even the Egyptians, who may have been taking revenge for the seizure of the Egyptian embassy in Ankara by Palestinian terrorists earlier in the month.

Similar confusion surrounds a 1992 attack in Paris on another senior Palestinian involved in planning the Munich Olympics operation, for which the Wrath of God unit may have been reactivated. Even though it was twenty years after the Fürstenfeldbruck massacre, Israel has a long memory.

The target in 1992 was Atef Bseiso, the forty-four-year-old head of intelligence operations for the PLO and a rising star within the organization.[44] Bseiso had driven from Berlin to Paris for a series of meetings with Palestinians and at least one meeting with officials from French intelligence. He booked into a room under a false name at the Hotel Meridien Montparnasse, a quiet luxury hotel on the Left Bank where he had stayed before and which he favored.

Middle age had made Bseiso careless. He made elementary security mistakes while travelling across Europe, such as driving an ostentatious Jeep that he had already driven to Marseilles when crossing to PLO headquarters in Tunisia by ferry.[45]

Bseiso was followed from his first moments in the French capital in early June 1992. The surveillance was so heavy Bseiso realized he was being watched. He contacted an acquaintance within French intelligence and requested protection. Bseiso was told there would be none available until the next morning.[46] He was on his own.

Later that same evening Bseiso was returning to his hotel from an evening meal with friends when two armed "European-looking" men in black jogging outfits jumped out on him as he emerged from a taxi by his hotel. One man, wielding a nine-millimeter pistol with a silencer, shot him three times from close range while the other kept guard, and then both men disappeared into the night. The gun used for the shooting had a small bag attached to the side to catch the spent cartridges, a clever trick designed to leave no evidence at the scene of the crime.[47]

Responsibility for the killing has never been clearly assigned to either side. Some French intelligence officials believe it was the work of rival Palestinians, probably men from the Abu Nidal terror gang, while others believe the killers were Israeli.

The Abu Nidal Organization was certainly killing nearly as many fellow Palestinians as the Israelis were in the 1980s and early 1990s, and Bseiso's assailants may have been sent by the that organization as part of a long-running feud.[48]

However, there is also strong circumstantial evidence of Israeli involvement in the execution. Within hours of Bseiso's killing a senior Israeli general gave a private briefing to a group of Israeli defense correspondents at which he allegedly told them Bseiso had been closely involved with the Munich massacre. The journalists then passed the news to the public that another terrorist guilty of the heinous crime had met his maker — two decades after the attack by Black September.

Sources within Abu Nidal's group and senior PLO officials have also consistently denied suggestions the killers were Palestinian.[49] Yasser Arafat himself had no doubt who was responsible for the killing. Mossad, Arafat told mourners during a wake for Bseiso at PLO headquarters, "has to know that the blood of our martyr will not go unavenged."[50] Arafat was furious at the attack. "Does Mossad have a free hand in European and French territories?" he asked angrily. Abu Daoud also blames the Israelis. "Even after Madrid, after the peace accord, the martyr [Bseiso] was killed in Paris by Mossad, under the pretext of involvement in Munich," he said.[51]

In truth, however, if Israel was responsible for the killing of Atef Bseiso, the attack may have had as much to do with Israeli elections on June 23, and the government's wish to show it was tough on Palestinian "terrorism," as with the twenty-year-old massacre in Germany. Yasser Arafat had warned PLO officials to be careful during the period leading up to the elections, and had given a particular warning to Bseiso: "I told him, 'You are going to Europe, so you need to be careful.' But Mossad was waiting to ambush him."[52]

The Cover-up

*A*lthough Operation Wrath of God was supposed to extract vengeance for the families of the athletes killed in Munich, few relatives wanted such a violent reckoning with the Palestinians. Instead the families have grieved for justice, and for the truth behind the events in Munich nearly thirty years ago.

Despite the spirited efforts of several of the Munich widows, the Bavarian and German governments have successfully sustained a massive cover-up since 1972. German officials made mistakes that cost Israeli lives, yet no one has been called to account. "The men died in Germany a second time, when we tried to find out the truth," said Ankie Spitzer, widow of the Israeli fencing coach Andre Spitzer.[1]

Ankie blames two groups for what happened to her husband: "Of course I blame the Palestinian terrorists, [but] secondly, and most of all, I blame the German authorities who were supposed to prevent the Palestinians coming to the Olympic village. And then after they did not prevent it, [the German authorities] should have rescued the Israeli athletes who were kept hostage. And they didn't do [that] either. They were the hosts of the Olympics, they should have been responsible for the well-being of their guests. And afterwards they should have rescued them and they botched up their whole rescue plan . . . I want justice from them."[2]

The relatives have been fighting a legal battle in Germany since just a few months after the massacre, demanding that the Bavarian and federal governments release all their files relating to the massacre. The families wanted to know how it was possible for every single athlete to die while they were supposed to be under German protection, and which officials should take responsibility for their deaths.

"I wanted from the Germans a full account of what happened," said Ankie. "I asked for ballistic reports, I asked for pathology reports, because nobody seemed to be able to explain to me what really happened, who was at fault. Who shot whom at the airport? Because everything was dark and there was total confusion." When the Germans finally responded, it was simply to say they could offer her no assistance. "They kept saying to me that we have nothing. And I couldn't believe it because the Germans are so thorough, I could not believe that they had nothing."

In the aftermath of her husband's death Ankie struggled to raise the couple's young daughter Anouk alone. The pressures of being a single parent meant she could not pursue the Germans or counter their persistent claims that they had no files or information for her.[3] But a desire for the truth never left Ankie. The German insistence that no reports existed began to rankle. "I felt very suspicious about the fact they said there is nothing."

As Anouk grew into a beautiful little girl, Ankie began to devote more of her time to discovering the truth behind the Munich massacre. As Ankie describes it, she began "pounding" people for information. "I went to every single German ambassador who resided in Israel since 1972, to every Israeli prime minister, to every Israeli president, to every Israeli foreign minister, to try to gather information because I had nothing. I said somebody did this, somebody has to pay a price, somebody has to say that they are responsible." However, "the journey was a futile one," she adds, "because every place I went I got the same answer: 'We have nothing.'"

Ankie even met Hans-Dietrich Genscher, German interior minister at the time of the massacre and later the country's foreign minister. "I met him personally. I asked him the same questions, if he could give me more information, if he could give me these reports."

Genscher told Ankie there were no more reports available, but added: "I'll go back to Germany and I'll check for you and I'll let you know."

The young widow never received a positive response from Genscher, so instead she flew to Germany herself and began asking questions. "I went to the Institute of Pathology in order to try to get the files out. I wanted to know, and I think I had the right to know, what happened to my husband? Who killed him? How did he die? The most basic question that I think every person has a right to know." Ankie received the same rebuttals in person as she had had by mail. "I was denied the answers. It was very frustrating."

As the months after the massacre became years, she grew ever more convinced that the Germans were hiding facts about the death of Andre and his friends. She also became convinced the Israeli government was acquiescing with the German cover-up, and searched in her mind for an explanation for the apparent Israeli indifference.

However, Ankie and other relatives became so incensed by the unofficial reports they heard of German incompetence in guarding and rescuing their loved ones that they eventually obtained the services of a lawyer and began legal action against the German and Bavarian governments. "The families decided to sue the German government and other defendants just because they think that they have the right to do it," said Pinchas Zeltzer, an Israeli lawyer working for the relatives. "They sent their beloved husbands [and] sons to Germany and they were not protected, or let's say the German authorities neglected to save their lives."[4]

Yet the relatives and their lawyers faced a difficult situation: they needed documents and official reports to back up their claims of incompetence and malpractice, but the Germans denied that any existed. The lawyer who represented them before Zeltzer formally applied to the German embassy in Israel, and to the government in Bonn, for access to official investigation documents. "He was refused," said Zeltzer. "The Bavarian government and the German government refused to give the documents and the evidence and to reveal everything that happened."

For years the German authorities stonewalled, claiming there was only one official document, a sixty-three-page published report with the title "Attack on the Israeli Olympic Team." For the Israelis, who knew only too well the meticulousness of the German authorities, it was inconceivable that there was only one document. "How could that be that in Germany there are [no documents]," said Ilana Romano, widow of the Libyan-born weightlifter Yossef. "It's a very neat nation. They know exactly where to put each word."

The families knew there would be ballistics reports, forensic reports, pathology reports, an endless stream of paperwork on every aspect of the attack, siege, and massacre. But without the documents the relatives' legal action withered, a victim of the German statute of limitations.

On their side, the German authorities seem to have been merely embarrassed by the Israeli relatives' constant demands for attention. They thought the relatives would eventually weaken — or grow old and die — and finally forget about the tragedy. They were wrong. "Maybe they thought these widows will go away some day, or they will leave it or they will tire or they will just let it go," said Ankie Spitzer. "But they forgot that we did not want to let it go because we have the right to know as families what happened to our loved ones."

Ilana Romano, who along with Ankie has led the assault on the German authorities, also had no intention of giving up.[5] "Don't forget that when I became widowed I was twenty-six, I had three tiny daughters. I didn't know where to start. And from then I'm searching and I'm digging. I'm looking for every little detail, together with Ankie." It was a struggle for them both, but "you fall and get to your feet again and again." She believes the "horrible scope of the crime" actually strengthened her. "Ankie and myself, we dug and got every last piece of information. We share the same tragedy. I swore I would find out what happened, for the sake of my daughters. After forty-eight hours, I asked to be told exactly what happened." Years later, "I am still searching for answers."[6]

All the relatives have felt a similar thirst for the truth. One of the first documents they asked to see was the ballistics report conducted on the helicopters and bodies at Fürstenfeldbruck. On June 30, 1976, several relatives met with Hans-Dietrich Genscher in Tel Aviv and formally requested compensation and documentation.[7] Nothing was forthcoming.

On September 5, 1977, the families wrote to the German embassy in Israel requesting copies of the ballistic and pathology reports.[8] Six months later, on March 9, 1978, the Germans finally responded, telling the families that although they could not have copies, it might just be possible for them to inspect the reports.[9] When the families requested permission for an inspection, they were ignored. They continued to harangue the German government, and that same year, Genscher met Ankie Spitzer and said that the ballistics report would be copied and passed to her lawyers. "He said that he could see no reason why the German government would hide this report," said Spitzer.[10]

Ankie left the meeting with Genscher satisfied that a senior member of the German government — someone who had personally witnessed the tragedy and could surely understand her quest for the truth — had promised her that the report would be made available for viewing. But she claims that Genscher failed to help.

The saga continued for another fourteen years, during which time Spitzer continually badgered the Germans for the report: "I can wallpaper my living room with the German government's responses to the request for the ballistics report."[11] Normally the Germans would not even bother to respond to her requests. Other times officials would give pathetic excuses for their inaction. Sometimes they would say "the investigation is still open," or give other "stupid answers," according to Pinchas Zeltzer. "They said, 'The documents do not exist any more,' 'We can't give you the documents,' 'The documents were destroyed,' or other stories like this, when we knew that it is impossible in any civil country with law and order. We were frustrated."[12]

Successive Israeli governments also failed to help the relatives. Ankie Spitzer asserted: "Well, we also have our theories about that. Of course Israel's position was also rather embarrassing in this whole thing because they should have never trusted the Germans with the security for their athletes in the first place."[13] Although Israeli gov-

ernment and Olympic officials told the relatives after the massacre
that Israel had not been "allowed" to send a security force with their
athletes, the East Germans, Egyptians, and several other nations sent
security officials to the Munich Games. "So it was quite embarrassing that they trusted the Germans with the security," said Spitzer.

The Israelis did accept a degree of blame for the attack. An inquiry was established under the leadership of Pinhas Koppel, a former Shin Bet officer and commissioner of police, to investigate the
catastrophic failure of security — indeed, the nonexistent security —
surrounding the Israeli athletes. He decided that the head of Shin
Bet's Protective Security Branch, which should have been responsible
for the athletes, should be fired.[14]

Nevertheless, in the eyes of Israelis most of the blame was directed first at the Palestinians, of course, and then in close second
place, the Germans. "Using the element of surprise, the terrorists were
able to enter the Israel pavilion and overpower its occupants because
the German authorities did not take the appropriate precautions," said
Golda Meir. "It was a grave error to provide mere routine security precautions for the Israel delegation."[15]

Many of the relatives believe that some sort of "deal" was done
between the Israeli and German governments after the massacre,
which explained why Israel did not aggressively pursue the truth
about the killings, or publicly castigate Germany for its extraordinary
series of blunders during the hostage crisis. "I don't know, I'm only
speculating," admitted one relative, who suspects the Germans have
"rewarded" Israel for its silence about the debacle.[16]

Yohanan Meroz, Israel's ambassador to Bonn from 1974 to
1981, has claimed there was never any deliberate attempt by the Israeli government to discourage negotiations between the relatives
and the German government. "We were instructed to help them
arrange meetings, but we never got involved in an active way. If there
is a fault, it lay in Jerusalem's clumsy handling of the situation . . .
There should have been a more pragmatic approach because, in fact,
the Germans were profoundly affected by the tragedy. The matter
should have really been taken up on a governmental level, not

between legal departments or lawyers. Because the damn bloody fact is that the Germans, through negligent handling of security, made the assault possible."[17]

The inaction of the Israeli government still puzzles and upsets many of the relatives. "What the real reason is, why Israel wasn't more pushy, we don't know, but believe me we asked every president, every prime minister, and every foreign minister if they could at least get the information out," said Ankie Spitzer.[18] It was all to no avail. The families thought the truth about the Munich massacre would never be known.

In early 1992, nearly twenty years after the killings at 31 Connollystrasse and Fürstenfeldbruck airfield, Ankie Spitzer was interviewed on German television, talking about the anniversary of the tragedy and her desperate desire to know the truth about the events of September 5, 1972. German officials had claimed there were no more reports available, she told viewers. Relatives were still suffering because they did not know what had happened to their loved ones.

The interview struck a deep chord with one German viewer, someone with intimate knowledge of the German and Bavarian government investigations into the Munich disaster. Two weeks after Ankie's television appearance, he rang her at her home in Israel. "It took twenty years after the events in Munich until finally there was a breakthrough and the breakthrough came from a side I never expected," she said.[19]

"There is information, you're absolutely right," the "anonymous German citizen" told Ankie. "I have access to the information, but I can never get this information to you in a normal way. I will have to try to slip it out of the archives and send it to you." Did Ankie really want the information, he asked?

"I've been waiting twenty years for it," she replied. "But who are you?"

"I can't reveal my identity, and I will never let you know who I am because I'm doing something which is illegal," said the man.

"Okay," said Ankie simply. "I'll have anything you can send me."

Two weeks passed and she heard nothing: "I wasn't sure whether to believe this guy," she recalled, remembering times in the past when she was contacted by hoaxers with a variety of conspiracy theories and explanations for the Munich massacre.

Then, finally, a courier arrived at her house carrying a parcel from Germany. It was everything the relatives could have hoped for. The contents proved that the German authorities had conducted major investigations into the massacre and then tried to cover up their findings.

"I saw eighty pages of all kinds of documents that I had never seen before," said Ankie. There were three pages of a pathology report, pages from a ballistics report. "I was amazed."

Still unable to believe the breakthrough had finally been made, lawyers for the relatives brought in Israeli experts to study the documents. A retired Israeli police officer and ballistics expert of German descent studied a thirty-page ballistics report, couched in typically technical language and dated September 6, 1972, which went as far as analyzing shrapnel removed from breastbones.

Experts even studied the actual paper on which the reports were written. Ankie said: "They came back and said, 'Look, Ankie, here you have papers that are indeed twenty years old, were written on a typewriter that's indeed twenty years old, and it looks like they're absolutely authentic papers.'"

The package revitalized the relatives in their quest for the truth. It included an index of a massive hoard of more than three thousand documents, reports, and files relating to the Munich massacre hidden in government archives in Bavaria. It was proof of a huge German cover-up.

Ankie's next step was to telephone a senior German politician in the Foreign Ministry. "I have here a number of papers relating to the Munich attack," she told him, "and I want you to give me the rest. I know there are a lot more."

"No," said the official, wearily trotting out the usual German line, "there are no more papers and no more reports."

Finally Ankie had proof. She launched herself verbally against the German: "The minister thought I was bluffing. So, over the phone, I quoted specific details from the documents. I said, 'Look at the ballistic report, dated 16 January 1973. Look at paragraph 1: a box contains one piece of shrapnel taken from my husband's back. Paragraph 2: three metal splinters were taken from his breastbone.'"[20]

Humbled, but perhaps also hoping the source of the leak could be discovered, the German official asked Ankie to take the papers to his ambassador in Israel, who would attempt to prove their authenticity.

"No, I'm not showing you anything," said Ankie. "I just want the rest of them."[21]

Several months of waiting ensued, as news of Ankie's claims spread among German politicians. Questions were asked in the Bundestag, the German parliament, and federal officials began a long battle with Bavarian officials in Munich, who blindly denied they had any further documents in their archives. Ankie recalled: "At one point we got to a certain level where Klaus Kinkel [the German foreign minister] was demanding that the minister of justice of the state of Bavaria [produce] the papers."

Finally, on August 29, 1992 ("A day I will never forget," says Ankie), the Germans capitulated. Ankie received a phone call. "They said, 'Okay, we've found the documentation that you were looking for. Please come to Munich with a lawyer and you can get all the papers that we have.'"

The next day the relatives' lawyer left Israel for Munich and was invited into the archives in Munich. Ankie recounted: "What did he see? There were 3,808 files of information, things that we were denied for twenty years, suddenly they showed up miraculously. Enormous amounts of papers, nine hundred pathology pictures. Suddenly everything was there. And I will never forget the feeling because I knew it all these twenty years. I knew that there is information that is being denied."

The files contained the full testimonies of everybody involved in the crisis, according to Pinchas Zeltzer: "The policemen, the people who took part in the action, people from the army, all the reports from the laboratories, the postmortems, photos that were taken, in the airport and also in other places, photos of the helicopters, photos of the Lufthansa airplane. I would say it was a full report of everything which happened."[22]

The information contained in the files was pure dynamite.

"It only became clear to us after we got the documentation how many mistakes were made," said Ankie Spitzer. The documents, according to Ankie, make the Germans look like "fools." "It is clear that what the Germans tried to do was to cover up all their failings. First in organizing the Games and not providing enough security for their guests. And then planning a rescue which they could not execute."[23]

Although the Munich police have since tried to claim no police force in the world could have dealt successfully with the terrorists, it is now clear that they were hopelessly ill-prepared for such a threat at the 1972 Olympics. They were equipped "with little lace-up shoes for patrolling, a tracksuit for sports, and a cap to keep the rain off," admitted Manfred Schreiber, the Munich police chief at the time. "That kind of equipment was inadequate for combating terrorism."[24]

Schreiber had come under political and official pressure to ensure policing at the Games was as light as possible. "The Federal State of Bavaria, the Federal Republic, the Olympic Committee of Germany, as well as the IOC wanted it [the Games] to be totally different from the 1936 Olympic Games. In other words, we wanted the Games to be peaceful ones, we wanted no policing of the Olympic venues." It put his men, he admits, "in a weak position." "As a result, we had plainclothes security officers in operation, about two thousand of them, covering all the Olympic venues, [but] none at the Olympic Village. Our police force was totally unprepared for a terrorist attack of this kind."[25]

German officials feared that armed guards in aggressive uniforms would evoke memories of the Nazi era. Therefore blue uniforms were specially designed for officers patrolling Olympia Park, while their "weapons" were limited to walkie-talkies. But Schreiber and the Munich police should have been more aware of the danger of a terrorist attack.

The Israeli team was concerned about security even before they arrived. Team officials had told the Germans they would prefer to be billeted at the top of one of the taller accommodation buildings. Before the Israeli team had left for Munich, military security specialists had flown to Germany to suggest ways of protecting the team. At the insistence of the Germans, all security protection was left to the host country.

However, the newly uncovered files reveal that German security officials were warned of a possible terrorist attack at the Olympics. A German psychologist told the Munich police that there was a danger of a terrorist assault on the Israelis, and Interpol issued an alert just weeks before the Games that Arab terrorists appeared to be grouping in Europe for a possible "spectacular" attack to coincide with Jewish New Year on September 2. The Munich police were warned explicitly that Palestinian terrorists might attack the Olympics. On August 21, 1972, the German secret police sent a letter to the Munich police warning of Palestinian plans to do "something" at Munich.[26]

The Germans also knew that Black September was active in Europe, and days before the Olympics Leila Khaled, a known terrorist who once tried to hijack an Israeli Boeing 707 airliner, had been seen at Schiphol Airport in Amsterdam. Interpol warned that terrorists might be "on the move" throughout Europe.[27] On Monday, September 4, German officials had been told that terrorists had entered Germany from Scandinavia, but they apparently thought the threat would be limited to parcel bombs or that an Israeli competitor might be kidnapped while wandering around Munich.

Some basic precautions were taken. Munich was home to a huge number of Middle Eastern "guest workers" (the police knew of 779 Jordanians alone,)[28] and officials compiled a list of approximately thirty potential terrorists on whom a special watch was supposed to be kept. But in a staggering underestimation of terrorists' likely objectives, nobody considered the possibility of an attack inside the Olympic Village.

The four thousand–odd files revealed to the families show that the incompetence and mistakes continued long after the attack began. Perhaps the most disastrous blunder involved intelligence about the number of terrorists. Throughout the siege, as deadlines ticked by and negotiations stretched to dusk, the German police stuck rigidly to their belief that there were just five Palestinians holed up in 31 Connollystrasse.

Yet the documentation confirms that six German postal workers told the police there were between eight and twelve men in the two groups that originally climbed over the fence.[29]

When the postmen heard about the attack they told their supervisor, a Herr N. Britz, about what they had seen at 4:10 A.M. and he immediately informed the police.[30] However, it was not until about 6:00 P.M. that detectives were sent to interview the postmen, and even when they explained that they had seen a large group of terrorists, this information was not passed to the crisis committee or police operations center. It was an astonishing breakdown in police procedure.

To make matters worse, German television journalists were reporting the postmen's account by 8:50 A.M., as did a special edition of the newspaper *Bild-Zeitung*, published on the fateful day.[31]

Even German policemen and women at the scene warned their superiors that the actual number of terrorists could be higher than five. One of the German marksmen watching the building suggested there were more than six terrorists, while Annaliese Graes told Hans-Dietrich Genscher and Manfred Schreiber that there were "at least" six terrorists.[32]

When the terrorists and hostages left 31 Connollystrasse, a German police officer, Kriminalinspektor Nachreiner, correctly counted nine living hostages and eight terrorists.[33] When he told Manfred Schreiber this figure, Schreiber allegedly responded that the number of terrorists was already known.[34]

The most amazing failure was that nobody thought to tell the police and snipers waiting at Fürstenfeldbruck. Even when Schreiber landed at the airfield with the rest of the crisis committee, just before the arrival of the terrorists and hostages, he allegedly did not tell his deputy Georg Wolf there were eight terrorists.[35] He later claimed: "I assumed that the transmitting of the number of terrorists was a little technical problem."[36] Lawyers for the relatives of the athletes describe this as "pure cynicism and a sign of incredible carelessness."[37]

The lawyers for the Israeli relatives are scathing about the obstinate manner in which the Munich police stuck to their belief that just five terrorists were opposing them: "There was no order to investigate the number of terrorists and to transmit the results immediately to the operations center; there was no order to transmit at least those numbers investigated when the terrorists left the accommodation or entered the bus; there was no precautionary higher estimate of the number of terrorists — one saw five terrorists; from a logical point of view an estimate had to be higher than five."[38]

When the terrorists and hostages arrived at Fürstenfeldbruck, as we have already seen, there were only five marksmen waiting for them, a hopelessly inadequate figure for the task at hand.[39] The Israeli legal campaign, however, has discovered there were more than fifty sharpshooters available to the Munich police on that day.[40] Relatives of the dead athletes want to know why the extra men were not rushed to the airfield.

In addition, lawyers for the relatives have also discovered that the entire staff of the 1. Polizei Abteilung der Bayerischen Bereitsschaftspolizei (the First Unit of the Bavarian Mobile Police) had been trained in precision sharpshooting with telescopic sights, since the debacle of August 24, 1971, when a young female bank teller being held hostage by robbers was accidentally killed in a "rescue" operation.[41] Why were they not used in the rescue operation, ask the relatives?

Without the extra snipers there was little hope the rescue operation could be successful. Manfred Schreiber now claims the German plan was to kill only Issa, as he thought this would then encourage the rest of the group to surrender. Other officials present at the Games ridicule the idea, as do lawyers for the relatives.

"I think this sort of plan is very, very dangerous," said Uwe Schlütter, a German lawyer for the relatives of the Israeli athletes. The plan, he says, should have been based on a "sure concept." "And a sure concept would have been to have enough sharpshooters to eliminate all at once. Sixteen or more sharpshooters would have been necessary and would have been available."

Schlütter does not know of a single police official punished or reprimanded for incompetence at any point following the Munich debacle. It is testimony to the speed with which Bavarian and Munich officials closed ranks to protect themselves from blame after the massacre at Fürstenfeldbruck.

Even Schreiber has since appeared keen to clear his own name. "I have to emphasize once more that the action area at Fürstenfeldbruck was mainly left to Dr. Wolf and [Alfred] Baumann [Wolf's right-hand man] for preparation and execution."[42]

The newly uncovered files confirmed many rumors Ankie had heard about the "rescue" operation at Fürstenfeldbruck airfield. "It is incredible that . . . that they had five sharpshooters, while there were eight terrorists, instead of having five hundred sharpshooters there trying to finish this hostage-taking drama," said Ankie with disgust. "They had no infrared apparatus in order to see in the dark. They had no walkie-talkies . . ." Her voice trailed off in horror.

The behavior of the German police has also upset Ankie Spitzer and other relatives, who are particularly shocked that the seventeen policemen who were supposed to spring a trap on the terrorists aboard the Lufthansa 727 at Fürstenfeldbruck "just abandoned the plane."[43] Ankie still cannot quite believe that the German police continued with their plan to rescue the hostages after terrorist leader Issa and his deputy Tony approached the 727 and discovered there were no pilots or cabin crew on board.

"Why continue? Why continue?" asked Ankie angrily. "Did [the Germans] really want to save them? That's my question. Did they really come out to finish this problem or did they just want to get this whole problem out of the Olympic Village, away from the eyes of the world? And then whatever happened at the airport . . . well, that's too bad."[44]

Many of the relatives, and even some German officials, allege that the police were pressurized into moving against the terrorists by Olympic officials who did not want the attack spoiling their Games of "Peace and Joy."

Avery Brundage allegedly told the Bavarian authorities that the crisis had to be resolved. "Avery Brundage . . . wished to settle it and to finish it, this was clear," said Walther Tröger, then mayor of the Olympic Village and the general secretary of the West German National Olympic Committee.[45]

The thousands of files and documents obtained by the relatives confirm many rumors about the massacre and paint an astonishing picture of the German response to the Black September attack. The files prove that David Berger, the Israeli-American wrestler, did not die when he was shot by the terrorists in the helicopter at Fürstenfeldbruck, but instead suffocated to death in the fire that followed.

Berger's family, who have already suffered the loss of a son, now have to suffer the knowledge that if the German police had moved faster when the first helicopter went up in flames, and quickly extinguished the blaze, his life might have been saved. Instead the young athlete was overcome by smoke.

Perhaps even more astonishingly, Ankie Spitzer believes the files suggest that one or possibly two of the Israelis were actually killed by German sniper fire rather than by the terrorists: "According to the ballistic reports that I saw, they were killed by fire of the Germans. Not on purpose, I didn't say that, but mistakenly."[46]

The Palestinians are certainly not averse to raising the possibility that the Germans killed some of the hostages. When Jamal Al-Gashey was asked directly how the Israeli athletes died, he responded cryptically: "It's hard to say. When the snipers opened fire on the leaders of the operation and they suddenly turned the lights on, the bullets were coming from all directions, and we shot back."[47]

Abu Daoud, one of the men who sent Al-Gashey on the attack, sings the same tune: "As to who actually killed the athletes and who actually killed the guerrillas, who knows after all this time? There were bullets flying everywhere, fired by the freedom fighters and by the Germans."[48]

As soon as the full extent of the German cover-up was exposed, the relatives approached a Munich law firm and asked whether they thought they had grounds for a legal action against the German and

Bavarian governments. The lawyers confirmed that they did. "Of course we decided to start a court case," said Ankie. "The documents showed us how big the failure was, what tremendous mistakes have been made."[49]

Still the German state tried to hamper their campaign. In Munich the courts threw out the case because of a three-year statute of limitations. Not surprisingly, the families were livid. "We said, 'How can you, even on the basis of statute of limitations, throw our case out after you hid all the documentation for twenty years?' "[50]

The families appealed on the grounds that the Germans had instigated a massive campaign of cover-up, disinformation, and deception to prevent the families and the outside world from knowing the full details of the Munich attack. The statute of limitations, said lawyers for the relatives, should start from the moment they received the documents. "And in that period of time we submitted our court case," said Ankie.

The case was thrown out of the lower Munich law courts, so the families went to a higher Bavarian court, where their case is still being heard, nearly three decades after the Munich Olympics. The relatives are suing the Federal Republic of Germany, the Free State of Bavaria, and the regional capital of Munich for mismanagement and misconduct at Fürstenfeldbruck.

"We are very optimistic that at last all the nonsense, all the details of statute of limitations, will be discarded and that people will finally start to focus on what really happened," Ankie concluded. "For us the facts are clear. Eleven Israeli athletes were killed on German soil . . . under the supervision of the German authorities by the Palestinian terrorists . . . somebody has to take responsibility . . . for what happened there and we are waiting for this to happen and I'm absolutely convinced that one day we will get the answer."

Many lawyers believe the relatives have an excellent case against the German authorities. Pinchas Zeltzer remains quietly confident: "It is rather a complex thing because it's not only that they were incompetent, there were so many things that they did wrong, so altogether of course it's gross negligence."[51]

The case has gone on for years and will probably continue for several more. Zeltzer believes the families will never give up their struggle. "I think the main point is that the families want to know the truth." Financial compensation is also being discussed. "The families were destroyed, financially, economically, and of course morally. Nobody can give life back, but the law has some tools to evaluate how [to] compensate somebody who has lost his father, somebody who has lost her husband. And this is a very fundamental point . . . These are the reasons why the families are struggling so long for this case."[52]

An end may now be in sight for the relatives who have battled on against German obfuscation. Even many senior German officials and police officers involved in the operation to rescue the Israelis are now prepared to admit it was a complete shambles. Heinz Hohensinn was one of the officers originally supposed to assault 31 Connolly-strasse and rescue the Israelis and was then one of the officers who abandoned the Boeing parked at Fürstenfeldbruck. "The weaknesses then were undoubtedly due to our training and the quality of the technical equipment. Our training at that time regarding terrorism was absolutely insufficient if existent at all. Today both training and equipment are at a completely different level."[53]

Hohensinn points out that there are now units, such as GSG-9, that exist almost exclusively to rescue hostages and defeat terrorism. "There have been continuous further developments and production of technical equipment specialized in terrorism," he adds. "There are now precision guns and infrared guns and blinding [stun] grenades. I'm sure the situation would be quite different today."

Ulrich Wegener, the founder of GSG-9, would doubtless agree. He describes the German handling of the Munich crisis as "one of the biggest mistakes the German government made at this time." It must, he adds forcefully, "never happen again."[54]

The relatives of the Israeli athletes have suffered endlessly since 1972. But they are not alone. The wounds from Munich run deep. Even the family of Ahmed Bouchiki, the innocent Moroccan waiter Israeli agents murdered in Norway, have been forced to wait decades for some semblance of justice. "To put it mildly, that Israel killed an innocent man is more than just an assumption. A Norwegian court has established this, but Israel has not faced up to it," said Björn Tore Godal, the Norwegian foreign minister, in 1996.[55]

Yet Israel has refused to accept moral responsibility for the death. "Israel will never take responsibility, because Israel is not a killing organization," responded Israeli prime minister Shimon Peres defiantly. "As a country we never took upon ourselves, we never shall go into the business of killing or accepting responsibility if somebody accuses us of killing."[56]

However, other Israeli politicians have been more open. "Norway is a friendly country. Bouchiki was not a terrorist. We killed him by mistake. Therefore, we should pay compensation provided the claim is submitted in an orderly fashion," said Shulamit Aloni, the Israeli communications minister, and the highest-ranking serving official ever to admit Israel was responsible for the murder.[57]

In 1996 Israel finally agreed to negotiate a still-undisclosed financial settlement with the widow, Turil Larsen-Bouchiki, and the couple's twenty-two-year-old daughter Malika.[58] "After twenty-three years, it is time to close the score," said Michael Shiloh, Israel's ambassador to Norway.[59]

But it is the campaign waged against the German authorities by the relatives of the Israeli athletes that is proving to be the real marathon. It was only in June 1998 that the German government finally relented and set aside the statute of limitations for the case to proceed. Senior German politicians have personally assured Ankie Spitzer that the time is now right, once and for all, for the case to be decided.

"I want those who were criminally negligent to have to face up to it, to take responsibility. If we don't learn from our mistakes we are bound to repeat them," said Ankie Spitzer. "I don't want money, I don't want revenge, I just want the truth to be known."

However, during investigations for the One Day in September documentary film, it has become clear that Germans officials are still determined to hide the truth. Documents and files are still being hidden from the relatives. "There are some documents that we did not receive," confirms Pinchas Zeltzer.[60]

Some of the missing evidence is believed to confirm that the

Black September unit received help from the East German Olympic delegation before their attack. A member of the German negotiating team has now stated that he believes East Germany was involved, the first time such a claim has been made by a senior German politician.[61]

The cover-up has also taken a more direct form. Even now, nearly thirty years after the massacre at Fürstenfeldbruck, photographs have vanished from files, documents have disappeared, and officials present at the Olympic Village and Fürstenfeldbruck have been cajoled or even threatened and ordered not to talk about the massacre.

For example, during investigations for the documentary it has been alleged that one of the pilots injured by "friendly fire" at Fürstenfeldbruck was visited in the hospital by a senior German official and offered a bravery medal on the strict condition that he never speak publicly or to the press about what happened. More recently several German police officers were threatened with losing their pension rights if they spoke to the *One Day in September* production team.

The only German police officer present at Fürstenfeldbruck who agreed to be interviewed was Heinz Hohensinn. Hohensinn does not have a police pension, so threats to silence him failed.[62]

But the most astonishing evidence of the depths to which the German and Bavarian authorities have sunk in their ongoing attempts to cover up details of the massacre concerns a film made by officials at Fürstenfeldbruck on the night of September 5, 1972, apparently to ensure there was an accurate record of what happened.

Sources contacted during the making of the *One Day in September* documentary state that the Fürstenfeldbruck film finally reveals exactly how Bavarian incompetence resulted in the deaths of the nine Israeli athletes and a German police officer.

Ever since the massacre the German authorities, both federal and Bavarian, have claimed that the seventeen German police officers stationed on the Lufthansa Boeing 727 at the airfield were there merely as backup in case the terrorists somehow managed to get onto the plane. What is now known, however, is that they were instead absolutely central to the rescue operation.

The German negotiators had agreed with Issa, the terrorist leader, that he and his deputy Tony would walk from the helicopters to the Boeing and check that they were happy with the plane. New investigations have revealed that the officers on the 727 were supposed to capture the two terrorists, and the five snipers at the airfield were then supposed to eliminate the remaining terrorists still standing by the choppers.

However, as has already been shown, the operation was thrown into chaos because the officers on the plane decided their mission was too dangerous and voted to leave the jet just seconds before the terrorists and hostages landed by helicopter. The German rescue plan then collapsed and five snipers were ordered to tackle eight terrorists, two of whom were already walking briskly back to the helicopter. A bloodbath ensued.

The film made at the airfield purportedly shows the entire operation. However, the main reels have disappeared and several German officials have since denied that the film even exists.

But the Fürstenfeldbruck film *does* exist. Extracts have been shown to German antiterrorist GSG-9 soldiers during their training (as an example of how *not* to rescue hostages), and during the making of the *One Day in September* documentary a senior serving member of the BundesNachrichten Dienst, or BND (the German equivalent of the CIA or MI6), illegally offered to provide a copy of the film. He demanded a large bribe, which was rejected.

Attempts to cover up the existence of the Fürstenfeldbruck film have resulted in further criminal behavior which should and must be investigated by the German and Bavarian governments.

When German federal prosecutors in Bonn recently demanded a list of files and evidence relating to the massacre from the Bavarian authorities — as part of new investigations into the crisis prompted by the lawsuit brought by the families of the athletes — they were promised full cooperation. The Bavarian authorities collected and dispatched dozens of files, folders, and photographs to the lawyers in Bonn. On the bill of loading there is an entry for the film made at Fürstenfeldbruck. When the haul arrived in Bonn, it was the only item missing.

German legal sources claim this is almost certainly an offense that could be prosecuted as criminal theft or perverting the course of

justice.[63] Nearly thirty years after the massacre, senior Bavarian officials continue to resort to subterfuge in their desperate attempts to
hide official failures in 1972.

The federal prosecutors in Bonn have promised to investigate
the theft but at the time of writing have made little progress. Nor
has an adequate investigation ever been conducted into the involvement of East Germany in the 1972 attack, despite the claim of a
member of the German negotiating team that agents of the communist state were culpable, and now presumably roam free in the unified
Germany.

The inescapable conclusion of this extensive thirty-year cover-up
is that German officers were unprepared to risk their lives for a group
of Jews, and that senior figures in successive German and Bavarian
governments have been frightened to reveal the true story for fear
that Germany would once again be accused of institutionalized anti-
Semitism.

The Survivors

13

Nearly thirty years after the massacre at Fürstenfeldbruck airfield, the effects continue to echo around the world. Nowhere is the tragedy felt more strongly than in a smattering of homes across Israel. The athletes left thirty-two dependents, including fourteen orphans and seven widows.[1]

Shlomo Freidman seeks a desperate solace from photograph albums, and tends a memorial to his son Zeev in Haifa. Ankie Spitzer works as a correspondent for Dutch television and newspapers and lives in Tel Aviv with her second husband, their three young children, and Anouk, her daughter by Andre, a twenty-seven-year-old who never knew her father. A pair of Andre's fencing foils grace the wall above Ankie's fireplace.

Ilana Romano, the widow of Yossef the weightlifter, runs an Italian restaurant in Tel Aviv. She has vowed that the world must never forget the tragedy. Her three daughters, Oshrat, Rachel, and Schlomit, were small children when their father was murdered. The tragedy enveloped other members of the family: three years later Yossef's mother (who had also lost two other sons) committed suicide by setting herself on fire.

Ilana's daughter Schlomit was just five months old when her father was killed. She does not even have the comfort of her own memories. Instead she relies on those of others. "It's like a puzzle," she said, "you take one piece from this person and another piece from that person and you build yourself an image of that person and you see pictures."[2]

When people discover that Schlomit is the daughter of Yossef Romano, they also share their memories: "They say, 'Oh, you know, when I was little I admired your father, and he was like this and like that'" . . . all the time I hear new stories and new things about my father. And that's how I know him."

Life has been hard for Schlomit. From an early age she was confronted by her loss, but one incident sticks in her memory: "I was very little. Most of the kids in school brought their fathers for one of the holy days, when everybody brings their parents and I brought my mom. When the evening was over the teachers asked fathers to stay behind and help to clean up. I just went home with my mom . . . that's the first time I really felt like something very [important was] missing. Like I don't have something that most of the kids have. It was hard."

Anouk Spitzer was also a tiny infant when her father died. She finds it unbearable that she does not have simple memories of her father walking, moving, talking.[3]

Yet at the same time, says Anouk, her father "was always there," because her memories of childhood are dominated by images of her mother desperately struggling to make sure the massacre at Munich would never be forgotten. "She decided to take his dream — my father really believed in the Olympic dream, and friendship and brotherhood between countries and people — and she decided to make something good out of this horrible thing." A year after Andre was murdered Ankie began organizing an international fencing competition for young people from all over the world. "So his memory was always with us but in a good and positive way."

Other children of the athletes were older than Schlomit and Anouk when they lost their father, but none had time to say goodbye. Alex Springer, the son of the weightlifting judge Jacov Springer, was travelling around Europe during August 1972 and arrived home just a few days before his father set off for the Munich Olympics.[4] He is left with memories of a gentle, caring sportsman who trained Jews and Palestinians alike. "They were his friends, he really loved them. To respect people and to honor them I think was a motto of his life."

Alex's sister Mayo was an adult by the time of her father's death. Age did not make her suffering any easier. "I couldn't cry for a long time. I couldn't let it out. In the end you never accept it, you just live with it. You continue with living your life and it follows you. That's what happened to me."[5]

Ten months after the Munich Games Mayo married. Still, the memories of her father's death haunted her. "There are many weird things in life that make you remember. There are things that make it sharper, like for instance my daughter was born on September 5, 1975, at 2:00 A.M. Exactly like the death certificate, three years' difference."

Such excruciating memories have made it too painful for some relatives of the athletes to remain in Israel. Judith Gutfreund–Salman and her husband Zohar emigrated to Toronto from Jerusalem and have no plans to return to the Middle East; even twenty years after Munich, Judith would demand that her children call her every single hour to reassure her they are safe. "If I don't hear from them for two hours, I think, 'They're finished, I don't have them any more.' Only when they phone am I happy."[6]

Judith's family was devastated by the death of her father Yossef. It was as if the Black September guerrillas had thrown a hand grenade into their home in Israel. Judith's grandfather Emile died just before midnight on October 3, 1972, four weeks to the hour after Yossef, while he was typing a letter to Willy Brandt; her mother Miriam died aged fifty-three in 1986, destroyed by grief.[7]

Perhaps surprisingly, Ankie Spitzer chose to stay in Israel after the massacre. "Everybody expected me to go back to Holland because I was Dutch, I had a little baby, and I was only married for a little bit over a year. But I did not come to Israel to run away."[8]

Ankie wanted to stay in Israel so "one day" Anouk could "know who her father was, why he was killed and who did it." It was not something that could be done from the comfort of northwest Europe. "I just [did not want] this to become something remote and go back to Amsterdam and tell her there was once a Palestinian ter-ror group or something. I wanted her to live this, I wanted her to un-derstand it. I wanted her to better understand who her father was and I felt that I could only do this in Israel."

Ankie may try to make staying in Israel seem like an obvious choice, but back in 1972 it was a brave decision for a young widow from Holland. It was also an inspired move, because she knew that few people in Holland had ever experienced a terrorist attack, or lost a relative in anything akin to the massacre at Fürstenfeldbruck. Ankie foresaw that in Holland Anouk would have been an oddity, perhaps even an object of pity. "In Israel she was not an exception. There were more of her kind and I thought it was healthier for her to grow up here in Israel and not to be an exception. And I've never regret-ted the decision."

According to Anouk, she never felt unusual or unique growing up in Israel without a father. "Almost every family in this country has lost somebody. So in that sense I wasn't different or special; . . . grief in this country is something very common so I was never treated like the poor orphan, or in a special way." But there were, of course, painful moments. "One time I came back from kindergarten and I was very upset because kids said that Arabs killed my father and I just said, 'No, he's abroad.'"[9]

Staying in Israel has not only helped Anouk to feel closer to her father but it has enabled Ankie to pursue a career in journalism and learn the background to the conflict between Palestinians and Is-raelis — the conflict that killed her husband. "This region that had so much hatred and so much conflict and so many wars . . . I said, 'I'm a little part of all this conflict with what happened in Munich, [so] I have to understand it better. I have to read about it, I have to under-stand it, and that's what I've been doing.'"

In 1981 Ankie remarried, taking as her new husband Elie Rekhess, a professor at Tel Aviv University specializing in Arab-Israeli affairs.[10]

Nevertheless, it took many years of heartache for Ankie and Anouk to come to terms with their loss. Mother and daughter have suffered together. Eventually their fury developed into a passionate desire to remember and commemorate the Munich massacre.

When Anouk was sixteen years old, she remembers going to high school on September 5, the anniversary of her father's death. "It was just a regular day, nothing special happened and nobody mentioned it," she said.[11] The lack of commemoration of such a crucial event in Israeli and Middle East history — especially given that Anouk was a pupil at the school — upset the youngster.

"I realized that my friends knew who my father was but they didn't really know exactly what happened there and many of them were born after the event." Anouk went to see the principal and obtained permission to hold an exhibition in the school commemorating and explaining the disaster.

The experience emboldened the teenager, and she has since visited Munich with friends to see where her father died. "It was interesting because I never thought I would end up going there by myself. I always imagined that I would do that with my mother."

It was, said Anouk, a "horrible feeling," wandering around the maze of apartment buildings — which were converted into public housing after the tragedy — trying to find the old Israeli residence at 31 Connollystrasse. The emotional trial was made worse because none of the Germans Anouk and her friends encountered knew where the Israeli quarters had been; or perhaps they pretended not to know. "Nobody knew what we were talking about. And I couldn't believe that something like that happened and nobody knew where it was."

As the young Jews walked through the old Olympic Village, one of them spotted a huge sunflower in a garden. "Oh, what a shame, I didn't bring flowers, because that's his favorite flower," Anouk said to her friends. The group walked on and eventually found the building which had once housed the Israeli delegation and eight Black September terrorists. Anouk was amazed by what she found.

"There was a little stone memorial that has the names on it. But it's just a regular house with the names of people who live there [inscribed outside]. And I just couldn't believe that the biggest thing of my life happened there, and people just lived there like nothing happened!

"At one point my friends left and suddenly they came back with the sunflower that they stole from that garden. My friends just stood up and they sang 'Hatikvah,' which is the national anthem. It was quite a moment."

Other relatives have also visited Munich. After suffering nightmares for eleven years after the massacre, Zeev Friedman's sister Nina eventually visited Fürstenfeldbruck in a bid to exorcize her visions.[12] It was a painful experience ("You could still see the oil stains on the tarmac," she recalled), but cathartic.

Time has also mellowed her anger. "At first I was ready to kill. But that feeling has gone. I've changed. I'm ready to understand the Palestinians have a cause to be heard."

For Anouk, the visit to 31 Connollystrasse sparked passion like her mother's for discovering the truth about the Munich massacre: she has become a campaigner for awareness and remembrance. "It's very important to me that people do talk about it and that it is made public. Because you know we always say that they didn't only murder eleven athletes and eleven Israelis but they murdered the Olympic dream, a dream that my father really believed in."

Anouk is desperate that her father's spirit should not be forgotten. "I think the world has to remember. He deserves, and his friends deserve, to be remembered."[13]

However, keeping the memory of the eleven Israeli athletes alive has been difficult. The relatives have had to cope not only with the human loss, and a vast German cover-up designed to hide the truth behind the incompetence of their rescue operation, but also with officials and bureaucrats who have appeared to wish they would just mourn quietly at home and let the Munich massacre be reduced to a footnote in history.

Four years after Munich the Olympic Games were held in Montreal, Canada, and Ankie, Ilana Romano, and Michal Shorr-Shahar travelled to the Games to ask the International Olympic Committee to commemorate the Munich massacre with a minute's silence. The request was rejected out of hand. The relatives have since been treated appallingly by Olympic and government officials around the world.

Even other Israelis seemed to want them to "stop raking up the past."
A senior Israeli sports official told Ilana and Ankie they should cry
over the graves of their dead husbands in Israel, not publicly in Montreal. "His comment hurt us terribly," said Ankie. "We walked out
feeling like insects everyone was trying to brush off."[14]

It is not only the widows who have been made to suffer. By
1992 Anouk felt she was old enough to represent her dead father at
the Barcelona Olympics, but the Israeli Olympic Committee did not
want her to attend. "She approached them on her own initiative,"
said Ankie. "At first they said 'No way, we are not prepared to have
you, certainly not in any official capacity, because that would be considered a political act, one which would not go down well with the
International Olympic Committee.' Eventually they came around
and offered to subsidize part of the trip."[15]

The manner in which German officials have treated relatives
since the Games has been so astonishingly insensitive that even Ilana
Romano remembers that even just after the massacre, as she was being shown around 31 Connollystrasse following a memorial service,
a policeman pointed to a wall in the room where the athletes were
held, not knowing that Ilana knew her husband had been shot in
front of it, and insisted on telling her it had been splattered with
blood during the firefight. It was, said Ilana, where her husband was
"destroyed."[16]

Other German officials seemed to hold the relatives to blame
for ruining their Games. "You are the Jews who brought the war to
our land. You, the Israelis, to be exact," one senior German official,
who called the terrorists "freedom fighters," told Ilana Romano.
Olympic officials have been craven in their desperate attempts to forget the massacre, trying to scuttle all efforts to create memorials to
the dead.

Yet the 1972 Black September attack is impossible to ignore. It
was a turning point in world sport; never again would it be possible
to separate major sporting events from politics. The Olympic ethos
itself suffered. The image of a family of nations competing together
away from politics was exposed as a fallacy. At the Montreal Olympics
in 1976 the Israeli delegation was sandwiched between several floors

of heavily armed Royal Canadian Mounted Police, and at every Olympics since, there have been more than twice as many security staff as officials and athletes.

But the IOC has deftly managed to avoid commemorating the Munich deaths. At the Atlanta Olympics in 1996, for example, Ankie Spitzer and other relatives demanded the Munich dead be given recognition. Juan Antonio Samaranch, the IOC president, a fascist minister in Franco's Spain, wanted to mention in his closing speech only the American killed in the Atlanta bombing.

Only after an emotional confrontation during which Ankie threw photos of her husband's mutilated corpse at Samaranch, and after she placed an advertisement in an Atlanta newspaper asking people to phone Samaranch in disgust at his actions, did the IOC agree to mention Munich in the closing speech. The relatives have been to every Olympics since Munich, campaigning to remind the world what happened to the Israeli athletes in 1972. "It must never happen again," said Ankie, "not anywhere, but especially not at the Olympic Games."

Official failure to recognize the dead athletes has only worsened the suffering of the relatives. Survivors of the 1972 Israeli Olympic delegation share the pain, for those who were at Munich also carry the scars of the events with them every day.[17]

At the Munich Olympics Esther Roth, then Esther Shahamurov, made it to the 100-meter semifinals, and lost her place in the final by just one-hundredth of a second. She was due to run in the semifinals of the 100-meter hurdles when Black September took hostage her trainer Amitzur Shapira. "We got to the Games and he was thrilled. He was so happy." When Esther made it to the second stage of the 100-meter hurdles he was waiting for her at the end of the track, his eyes shining. His death ripped apart her life for decades to come. She pulled out of the semifinals and flew back to Israel with Shapira's body. She did not put on another pair of training shoes for two years.

"After an incident like that . . . you ask yourself, 'What am I doing it for?' You are programmed to get to the Olympic Games. And then you get there. Look what happened at the Games. What kind of a thing is it? I couldn't even dream that this sort of thing could happen. You know with cars there are accidents. In Israel people die in wars. All kinds of events . . . but the Olympic Games?" Roth asks, searching for an explanation for the brutality. "The whole idea is unity, freedom, equal opportunities. There was nothing to come back to. For me sport was connected with murder."[18]

Roth's husband Peter, whom she married three months after returning, slowly brought her out of her shell. "We used to go to places where there was no memory of Amitzur, stadiums Amitzur hadn't been to," she said. "Step by step I recovered emotionally." And yet her life is still dominated by memories of her dead coach: "He was like a father to me."

For Gad Tsabari life after the Munich Olympics has been one long struggle. He saw a psychiatrist once a week in the early days, then received call-up papers for the Israeli Defense Forces and was subjected to a battery of psychological and physical entrance tests. The highest possible grade was 97, the lowest 21. Gad was in such bad shape he scored just 24.[19]

Shaul Ladany, who escaped from 31 Connollystrasse as the terrorists forced their way inside, has also had to live with the guilt of a survivor. But for him the Munich attack was just one appalling experience in a lifetime of Jewish suffering: "When I was just five, the family home, a villa in Belgrade, was bombed above our heads — a direct hit. We all survived in a basement laundry room, but our neighbors, who were in another cellar of our home, were killed. At eight and a half I was in Bergen-Belsen. My mother, father, sisters, and I all survived, but my grandmother and grandfather were made into soap at Auschwitz. I also served as an officer in several Israeli wars. There have been lots of bad experiences."[20]

It was, perhaps, the cruellest irony that the 1972 massacre happened on German soil. For the attack might never have happened if the Games had been held in another country. Security at the Munich Olympics was light precisely to avoid reminding the world of

Germany's Nazi past. Black September — a group that existed ultimately because German annihilation of the Jews had encouraged the
creation of the state of Israel — took immediate advantage of the lapse.

Senior German officials present in Munich on September 5, 1972,
demonstrate a variety of emotions when remembering the tragedy.
Some have clearly tried to block any sense of guilt from their minds by
maintaining a desperate belief that the massacre was unavoidable. Others are still pained by the events but draw comfort from the erroneous
belief that it could have happened anywhere, and they were merely
unwilling participants as a Middle East tragedy was played out on their
soil.

However, it would be wrong to portray all the German officials
as figures desperately trying to forget the past. "I deeply regret what
happened to my friends from Israel," said Walter Tröger sadly.[21] "I
have been in the war and I have seen death. But I will never forget
what happened in Munich."

For Hans-Jochen Vogel, who was responsible for securing the
Games for the city, the "happy memory" of the 1972 Olympics has
"a dark shadow." It still devastates him that "Israelis, Jewish people,
have been killed on German territory."[22]

Several German officials suffer the same visions as Zvi Zamir,
who watched as Jews shuffled to their doom. He still finds memories
of the dead athletes haunting his dreams. "I sleep with it," he said.[23]

Even now, nearly thirty years after the attack, the terrorists involved
in the operation have no regrets. The morality of their assault is un-
questioned. "In the Palestinian movement, we have a saying: every
crisis has its own morals," said Abu Daoud. "At that time, a state of
war existed between us and the Israelis. They were killing us, and we
were killing them, except they were killing many times more of us
than we were killing of them, and they were undermining our resources much more effectively than we were undermining theirs."[24]

Abu Daoud remains an eloquent and vociferous believer in the
righteousness of the Palestinian terrorist movement: "They were a
country that was armed to the teeth and we were just a resistance
movement with nothing more than our guns and our bodies."

The world, he believes, should not focus on the Munich massacre but on the thousands of Palestinians who, he claims, have been killed by Israel. The rest of the world, says Abu Daoud, "looks on as if the only thing that matters is this thing that happened twenty-five years ago, the Munich operation." It is certainly true that, at the start of a new millennium, the UNRWA (United Nations Relief and Works Agency for Palestinian Refugees) still claims to be supporting 3.6 million Palestinian refugees. Many of the Arab states housing the Palestinian refugees have done practically nothing to improve their living conditions, for fear temporary camps will become permanent towns.

While former members of Black September continue to defend the morality of their operation years after the deaths at Fürstenfeldbruck, nobody can doubt the "success" of the attack in raising the profile of the Palestinian cause.

Abu Iyad has claimed that "world opinion was forced to take note of the Palestinian drama, and the Palestinian people imposed their presence on an international gathering that had sought to exclude them."[25]

Jamal Al-Gashey, the only terrorist still alive, also believes the attack achieved its aim. "The name of Palestine was repeated all over the world that day. A lot of the people of the world who had never heard of Palestine knew then that there was a deprived people with a cause to fight for."[26]

A week after the attack, the following announcement appeared in the Beirut newspaper *Al-Sayad,* purportedly from senior officials of Black September:[27] "In our assessment, and in light of the result, we have made one of the best achievements of Palestinian commando action. A bomb in the White House, a mine in the Vatican, the death of Mao Tse-tung, an earthquake in Paris could not have echoed through the consciousness of every man in the world like the operation at Munich. The Olympiad arouses the people's interest and attention more than anything else in the world. The choice of the Olympics, from the purely propagandistic viewpoint, was 100 percent successful. It was like painting the name of Palestine on a mountain that can be seen from the four corners of the earth."[28]

Even the relatives of the fedayeen who died at Fürstenfeldbruck agree. Mahmoud Mohammad Jawad, the brother of young Khalid

Jawad, says the operation "informed the world."[29] "In the West, for a long time [prior to Munich], they said Israel, not Palestine," added his brother Adel. "They didn't know where it was. The only Arab they knew was Nasser. Those who had heard of Palestine thought it was next to Israel."[30]

In truth, the Palestinians are right: Munich was one of the most successful terrorist attacks in history. As Bruce Hoffman, a leading authority on terrorism, points out: "The premier example of terrorism's power to rocket a cause from obscurity to renown . . . was without doubt the murder of eleven Israeli athletes seized by Palestinian terrorists at the 1972 Munich Olympic Games."[31]

Most of the world had forgotten the Palestinians existed before the attack at Munich. Within two years of the massacre at Fürstenfeldbruck, Yasser Arafat was being feted by world leaders and invited to address the General Assembly of the United Nations, to which the Palestinians were later given special observer status.

It was not enough for Arafat and the PLO, but it was a start, and there can be little doubt that the killing of eleven Jewish athletes in Munich helped persuade the world that the Palestinian struggle needed to be taken seriously. By the end of the 1970s the PLO had established diplomatic relations with eighty-six countries around the globe, compared with seventy-two for Israel.[32]

Memories of the Black September attack on the Munich Olympics affect many people around the world. Like the assassination of President Kennedy in Dallas or the death of Diana, Princess of Wales, in a Paris car crash, it was an event that had a global impact.

Millions still remember the shock they felt seeing pictures of the first live televised terrorist attack in history. It was as if the entire world was reading the same book.[33] "The whole world was watching," agrees Ankie Spitzer. "It was on the international stage."

But the world has changed dramatically since 1972. In recent years the Intifada uprisings, which erupted in the Gaza Strip and West Bank spontaneously in December 1987, encouraged a peace process between the two sides that finally brought the men of violence in from the cold.

In 1996, under the terms of the Israeli–Palestinian peace accords, even Abu Daoud was among a group of activists allowed to return from abroad to live in the autonomous Palestinian areas. A graying grandfather, he settled in the town of Ramallah on the West Bank, near Jerusalem, and was given a comfortable job as director of Fatah membership, with a suite of bare white rooms at the bottom of a marble staircase in the town's Civil Affairs building.

Age and time have mellowed this once violent man. "We were certainly not angels in our actions, but neither were the Israelis," Abu Daoud now says reflectively. "For a long time — too long a time, perhaps — we thought that resorting to violence, which worked so well for the Zionists, could also succeed for us." Now, more than a quarter of a century later, with the Middle East peace process in place, times have changed. "We have agreed to share Palestine [and] we must bury the past. That means we shake hands, even if our partner has blood on his hands."[34]

Finally, there is hope for a future peace in the Middle East. The endless cycle of violence between Israelis and Palestinians may one day draw to a close. Many survivors, relatives of the dead athletes, and even the terrorists, pray for such a new dawn. They want peace, and although reconciliation takes time, progress is being made.

Working as a journalist, Ankie Spitzer regularly spends time among the Palestinians in the Gaza Strip and the West Bank. "In the beginning I must say that sometimes it was very difficult," she admitted. However, "I think that I did manage to grow above [distrust] and to understand also the rights of the Palestinians. I am a realistic person, I think. I can see their plight, I can see their struggle, I can understand their struggle."

Above all, says Ankie, she will not allow the bitter hatreds that caused the massacre to be perpetuated into another generation. "I have never raised my daughter, Anouk, with hate in her heart. I have never told her to hate the Palestinians. I do think that I have very hateful feelings against those people that did what they did to Andre and I think this is natural. But I don't hate the whole Palestinian people for this, not at all."[35]

Ankie retains her passionate desire for justice: "I think that justice has to be done. And this has nothing to do with the Palestinian people as a whole, but I think that the perpetrators, the ones that did kill and did maim people, that they should pay the price."

The terrorists, not surprisingly, have no intention of "paying the price" for their crimes. They see what happened in Munich as a consequence of war. The PLO have still never apologized for the massacre. Abu Daoud's enigmatic message to the families, on both sides, Israeli and Palestinian, of those who died at Munich is that "fate had written it so." They all died, he says "for the sake of a just and lasting peace, in which their children could live as a result of what their fathers did."

Jamal Al-Gashey, however, is more contrite, and claims to understand the pain of the Israeli relatives: "I feel sorry for what they suffered. I can sympathize because I have lost people who were close to me at the hands of the Israeli army. I know what it's like on a human level to lose someone who is close." But, he adds, "we were in a state of war caused by the expropriation of my land by the Israelis and their denial of my rights, even my existence."

Al-Gashey still describes himself as a "soldier" carrying out orders during the Munich attack. He has lived in the shadows since the massacre. Even now, he refuses to be publicly identified to avoid possible assassination by an Israeli Wrath of God hit team. "But I don't regret it. I have always lived cautiously, not for myself but for my family, my wife, who agreed to marry me after the operation and in the knowledge of the danger I was in, and my children. My family has paid a big price, but we think it is the price that every Palestinian family has to pay to get what it deserves."[36]

As a combatant who committed his youth to fighting what he sees as Israeli occupation of his land, Al-Gashey has found it difficult to adapt to the peace process. The Palestinians, he pointed out, agreed to negotiate "even with people who had committed atrocities against our people," including Israeli politicians and military leaders responsible for heinous crimes "in which relatives of mine died."

But Al-Gashey says he now wants peace. "The most important thing to me now is ensuring that my family can live [in] peace, security, and independence like all families in the world, enabling my children to get into the best universities and graduate from them and achieve everything they dream of. As you can see, my dreams are those of any other person, but the barrier to achieving them is that, as a Palestinian person, I am deprived of all my rights."

Al-Gashey's hopes for his children are now pinned on the Middle East peace process, resurgent since the election of Ehud Barak, the former commando, as Israeli prime minister in 1999. The wheel has come full circle. Barak was the leader of the elite unit that murdered three of Al-Gashey's Palestinian commanders as part of Operation Spring of Youth in Beirut in 1973. Now he is seen as a moderate political leader, and there is some semblance of hope that an era of violence, in which the Munich massacre was such a milestone, can be lain to rest, and once bitter enemies can learn to live together in their ancient land.[37]

So can there be peace between the warring sides and reconciliation between the families of the dead Israeli athletes and the fedayeen? Hajja Hamid, the mother of Black September guerrilla Afif Ahmed Hamid, said that if she was to meet the family of one of the Israeli athletes, "I would say, 'Welcome.'" Her husband, Afif's father, interjected, "They are bereaved, just like us."[38]

Many of the families of the fedayeen still live in the same tin shacks they have always occupied in refugee camps, yet they still want reconciliation. "We want peace," said Hajja Hamid. "Who wants war?"[39]

Many of the dead athletes' children have the same belief. "Even though the Palestinian people are responsible for the killing . . . I can't really feel hate against all the Palestinian people," said Alex Springer. "Because of the pain of the war and the killing, the most important thing is to make a peace with them and not to kill one another."[40]

Anouk Spitzer wholeheartedly backs the peace process, despite knowing it has a price. "It's very difficult for us as families to see the peace process and see people like Arafat being welcomed and seeing [former Israeli prime minister Yitzhak Rabin] shaking Arafat's hand. But on the other hand we know that that's the only way, and I believe in it with all my heart because I don't wish that my children or my grandchildren will ever know what it means to grow up like I did without a father. I have to believe that there's another way."[41]

Schlomit Romano feels much the same: "You have to understand, since I was little I was raised under the values of peace. Never for revenge. Never for hatred. Always for a better world without murderers."[42] However, she cannot forgive the terrorists who killed her father Yossef, the men "with blood on their hands."

"I want them to stand trial and to get what they deserve for what they did," she said. "First I want them to spend some time [in prison] and to feel what they did was wrong." It upsets her that Jamal Al-Gashey may think her father was killed in the name of freedom for the Palestinians. "It wasn't a war," the athletes were not "soldiers," they were innocent people. She wants to sit down with Al-Gashey and explain to him her suffering, her sense of loss. However, she stressed again that she does not want revenge, repeating it like a mantra.

"I really don't want anyone to grow up like I grew up [without a father]. I'm eager for peace." Schlomit even said she would like to meet Jamal Al-Gashey's daughter "and tell her that together we can build a very new world of people that can live together."

"But as for her father," she added, "I'm not going to forgive . . . Never."

Notes

Introduction

1   Filmed interview with Hans-Jochen Vogel.
2   Filmed interview with Gerald Seymour.
3   Filmed interview with Shmuel Lalkin.
4   Ibid.
5   Filmed interview in Hebrew with Henry Herskowitz.
6   Ibid.
7   This and following quotes from filmed interview in Hebrew with Esther Roth.
8   The last American ground combat unit in South Vietnam, the Third Battalion of the Twenty-first Infantry, left the country on August 11, 1972. However, it was not until the week of September 22 that the U.S. suffered no military fatalities — the first time since March 1965. Even after U.S. forces left, the war continued.
9   This and following quote from Peter Taylor, *States of Terror* (London: BBC Books, 1993), pp. 7–8.
10 This and following quotes from filmed interview in Hebrew with Esther Roth.

1 The Takeover

1   The true identity of the terrorists in the Black September unit has never been confirmed. During the making of the *One Day in September* documentary film, on which this book is largely based, nearly half a dozen identities were suggested for "Issa." Based on information from the only surviving terrorist (Jamal Al-Gashey), a surviving Black September leader (Abu Daoud), German police interrogations, investigations by lawyers working for the relatives, and numerous Palestinian sources, I believe the names used in this book are the most accurate published to date.

2   This and following account from filmed interview with Jamal Al-Gashey, the only surviving terrorist.

3   He also made this claim during his interrogation (under the alias "Abdull Samir," a.k.a. "Jamal") by Georg Wolf of the Munich police in 1972, but the unwitting help of the U.S. athletes was covered up.

4   "Grounds of the Appeal," filed by the relatives of the Israeli athletes, quoting the testimony of Hein-Peter Gottelt, Arno Thomas, and Karl Weber, all in the Leitz-file StA 1 of the investigation record, chapter "Kontaktpersonen, Postbeamte," LKA-report (annex K 8, p. 29).

5   Filmed interview with Jamal Al-Gashey.

6   Ibid.

7   Another identity has also been suggested for Tony. Several sources state he was actually called Hamid Kartout and was a law student in Munich. Although the true identities of the Black September terrorists have been systematically concealed by the Palestinian liberation movement and the German and Bavarian governments, Bruno Merck, the Bavarian interior minister, did confirm several details about the leaders of the attack in interviews broadcast on German television immediately after the Munich crisis. He confirmed that one of the terrorists had worked as a civil engineer inside the Olympic Village and that another worked as a cook. Further details of their identities have been compiled by Palestinian researchers and from interviews with Jamal Al-Gashey, Abu Daoud, and other Palestinian sources; Manfred Schreiber and Zvi Zamir; and from the writings of Abu Daoud and Abu Iyad, the leader of Black September in the early 1970s.

8   Filmed interview with Jamal Al-Gashey.

9   Peter Taylor, *States of Terror* (London: BBC Books, 1993), pp. 7–8.

10   "Coach Tells of Escape from Assailants," *Jerusalem Post,* September 6, 1972.

11   Peter Taylor, op. cit.

12   Ibid.

13   From the interrogation of "Abdull Samir," a.k.a. Jamal [Jamal Al-Gashey], by Georg Wolf of the Munich police.

14   This and following account from Peter Taylor, op. cit.

15   Sokolovsky stayed there for perhaps ten minutes, then began running again. "I just ran and ran — into the arms of a policeman who was making a routine tour of the village. I broke down and cried. I thought maybe I had been very close to death," he said. (Source: ibid.)

16   Filmed interview with Jamal Al-Gashey.

17   This and following account from filmed interview with Gad Tsabari.

18   Ibid.

19   Peter Taylor, op. cit., p. 8.

20   Ibid.

21 Filmed interview with Abu Daoud.

22 Ibid.

23 Filmed interview with Jamal Al-Gashey.

24 From the interrogation of "Abdull Samir," a.k.a. Jamal [Jamal Al-Gashey], by Georg Wolf of the Munich police.

25 Ibid.

26 Filmed interview with Jamal Al-Gashey.

27 Ladany's account taken from Kenny Moore, "Munich's message," *Sports Illustrated* 85 (6), August 5, 1996.

28 Ibid.

29 Filmed interview with Jamal Al-Gashey.

30 This quote and following account from filmed interview in Hebrew with Henry Herskowitz.

31 Serge Groussard, *The Blood of Israel* (New York: William Morrow & Company, 1975), p. 5.

32 This account from filmed interview with Manfred Schreiber.

33 Filmed interview with Hans-Dietrich Genscher. This is the first time Genscher has spoken publicly about the Munich crisis since 1972.

34 This and following account from filmed interview with Shmuel Lalkin.

35 Filmed interview in Hebrew with Henry Herskowitz.

36 Ibid.

37 This and following account from filmed interview with Shmuel Lalkin.

38 Filmed interview with Walther Tröger. He had been a guest in Olympic Villages since 1964 and was seen as the perfect choice to run the Munich Village. "It was a great task and it still is the most important issue in my life so far," said Tröger.

39 Morley Myers, "Olympic Massacre: When Talks Failed," United Press International, September 4, 1987.

40 Filmed interview with Walther Tröger.

41 This and following account from testimony of Annaliese Graes to the official Bavarian pre-criminal investigation into the Munich crisis.

42 This exchange from Serge Groussard, op. cit., p. 74.

43 Stasi file located for *One Day in September:* "Documentation regarding the events of September 5, 1972, in the Olympic Village by Martin Kramer, Dieter Wales, Wolfgang Gitter." The files provide an extraordinary minute-by-minute chronology of events as seen through the eyes of the East Germans.

44 Testimony of Annaliese Graes, op. cit.

45 This and following from Stasi file, op. cit.

46 Filmed interview with Ulrich Wegener. At the time Wegener had just returned from a course at a NATO defense college in Rome.

47 Filmed interview with Shmuel Lalkin.

48   Ibid. The Israeli government was adamant there would be no prisoner releases. "The Israeli policy was not to give in," said Zvi Zamir, then head of the Israeli secret service, Mossad. (Source: filmed interview with Zvi Zamir.)

49   This and following quotes from filmed interview with Gad Tsabari.

50   Ibid. Tsabari said: "I didn't know there were eight terrorists." The police may have relied on his information, causing possibly fatal mistakes later in the day.

51   This and following account from filmed interview with Esther Roth.

2 Black September

1   Quoted by Christopher Dobson, *Black September* (London: Robert Hale & Company, 1975), pp. 9–10.

2   Ibid., p. 11. Also quoted in Egyptian newspaper reports of the attack.

3   Ibid., pp. 20–21.

4   This has recently been disputed by Zeev Herzog, an archaeologist at Tel Aviv University. He claims that Jerusalem was at best a small fiefdom, and the seeds of the Jewish state can be found in the ninth century B.C., when groups of shepherds established the two rival states of Judah and Israel. For further information, see an article by Herzog in the Israeli daily *Ha'aretz,* October 28, 1999.

5   Possibly as many as two hundred thousand Jews were expelled from Spain.

6   If Abd ar-Rahman, governor of Spain, had not been defeated at Poitiers in 732 A.D. by Charles Martel, the Arabs would have taken Paris and probably conquered large tracts of northern Europe.

7   Many Jews opposed the Zionists, saying that the idea fed anti-Semitism, and they were happy with their British, French, or German nationality.

8   The first Arab protests against Jewish settlements in Palestine occurred in 1891. Major anti-Zionist Arab riots followed in 1919 and 1921.

9   The declaration read in part: "His Majesty's Government view with favour the establishment in Palestine of a national home for the Jewish people, and will use their best endeavours to facilitate the achievement of this object, it being clearly understood that nothing shall be done which may prejudice the civil and religious rights of existing non-Jewish communities in Palestine, or the rights and political status enjoyed by Jews in any other country."

10   Abu Iyad with Eric Rouleau, *My Home, My Land* (New York: Times Books, 1981), p. 12.

11   Other groups which emerged included the National Liberation Army, the National Liberation Front, the Organization for the Liberation of Palestine, the Palestinian Liberation Army, and the Popular Front for the Liberation of

Palestine. Nasser also dramatically increased support and training for the fedayeen after an Israeli assault on the Egyptian army headquarters (which was in turn revenge for the occasional fedayeen cross-border strikes) on the night of February 28, 1955, ended with thirty-eight deaths. Later Israeli raids into Gaza resulted in dozens, possibly hundreds, of Palestinian deaths, and Israeli soldiers looted and burnt Palestinian homes.

12 Neil C. Livingstone and David Halevy, *Inside the PLO* (New York: William Morrow & Company, 1990), pp. 59–60.

13 *The Times,* April 15, 1968, and *The New York Times,* October 22, 1968.

14 Ibid. Also Tabitha Petran, *Syria* (London: Ernest Benn, 1978), p. 199; and Nadav Safran, *Israel* (Cambridge: Belknap Press of Harvard University Press, 1978), p. 246.

15 This and following quote from filmed interview with Jamal Al-Gashey.

16 John K. Cooley, *Green March, Black September* (London: Frank Cass, 1973), p. 149.

17 There were several other actions attributed to the PFLP. At Zurich airport on February 18, 1969, the pilot of an El Al jet was fatally wounded, and his co-pilot seriously injured, in a gun attack by guerrillas. An armed Israeli security guard, Mordecai Rachamin, shot one of the attackers and was then tried by a Swiss court but later acquitted. Two days after the Zurich attack a Jerusalem supermarket was bombed, killing two Israelis and wounding another twenty.

18 Habash was interviewed by the Italian journalist Oriana Fallaci. Quoted in John K. Cooley, op. cit., pp. 39–40.

19 The 007 Squad carried small .22 pistols, which fired bullets that could kill a human without passing through the target and penetrating the outer shell of a plane.

20 This and following quotes from filmed interview with Abu Daoud.

21 Excerpts from testimony of Abu Daoud before the military prosecutor on February 15, 1973. Amman radio report of confession, broadcast on the Amman Home Service, 16.00 GMT, March 24, 1973, and published in the *BBC Summary of World Broadcasts, Part 4: The Middle East and Africa,* Second Series ME/4255, March 27, 1973.

22 Charles Richards, "Defending a Palestinian State of Mind," *Independent,* July 26, 1989.

23 Deeper in the background of those behind Black September was Fuad Shemali, a Lebanese Christian who helped to plan the assault on Connollystrasse and organized the terrorists before they arrived in Munich. Shemali died of cancer in Geneva in August 1972, before the assault was even launched, but his contribution was still significant. Before the Munich attack Shemali was even quoted in a Cairo newspaper as saying: "We have to hit their weak spots.

Bombing an El Al office does not serve our purpose. We have to kill the most famous. Since statesmen are difficult to kill, we have to kill artists and athletes."

24 Based on a pretrial interrogation of Therese Halsa by General Rehaven Zeevi, commander of Israel's Central District, an area which includes Lod Airport.

25 She later claimed she had been raped and was recruited into Fatah by a doctor with whom she was having a passionate affair. The doctor introduced her to morphine, to which she rapidly became addicted, and she then became a "robot" under the command of Fatah and Black September. (Based on comments and claims made during the trial of the two women.)

26 Christopher Dobson, op. cit., p. 75.

27 Ibid. p. 74.

28 Ibid. p. 81; quoting from Kozo Okamoto's later interrogation by General Rehaven Zeevi.

29 Abu Iyad with Eric Rouleau, op. cit.; the Munich operation is covered on pp. 106–12.

30 When questioned back in 1973 by the Jordanian secret police about the Munich attack, Abu Daoud initially claimed his involvement was limited. He was in Sofia, Bulgaria, when Abu Iyad arrived from Geneva with Fakhri al Umari and explained they were developing a plan to attack the Israeli team at the Munich Olympics. "At the hotel Abu Iyad informed me . . . that they intended to attack the Israeli delegation to the Olympic Games in Munich," said Daoud, "to detain the Israeli athletic delegation and to ask the German government to ask for the release of the Arab prisoners in Israel in return for the release of the Israeli athletic team." Daoud claims Abu Iyad asked him to give his false Iraqi passport to al Umari because it contained a valid German visa, and he then had nothing more to do with the Munich attack. Even at the time German and Israeli investigators doubted his version of events. German detectives soon decided Abu Daoud had been one of the central figures behind the plot. They discovered that Fakhri al Umari had been in the city at the same time as a man called Saad ad-Din Wali, who stayed in a small hotel on the outskirts of the city from June 1972 until the Olympic attack and was, the German police believed, Abu Daoud. (Source: excerpts from testimony of Abu Daoud before the military prosecutor on February 15, 1973. Amman radio report of confession broadcast on the Amman Home Service, 16.00 GMT, March 24, 1973, and published in the BBC Summary of World Broadcasts, Part 4: The Middle East and Africa, Second Series ME/4255, March 27, 1973.)

31 Abu Iyad with Eric Rouleau, op. cit., pp. 106–12

32 These and the following details of Issa's life from testimony of Annaliese Graes to the official Bavarian pre-criminal investigation into the Munich crisis. Graes spent long periods talking with Issa during the day-long siege in

Connollystrasse. While most of what he told her must be treated with skepticism, Issa did appear to see Graes as an independent intermediary he could trust, and much of what he said has been corroborated by other Palestinian sources. Issa told Graes that "Tony," his second-in-command, was actually his "brother," but there is confusion over whether Issa meant sibling, or brother Palestinian.

33 Issa told Graes he had "a good life" in France.

34 Abu Iyad with Eric Rouleau, op. cit., pp. 106–12.

35 Ibid.

36 Filmed interview with Jamal Al-Gashey.

37 Ibid.

38 Filmed interview with Abu Daoud. The terrorists chosen for the operation were, according to Abu Daoud: "all children of the camps, the Lebanese camps which were attacked every day by Israel. Therefore they were all part of the Palestinian experience and they had all known suffering, if not them directly then their relatives, their children, their communities. They were victims of Israeli aggression on a daily basis, and we could do nothing about it since we had no air force, no ground-to-air weapons, no long-range missiles like the Israelis. So our children suffered aerial bombardment and were keen for revenge, for their dignity and their suffering."

39 Arabic for "young men" or "lads," but often used to describe young freedom fighters.

40 Filmed interview with Adel and Mahmoud Mohammad Jawad, the brothers of Black September commando Khalid Jawad.

41 Ibid. Khalid was sent home from West Germany by his brother because he "couldn't fit in."

42 Filmed interview with the parents of Black September commando Afif Ahmed Hamid.

43 This and following quotes from filmed interview with Mrs. Al-Gashey. "He won a scholarship to attend the university, and a doctor at the AUB paid the rest," she said.

44 Following exchange related in filmed interview with Hajja Hamid, the mother of Black September commando Afif Ahmed Hamid.

45 Filmed interview with Mahmoud Mohammad Jawad, the brother of Black September commando Khalid Jawad.

46 Filmed interview with Jamal Al-Gashey.

47 In 1951 the Israeli Supreme Court ruled that the families could return to the villages, but on Christmas Eve that year the Israeli army burnt all their homes, leaving only some Roman ruins, the church, and a graveyard. For more than fifty years the Arab Christians thrown out of their homes have raised their children in neighboring villages, returning to the church to marry, bury their

dead, and commemorate their loss. At press, a lawsuit on behalf of the Arab Christians against the Israeli government was continuing.

48   For years Palestinians claimed Black September was separate from Fatah, and thus Arafat had no idea what terrorist attacks were being planned. More recently it has become clear that Black September was an integral part of Fatah, but senior Palestinians have still sought to distance Arafat from terrorism.

49   According to Alan Hart, author of *Arafat: Terrorist or Peacemaker?*, "the decision to play the terror card came from the bottom of the PLO on up. The simple militiamen were desperate concerning their situation and the indifference of public opinion. Many people said 'The world doesn't care about us, so we'll have to make sure it does.' Arafat and his leaders approved an operation, the one in Munich. For Arafat it was a kind of crisis management. He wanted to carry out a successful operation with the purpose of being able to put his hand on the terror tap and control it and turn it off." (Source: Alan Hart was interviewed for *Wanted: The Secret behind the 1972 Olympic Assassinations,* a film by Wilfried Huismann, broadcast in England on July 15, 1996.)

50   From the interrogation of "Abdull Samir," a.k.a. Jamal [Jamal Al-Gashey], by Georg Wolf of the Munich police. Also based on an interview with the parents of Black September commando Afif Ahmed Hamid.

51   Interrogation of "Abdull Samir," op. cit.

52   Ibid.

53   This and following quotes and account from filmed interview with Jamal Al-Gashey.

54   Abu Daoud travelled with them and helped the last Palestinian over the fence, then he took a taxi back to his hotel, packed his bags, and fled the city. (Source: interview with Abu Daoud.) Ali Hassan Salameh had already left West Germany to establish a forward command post in a flat in East Berlin with the connivance of the East German government. (Source: interview with Israeli intelligence source, and Michael Bar-Zohar and Eitan Haber, *The Quest for the Red Prince* [London: Weidenfeld & Nicolson, 1983], p. 124.)

3 Negotiations

1   This and following quotes and account from filmed interview with Manfred Schreiber.

2   Filmed interview with Walther Tröger.

3   Filmed interviews with Jamal Al-Gashey and Abu Daoud.

4   Filmed interview with Manfred Schreiber.

5   This and following account and quotes from filmed interview with Ankie Spitzer.

6   Dudley Doust, "Munich: The Gunfire Still Echoes Today," *Daily Telegraph*, February 29, 1992. An excellent magazine article about the tragedy.

7   This and following account and quotes from filmed interview with Ilana Romano.

8   This and following account and quotes from filmed interviews with (separately) Rosa Springer, Alex Springer, and Mayo Springer.

9   Filmed interview with Ulrich Wegener.

10 This and following quotes and account from filmed interview with Walther Tröger.

11 This and following account and quotes from testimony of Annaliese Graes to the official Bavarian pre-criminal investigation into the Munich crisis.

12 Golda Meir, *My Life* (New York: Dell Publishing,1975), p. 11.

13 Quoted by Ian Black and Benny Morris, *Israel's Secret Wars* (London: Warner Books, 1996), p. 270.

14 Testimony of Manfred Schreiber to the official Bavarian pre-criminal investigation into the Munich crisis.

15 Filmed interview with Manfred Schreiber.

16 "Grounds of the Appeal," filed by the relatives of the Israeli athletes, quoting the report of the Landeskriminalamt (annex K 8, p. 111); testimony of Dr Schreiber (annex K 30, p. 12).

17 Stasi file located for *One Day in September:* "Documentation regarding the events of September 5, 1972, in the Olympic Village by Martin Kramer, Dieter Wales, Wolfgang Gitter." The files provide an extraordinary minute-by-minute chronology of events as seen through the eyes of the East Germans.

18 Filmed interview with Ulrich Wegener.

19 This and following account and quotes from filmed interview with Magdi Gohary.

20 "Grounds of the Appeal," filed by the relatives of the Israeli athletes, quoting from the report of the Landeskriminalamt (annex K 8, p. 41, 51); testimony of Dr. Wolf (annex K 14, S.2); testimony of Dr. Schreiber (annex K 30, p. 10).

21 Allen Guttmann, *The Games Must Go On: Avery Brundage and the Olympic Movement* (New York: Columbia University Press, 1984), pp. 250–55. Professor Guttmann sources the information to an interview with Willi Daume in Cologne, December 16, 1981.

22 Filmed interview with Gerald Seymour.

23 This and following account and quotes from filmed interview with Jamal Al-Gashey, the only surviving terrorist.

24 This and following account and quotes from Kenny Moore, "Munich's Message," *Sports Illustrated* 85 (6), August 5, 1996.

25 Filmed interview with Gerald Seymour. Seymour had been awakened at 6:30

A.M. and ran down to the Olympic Village with a camera crew. His crew slipped under the fence, Seymour climbed over, and they followed him through the Village as he shouted importantly into a walkie-talkie to discourage anyone from trying to stop him. He ran right through a police cordon — brushing off the officials who tried to stop him — and suddenly emerged just meters from the Israeli building. Eventually he found a spot overlooking the Israeli building on the balcony of the Puerto Rican team with, ironically, two members of the national sharpshooting squad.

26 Filmed interview with Peter Jennings.

27 Ibid. When the German police finally swept the buildings looking for the press, the Italians stashed Jennings in their bathroom, "so the German police missed me as they went through," he said.

28 Filmed interview with Roone Arledge.

29 Filmed interview with Peter Jennings.

30 Filmed interview with Roone Arledge. The camera on the TV tower "ultimately turned out to be the only camera that could see the building where the terrorists were," said Arledge. Part of the reason the camera was never moved from pointing at the outside of 31 Connollystrasse was that Arledge had memories of the assassination of John F. Kennedy in his head, when NBC beat ABC to crucial footage by keeping a camera at the jail when the assassin Lee Harvey Oswald was moved. NBC caught Jack Ruby shooting him dead. Arledge didn't want to risk moving the camera and missing a crucial event.

31 Ibid.

4 Operation Sunshine

1 Manfred Schreiber's account from his testimony to the official Bavarian pre-criminal investigation into the Munich crisis.

2 Testimony of Annaliese Graes to the official Bavarian pre-criminal investigation into the Munich crisis.

3 Filmed interview with Ulrich Wegener.

4 This and following quotes and account from filmed interview with Hans-Dietrich Genscher. This is the first time Genscher has spoken publicly about the Munich crisis since 1972.

5 Filmed interview with Ulrich Wegener.

6 Based on filmed interviews with Ulrich Wegener and Walther Tröger. Ulrich Wegener now claims it was a mistake for Genscher, Tröger, and Vogel to offer themselves as hostages. "I told him [Genscher] later, we were talking about the affair in Munich, and I said that this was another mistake and he said, 'Yes, I know today.'"

7 Filmed interview with Hans-Dietrich Genscher.

8   The Black September terrorists were given complete authority by the PLO leadership to take whatever action they saw fit during the attack. Jamal Al-Gashey claims Issa was not even able to make contact with the PLO by phone or any other means: "There was no communication with anyone . . . That meant that we were in a position to make decisions on the ground, based on situations that arose." (Source: filmed interview with Jamal Al-Gashey.)

9   Filmed interview with Walther Tröger.

10 Tröger claims that Genscher did not offer himself as a hostage: "No, it was not Mr. Genscher, it was Mr. Vogel, the former mayor of the Olympic Village of Munich, who later on was a minister, he offered himself and I offered myself. It was not Genscher but maybe Genscher would have done it as well." Several other sources, however, state that Genscher did offer himself to the terrorists.

11 Testimony of Manfred Schreiber, op. cit.

12 "There was little I could do on the spot," Brandt wrote subsequently. "The Bavarian authorities were in charge, backed up by the Federal Minister of the Interior and Federal police. All concerned were at full stretch, and it is only too easy to be dogmatic, after the event, about how such situations could have been better handled." (Source: Willy Brandt, *People and Politics* [Boston: Little, Brown and Company, 1978], pp. 439–41.) The crisis was a personal tragedy for Brandt, who had been an active anti-Nazi from his teens, and had spent the years immediately before, during, and after the Second World War in exile, working in the Resistance and as a journalist. (Source: Willy Brandt, *My Life in Politics* [London: Hamish Hamilton, 1992].) Brandt had desperately wanted to secure better relations with Israel and had always called for maximum restitution to those Jews who survived the Holocaust. He had been awarded the Nobel Peace Prize in 1971, and in February 1972 had been invited to visit Israel. (Source: Terence Prittie, *Willy Brandt* [New York: Schocken Books, 1974], p. 287.) Brandt finally made the visit in June 1973.

13 Muki Betser with Robert Rosenberg, *Secret Soldier* (London: Pocket Books, 1997), pp. 148–51.

14 Ibid., p. 150.

15 This and following quotes and account from filmed interview in Hebrew with Muki Betser.

16 Muki Betser with Robert Rosenberg, op. cit, p. 154.

17 Filmed interview with Ulrich Wegener, and *Wanted: The Secret behind the 1972 Olympic Assassinations,* a film by Wilfried Huismann, broadcast in England on ARD, 9:45–10:30 P.M., July 15, 1996.

18 This and following account from filmed interview with Zvi Zamir.

19 This and following account and quotes from filmed interview with Victor Cohen.

20 Filmed interview with Zvi Zamir.

21 Testimony of Annaliese Graes, op. cit.

22 Ibid.

23 Testimony of Manfred Schreiber, op. cit.

24 Testimony of Annaliese Graes, op. cit.

25 According to Stasi files located for *One Day in September:* "Documentation regarding the events of September 5, 1972, in the Olympic Village by Martin Kramer, Dieter Wales, Wolfgang Gitter."

26 This exchange from Serge Groussard, *The Blood of Israel* (New York: William Morrow & Company, 1975), p. 164.

27 Filmed interview with Walther Tröger.

28 Testimony of Annaliese Graes, op. cit.

29 Abu Iyad with Eric Rouleau, *My Home, My Land* (New York: Times Books, 1981); the Munich operation is covered on pp. 106–12.

30 Annaliese Graes confirmed she arranged for Issa to telephone Tunisia 276277, but he was unable to get through to his contact. (Source: testimony of Annaliese Graes, op. cit.)

31 Abu Iyad with Eric Rouleau, op cit.

32 Filmed interview with Jamal Al-Gashey.

33 Stasi files, op cit.

34 Testimony of Annaliese Graes, op. cit.

35 Serge Groussard, op. cit., p. 201.

36 Filmed interview with Manfred Schreiber.

37 Serge Groussard, op. cit.

38 Testimony of Annaliese Graes, op. cit.

39 Filmed interview with Manfred Schreiber.

40 Ibid.

41 Terence Prittie, op. cit., p. 288.

42 Filmed interview with Manfred Schreiber.

43 Testimony of Annaliese Graes, op. cit.

44 Filmed interview with Ankie Spitzer.

45 Ibid.

46 Filmed interview with Walther Tröger.

47 Filmed interview with Hans-Dietrich Genscher.

48 Filmed interview with Ilana Romano. Walther Tröger, however, does not believe the Israelis were tortured, describing their treatment more as that of prisoners of war: "I didn't have that idea when I saw them personally in that room, they were not tortured, they had no signs of torture." (Source: interview with Walther Tröger.) Perhaps not surprisingly, Jamal Al-Gashey also denies any suggestion that Yossef Romano was tortured: "That's just a complete lie." According to Al-Gashey: "those German police reports set out to portray us as a criminal gang of murderers to German, Israeli, and international opin-

ion in order to justify their deceit and . . . the carnage that ensued. The German government wanted to say that we were a gang of dangerous murderers and that there was only one way of dealing with us, which was to carry out a military attack to prevent us from killing the athletes." (Source: interview with Jamal Al-Gashey.)

49 Filmed interview with Hans-Dietrich Genscher.

50 This and following account and quotes from filmed interview with Walther Tröger.

51 Filmed interview with Hans-Dietrich Genscher.

52 Filmed interview with Ulrich Wegener.

53 Filmed interview with Manfred Schreiber.

54 The following account from filmed interview with Ilana Romano.

55 Filmed interview with Ankie Spitzer.

56 Filmed interview with Jamal Al-Gashey. In a briefing before the Olympics it was Abu Daoud who apparently suggested that the terrorists should aim for Egypt. "[Egypt] was chosen before, with a number of other Arab states," said Daoud. "But there was no collusion with the Egyptian government or any other government. As I said, our goal and our hope was that Golda Meir would use her head and bow to world pressure that came from the Olympics and release our prisoners in a sportsmanlike way." (Source: filmed interview with Abu Daoud.)

57 Ibid.

58 Filmed interview with Walther Tröger.

59 Filmed interview with Ulrich Wegener.

60 This and following account and quotes from filmed interview with Heinz Hohensinn.

61 Filmed interview with Peter Jennings.

62 This and following quotes from filmed interview with Heinz Hohensinn.

63 Hohensinn does claim he was told an elite Israeli hostage rescue unit might replace the Munich officers and assault the building. "There was a special commando [unit] of the Israelis who were to come and replace us on the roof," he said. "We would have had no objections in being replaced. But it was cancelled because of the filming. After we didn't hear anything about it anymore."

64 Stasi files, op. cit.

65 Not everyone agrees. Dr René Burger, a physician with the Luxembourg delegation to the Games, said there had been an earlier chance in the Village. He had been standing across the street from the besieged house and believes there was a chance for the police to have "wiped out" most of the group simultaneously: "The chief negotiator was outside the door. Another stood at a second floor window. A third looked down from the balcony on the third floor.

Two were out in the open on the lower level. With sharpshooters all in position — and I saw them — the police could have done the whole job quickly and cleanly with five shots." (Source: Brian Arthur, "How Hostages Died Remains Unclear; 'A chance to prevent it,'" *Jerusalem Post,* September 7, 1972.

66 Brandt tried to ring at least a dozen times.

67 Willy Brandt, *People and Politics,* op. cit.

68 Filmed interview with Aziz Sidky for *Wanted: The Secret behind the 1972 Olympic Assassinations,* a film by Wilfried Huismann, broadcast in England on July 15, 1996.

69 An anguished Willy Brandt told his senior officials the terrorists had to be stopped by force — it was inconceivable they could allow the Jews to be flown out of the country "like an airmail packet."

70 Filmed interview with Esther Roth.

71 This and following quotes from filmed interview wih Ankie Spitzer.

5 The Deception

1 Filmed interview with Walther Tröger.

2 Tröger's suggestion was seized upon by the other officials, particularly Bruno Merck, the Bavarian interior minister. He had been concerned that the terrorists might refuse to take a helicopter to Riem, just five miles from Munich, and might instead insist on travelling by bus. It would have presented the officials with a security nightmare.

3 This and following account and quotes from filmed interview with Zvi Zamir.

4 Filmed interview with Victor Cohen. In a speech to the Knesset, the Israeli parliament, on October 16, 1972, Prime Minister Golda Meir affirmed: "The Germans alone were responsible for the preparation as well as the execution of the operations they carried out; they alone made all the decisions, and never asked for the approval of any Israeli representative."

5 Netty C. Gross, "They Died a Second Time," *Jerusalem Post,* July 17, 1992. (Perhaps the most comprehensive media article written on the tragedy since the 1970s.)

6 This and following account and quotes from filmed interview with Zvi Zamir.

7 Filmed interview with Walther Tröger.

8 Testimony of Ulrich Wegener to the official Bavarian pre-criminal investigation into the Munich crisis.

9 Filmed interview with Ulrich Wegener.

10 Most members of the Olympic committee were in Munich on the day of the crisis, but several more — including the Irish Lord Killanin, who was due to

take over the reins of the International Olympic Committee from Avery Brundage after Munich — were in northern Germany, in Kiel, watching competitors in the yacht races. Most members of the executive board wanted to return to Munich immediately and hold an emergency summit on the hostage crisis, but Brundage, who thought of the entire Olympic movement as his creation, arrogantly decided he alone could handle the situation, perhaps the gravest in the history of the Games. Lord Killanin was having none of it, and flew back to Munich in a plane loaned by Berthold Beitz, a German member of the IOC. By the time he returned to Munich, Killanin was raging at Brundage. (Source: Allen Guttmann, *The Games Must Go On* [New York: Columbia University Press, 1984], pp. 250–55.)

11   Ibid.

12   Threats to boycott the Games followed the Russian invasions of Hungary and Czechoslovakia (in 1956 and 1968), the inclusion of South Africa and Rhodesia in the Olympic family, and the battle between the Chinese communist government and the nationalist regime in Formosa (Taiwan). Then there were the ever-present tensions between North and South Korea, and East and West Germany, and evidence of the increasing use of performance-enhancing drugs by competitors. They were difficulties that would have mired a less abrasive or arrogant IOC president, but Brundage pushed the Olympics forward, increasing its size and scale, and refusing to allow petty political differences to demean or interfere in any way with the Games.

13   Brundage blindly followed the same path during the catastrophic events preceding the Mexico Olympics of 1968, when more than 350 student protesters were killed by the Mexican police.

14   Filmed interview with Manfred Schreiber.

15   Serge Groussard, *The Blood of Israel* (New York: William Morrow & Company, 1975), p. 234.

16   Filmed interview with Manfred Schreiber.

17   This and following account from testimony of Annaliese Graes to the official Bavarian pre-criminal investigation into the Munich crisis.

18   Filmed interview with Magdi Gohary.

19   Testimony of Annaliese Graes, op. cit.

20   Filmed interview with Manfred Schreiber.

21   Filmed interview with Walther Tröger.

22   This and following account and quote from filmed interview with Manfred Schreiber.

23   Interviews with Zvi Zamir and Victor Cohen.

24   Filmed interview with Manfred Schreiber.

25   Filmed interview with Jamal Al-Gashey.

26   Stasi files located for *One Day in September:* "Documentation regarding the

events of September 5, 1972, in the Olympic Village by Martin Kramer, Dieter Wales, Wolfgang Gitter."

27   Filmed interview with Magdi Gohary.

28   Filmed interview with Zvi Zamir.

29   Filmed interview with Esther Roth.

30   Filmed interview with Gad Tsabari.

31   Filmed interview with Zvi Zamir.

32   Victor Cohen remembers how the realization of the true number of terrorists surprised the Germans: "They talked between themselves, and they told me, 'Look, there are eight people, not five people,' and there were [three] they didn't know of," he said. (Source: filmed interview with Victor Cohen.)

33   Filmed interview with Peter Jennings.

34   Filmed interview with Esther Roth.

35   "It was a horrible night with nightmares," said Roth. "I wished 'If only Amitzur is safe and alive I'll do anything . . . if only they come back alive.'" (Source: filmed interview with Esther Roth.)

6 Fürstenfeldbruck

1   Filmed interview with Zvi Zamir.

2   According to pilot Ganner Ebel: "It was agreed that my 'copter and Praus's [the other pilot] should go in a large circle to give time for the crisis committee to arrive." (Source: testimony of Ganner Ebel to the official Bavarian pre-criminal investigation into the Munich crisis.)

3   Filmed interview with Jamal Al-Gashey.

4   Ibid.

5   Testimony of Ulrich Wegener to the official Bavarian pre-criminal investigation into the Munich crisis.

6   These details from "Grounds of the Appeal," filed by the relatives of the Israeli athletes, Israeli version prepared by Israeli lawyers.

7   Sniper testimony to the official Bavarian pre-criminal investigation into the Munich crisis.

8   Ibid.

9   Ibid.

10   This and following account from filmed interview with Heinz Hohensinn.

11   Testimony of Friedrich Liebold to the official Bavarian pre-criminal investigation into the Munich crisis.

12   Filmed interview with Heinz Hohensinn.

13   Testimony of Rheinhold Reich to the official Bavarian pre-criminal investigation into the Munich crisis.

14   Ibid.

15 German officials had decided to ask for a plane with enough fuel for a trip to Cairo, rather than one with empty tanks. They feared news of the empty tanks would leak out, thus alerting the fedayeen to a trap.

16 Testimony of Rheinhold Reich, op. cit.

17 Testimony of Friedrich Liebold, op. cit.

18 Filmed interview with Heinz Hohensinn.

19 Filmed interview with former ITN reporter Gerald Seymour, recalling Wolf's comments to him after the crisis.

20 Dudley Doust, "Munich: The Gunfire Still Echoes Today," *Daily Telegraph,* February 29, 1992.

21 "Grounds of the Appeal," filed by the relatives of the Israeli athletes, quoting the opinion of the *Deutsche Wetterdienst* from September 13, 1972, p. 2 (annex K7).

22 The commanders of the operation at Fürstenfeldbruck had had hours to realize the lighting was inadequate, and the Bavarian Mobile Police had three powerful sets of floodlights at their disposal which were not brought into action. (Source: "Grounds of the Appeal," filed by the relatives of the Israeli athletes, quoting testimony of Mr. Löffelmann [investigation records Bd. II interrogations, p. 378].)

23 Filmed interview with Jamal Al-Gashey.

24 Allegation made during an interview with Uwe Schlütter, the German lawyer for the relatives of the Israeli athletes, who has conducted an extensive investigation into the events of the night.

25 Sniper's testimony, op. cit.

26 Testimony of Ulrich Wegener, op. cit.

27 Testimony of Ganner Ebel, op. cit.

28 Sniper's testimony, op. cit.

29 Filmed interview with Ulrich Wegener. The Germans maintain they had no time to change the flawed rescue plan. "The hypothetical crew — they were police officers — was supposed to feign our readiness for departure, thus lending support to our pretense of intending to fly them out. In other words, they were supposed to encourage [Issa's] euphoria at the idea of having achieved his goal," claims Manfred Schreiber. "We had decided to shoot [Issa] as he was returning from inspecting the plane, at a point when his concentration would have lapsed somewhat and he would be feeling rather euphoric, assuming that the departure was imminent." (Source: filmed interview with Manfred Schreiber.)

30 Only Issa went into the plane. Tony waited outside.

31 Filmed interview with Ulrich Wegener.

32 According to Georg Wolf, the two sharpshooters not in the tower were ordered to shoot at recognized terrorists. Wolf allegedly said later that he had

not checked whether they had walkie-talkies, as "I had not to take care about this detail." (Source: "Grounds of the Appeal," filed by the relatives of the Israeli athletes, quoting testimony of Dr. Wolf [annex K 14, p. 9].)

33   If there had been more snipers spread around the airfield they could have shot into the chopper and killed the terrorists.

34   Filmed interview with Ulrich Wegener.

35   "Grounds of the Appeal," filed by the relatives of the Israeli athletes, quoting report of interrogation of the terrorists (Leitz–file Bd. VII of the investigation records, pp. 79, 96, 194, 199, and 282).

36   This and following quotes from sniper's testimony, op. cit.

37   The pilot later told the sniper he had been informed all the sharpshooters would be posted on the tower — so he had therefore not realized he was running into the line of fire.

38   Sniper's testimony, op. cit.

39   Filmed interview with Jamal Al-Gashey.

40   Filmed interview with Ulrich Wegener.

41   Filmed interview with Heinz Hohensinn.

42   Filmed interview with Manfred Schreiber.

43   Ibid.

44   Sniper's testimony, op. cit.

45   "Grounds of the Appeal," filed by the relatives of the Israeli athletes, quoting testimony of Sniper 1 (annex K 2, p. 5) and testimony of Sniper 2 (annex K 3, pp. 3, 5).

46   Ibid., which in chapter 2: Operation at the airport in Fürstenfeldbruck, Part B, Section V: No unified order to shoot because of a lack of walkie-talkies (pp. 28–33), states that written in the LKA-report is the claim "that despite several demands 'in this short time an obtaining of other (??) [sic] walkie-talkies'" was not possible. German officials have since argued that walkie-talkies might have made noises that could have been heard by the terrorists, thus alerting them to the position of the snipers and the possibility of a trap. However, even in the early 1970s noise-suppression devices were readily available, and earphones could have silenced incoming voices.

47   Ibid., quoting LKA-report (annex K 8, p. 40).

48   Ibid., quoting the testimony of Georg Wolf (annex K 14, p. 3), and LKA-report (annex K 8, p. 53).

49   Ibid., quoting the testimony of sniper 3 (annex K 4, p. 6).

50   This and following specifications from ibid., based on a map of the airfield Fürstenfeldbruck, Reg. Nr. 91462/72 (northern view of the building complex) as annex K 49 and four copies from photographs of the investigation records as annex K 50 a–d.

51   Sniper's testimony, op. cit.

52 These quotes from filmed interview with Zvi Zamir.

53 This and following account and quotes from filmed interview with Zvi Zamir.

54 Filmed interviews with Zvi Zamir and Victor Cohen.

55 Filmed interview with Zvi Zamir.

56 This account from filmed interview with Ulrich Wegener.

57 "Grounds of the Appeal," filed by the relatives of the Israeli athletes, quoting
LKA-report (annex K8, p. 81); testimony of Dr. Wolf (annex K 14, p. 16).

58 Sniper's testimony, op. cit.

59 Filmed interview with Manfred Schreiber.

60 "Grounds of the Appeal," filed by the relatives of the Israeli athletes; early Israeli legal document prepared by Israeli lawyers.

61 Filmed interview with Ulrich Wegener.

62 Filmed interview with Zvi Zamir.

63 Filmed interview with Manfred Schreiber.

64 Sniper's testimony, op. cit.

65 Testimony of Ganner Ebel, op. cit.

66 Sniper's testimony, op. cit.

67 Testimony of Ganner Ebel op. cit. During that time "several" armored cars
stopped to check he was alive but did nothing to help.

68 Filmed interview with Zvi Zamir.

69 Filmed interview with Victor Cohen.

70 Filmed interview with Manfred Schreiber.

71 Ibid.

72 This and following quotes from filmed interview with Heinz Hohensinn.

73 Filmed interview with Zvi Zamir.

7 Champagne Celebrations

1 Filmed interview with Peter Jennings.

2 Filmed interview with Gerald Seymour.

3 Ibid.

4 Ibid.

5 "As soon as the first shot was fired there was absolute silence among the spectators," said Seymour. (Source: ibid.)

6 This and following account from filmed interview with Hans-Jochen Vogel.

7 Ibid.

8 Ibid.

9 Filmed interview with Shmuel Lalkin.

10 Filmed interview with Hans-Jochen Vogel.

11 Ibid.

12   The following from Conrad Ahlers, interviewed by Jim McKay on ABC television on the night of September 5, 1972.

13   Filmed interview with Walther Tröger.

14   *Jerusalem Post,* September 6, 1972.

15   Filmed interview with Rosa Springer.

16   Filmed interview with Alex Springer.

17   Filmed interview with Mayo Springer.

18   The following account from filmed interview with Ankie Spitzer.

19   The following exchange from filmed interview with Zvi Zamir.

20   Filmed interview with Peter Jennings.

21   Filmed interview with Shmuel Lalkin.

22   Filmed interview with Ankie Spitzer.

23   Neil Allen, "Retracing the Last Steps of a Brave Man in Munich," *The Times,* September 7, 1972. Allen visited 31 Connollystrasse with Dov Atzmon.

24   Filmed interview with Ankie Spitzer.

25   Filmed interview with Rosa Springer.

26   Filmed interview with Mayo Springer.

27   Filmed interview with Hans-Jochen Vogel.

28   This and following quotes from filmed interview with Abu Daoud.

29   Willy Brandt, *People and Politics* (Boston: Little, Brown and Company, 1978), pp. 439–41.

30   Filmed interview with Shmuel Lalkin.

31   The following account from filmed interview with Ankie Spitzer.

32   Filmed interview with Gad Tsabari.

33   Filmed interview with Esther Roth.

34   Filmed interview with Ankie Spitzer.

35   This and following quotes from filmed interview with Shmuel Lalkin.

36   Under a torrent of criticism, Brundage later apologized, at least to some extent: "As president of the International Olympic Committee we regret any misinterpretation of the remarks made during the solemn memorial service in the stadium yesterday. There was not the slightest intention of linking the Rhodesia question, which is purely a matter of sport, with an act of terrorism universally condemned." But the damage had already been done.

37   Lord Killanin, *My Olympic Years* (New York: Morrow, 1983).

38   This and following account from filmed interview with Ankie Spitzer.

8 The Mourning Begins

1   Filmed interview with Esther Roth.

2   Peter Taylor, *States of Terror* (London: BBC Books, 1993), pp. 7–8.

3 Filmed interview in Hebrew with Henry Herskowitz.

4 Although the other athletes were buried that day, in accordance with Jewish traditions, Andre's mother was abroad and could not get to Israel in time, so his funeral was delayed until the following day.

5 Filmed interview with Mayo Springer.

6 Filmed interview with Rosa Springer.

7 This and following account from filmed interview with Ilana Romano.

8 This and following account from filmed interview with Hajja Hamid, the mother of Black September commando Afif Ahmed Hamid.

9 Filmed interview with Mahmoud Mohammad Jawad, brother of Black September commando Khalid Jawad.

10 Filmed interview with Hajja Hamid.

11 Filmed interview with Israeli intelligence source.

12 Incident quoted in Michael Bar-Zohar and Eitan Haber, *The Quest for the Red Prince* (London: Weidenfeld and Nicolson, 1983), p. 132.

13 Filmed interview with Walther Tröger.

14 Filmed interview with Ulrich Wegener.

15 Filmed interview with Shmuel Lalkin.

16 Filmed interview with Roone Arledge.

17 Abu Iyad with Eric Rouleau, *My Home, My Land* (New York: Times Books, 1981), pp. 106–12.

18 Kenny Moore, "Munich's Message," *Sports Illustrated* 85 (6), August 5, 1996.

19 Ibid.

20 Liberal Germans admitted the massacre was a devastating reminder of their country's past. The *Süddeutsche Zeitung* newspaper expressed the mood of the nation. Was Munich cursed? it asked. "There may not exist a great city whose people are less imperialistic, less aggressive, more peaceable, more full of simple human qualities than those of the Bavarian metropolis. However, various slogans have stuck to the name 'Munich.' Capital of the [Nazi] 'movement.' Originator of politically ideological lawlessness. Site of the capitulation of the law before naked power. 'Brown' Munich. Bulwark of vengeance. However contourless and emotional these notions have seemed to us, they now appear to be confirmed." (Source: *Süddeutsche Zeitung,* Munich, September 7, 1972.) Zvi Zamir, who had been forced to watch as fellow Jews died at Fürstenfeldbruck, had nothing but scorn for the Germans. Those who thought the "new Germany" was inhabited by "new Germans" should be disappointed, he said. "I've seen the German hierarchy from the chancellor down, leaders of Germany of 1972, their sense of responsibility about human beings, not necessarily Jews," said Zamir, who concludes stingingly: "I doubt very much if Germany 1972 was a different Germany [from the Nazi era], it was not." (Source: interview with Zvi Zamir.)

21 Further details of the attack are given in *The Economist,* September 23, 1972.

22 Yariv was interviewed for *States of Terror,* BBC Television, 1993. The text of the interview was published in Peter Taylor, op. cit., pp. 15–28. Further questioning of Yariv is now impossible, as he has since died.

23 Ibid.

24 Ibid.

25 This was not the first time the Israeli state advocated assassination as a policy for preventing "terrorist" attacks. In the 1950s, when President Nasser of Egypt was supporting fedayeen attacks on Israel, a Mossad investigation discovered that the head of Egyptian intelligence in Gaza, Lieutenant-Colonel Mustapha Hafez, was the main person responsible for organizing the cross-border raids. A Mossad hit team swung into action, and when Hafez met one of his informants — who just happened to be a double agent working for Mossad — on July 11, 1956, he was given a package that later exploded and killed him. With typical attention to detail, Mossad then decided to kill Hafez's likely successor, Colonel Salah Mustapha, the Egyptian military attaché in Jordan and the man they had identified as being the deputy to Hafez in organizing the fedayeen raids. Three days after the death of Hafez a book arrived, apparently from someone at the United Nations, for Colonel Mustapha. It exploded in his face, killing him instantly. The Israelis also used parcel bombs in a campaign of terror against German and Nazi scientists who began working for the Egyptian government after the Second World War. The policy backfired when Mossad sent a bomb to a German at the Heliopolis missile factory and it killed five Egyptians.

26 Willy Brandt, *People and Politics* (Boston: Little, Brown and Company, 1978), pp. 439–41.

27 Filmed interview with Jamal Al-Gashey.

28 This and following account from filmed interview with Heinz Hohensinn.

29 Filmed interview with Jamal Al-Gashey.

30 Ibid.

31 Filmed interview with Ulrich Wegener.

32 Interview with Israeli intelligence source. Incident also quoted in Michael Bar-Zohar and Eitan Haber, op. cit., pp. 6–7.

33 Golda Meir, *My Life* (New York: Dell Publishing, 1975), p. 385.

34 Meir was interviewed for an Israeli television film, *Sportaim al Capaim,* September 4, 1983.

35 Interview with Israeli intelligence source.

36 Ibid.

37 Ibid.

9 Operation Wrath of God

1 Interviews with Israeli officials; and Dan Raviv and Yossi Melman, *Every Spy a Prince* (Boston: Houghton Mifflin, 1991), p. 186 (perhaps the definitive account of the Israeli intelligence community). Further details were also reported by Yoel Marcus in the Israeli newspaper *Ha'aretz*, most notably on June 10, 1986.

2 Bibliographic detail taken from "Aharon Yariv: Obituary," *The Times*, May 18, 1994; "Laurence Joffe: Obituary," *Guardian*, May 13, 1994; and "General Aharon Yariv: Obituary," *Daily Telegraph*, May 23, 1994. Some sources, notably the *Daily Telegraph*, state that Yariv was born in Latvia.

3 This and following explanation of revenge plans from Yariv interview for *States of Terror*, BBC Television, 1993. The text of the interview was published in Peter Taylor, *States of Terror* (London: BBC Books, 1993), pp. 15–28.

4 David B. Tinnin with Dag Christensen, *The Hit Team* (Boston and Toronto: Little, Brown and Company, 1976), pp. 49–50.

5 Victor Ostrovsky and Claire Hoy, *By Way of Deception* (New York: St. Martin's Press, 1990), p. 179.

6 Ali Hassan Salameh had an illustrious heritage. Legend has it that in 1936 his father Sheikh Hassan Salameh fired the first shot in an Arab attack against the British rulers of Palestine. The British eventually offered a £10,000 reward for his capture, as their prey flitted apparently at will between Arab villages encouraging Palestinian nationalism and organizing resistance against the British occupiers. The Sheikh was eventually killed in 1948 at the age of thirty-seven, as he led an attack on Irgun fighters at Ras el Ein on the road to Jerusalem. Even official Israeli historians pay tribute to his memory, noting that he fought at the head of his soldiers. For more information: Michael Bar-Zohar and Eitan Haber, *The Quest for the Red Prince* (London: Weidenfeld and Nicolson, 1983).

7 Interview by Nadia Salti Stephan, *Monday Morning Magazine* (Beirut) 5, no. 202, April 26–May 2, 1976. The family is still held in high esteem in the Middle East, and Ali Hassan Salameh's mother, Um Ali, recalls the defining moments of Palestinian history with ease. When her family lived in the small village of Kulleh, thirty miles from modern Tel Aviv, Um Ali says the Jews who were living in Palestine represented just 10 percent of the population. "We lived in peace with them," she said. "In those days, when my husband [Sheikh Hassan Salameh] was alive, our country was occupied by the English. They called it the British mandate. They brought the Jews to Palestine from all over Europe without consulting us. When the mandate ended, they deceived us and handed over our country to the Jews. We, as a Palestinian people, were supposed to get possession of Palestine. The British army was

supposed to hand over our country to us but we were surprised when they handed over everything to the Jews. Zionism was imposed upon us. Aren't we entitled, then, to defend our country? My husband had no choice but to fight." (Source: interview in Peter Taylor, op. cit., p. 30.)

8   Interview with Israeli intelligence source.

9   Filmed interview with Abu Daoud.

10 After Zwaiter's death one Beirut obituary mourned him as one of the Palestinian movement's "best combatants."

11 Interview with Israeli intelligence source.

12 Michael Bar-Zohar and Eitan Haber, op. cit., p. 148.

13 Interview with Israeli intelligence source.

14 Ibid.

15 The message was apparently discovered amid a mass of communications seized by the Israelis after their invasion of Lebanon in 1982, a fact revealed in Victor Ostrovsky and Claire Hoy, op. cit., p. 181 (a devastating exposé of Mossad by Ostrovsky, a former Mossad "katsa" or case officer).

16 Ibid., p. 186.

17 Ibid., p. 186.

18 Ibid., p. 191.

19 Ibid., p. 192.

20 Ibid., p. 196.

21 Ibid.

22 Ian Black and Benny Morris, *Israel's Secret Wars: A History of Israel's Intelligence Services* (London: Warner Books, 1996), p. 266; and Dan Raviv and Yossi Melman, op. cit., p. 187.

23 Her comments were reported in *Monitin* 113, February 1988.

24 Abu Iyad, with Eric Rouleau, *My Home, My Land* (New York: Times Books, 1981), p. 113.

10 Operation Spring of Youth

1   Following section based largely on a filmed interview in Hebrew with Muki Betser, and from Muki Betser with Robert Rosenberg, *Secret Soldier* (London: Pocket Books, 1997), pp. 155–75.

2   Filmed interview in Hebrew with Muki Betser.

3   Ibid.

4   Muki Betser with Robert Rosenberg, op. cit., pp. 158-59.

5   Filmed interview in Hebrew with Muki Betser.

6   The Khartoum attack was almost certainly Palestinian and Arab revenge for this Israeli atrocity. On February 21, 1973, a massive sandstorm confused the

pilot and navigator on a Libyan Boeing 727 flying from Benghazi to Cairo, and the plane accidentally flew over the Israeli-occupied Sinai Desert. As Israeli fighters appeared in the sky the pilot immediately realized the gravity of his mistake and began turning back towards Egypt. Without warning the Israelis opened fire on the plane, sending it crashing to the ground and killing its 106 passengers. The Israelis later claimed their pilots were concerned the plane might be loaded with explosives and flown into an Israeli city on a suicide mission. But the plane was only 10 miles inside Israeli "territory" when attacked; it was an astonishing example of Israeli overreaction to a perceived military threat, and the pilots and their controllers were condemned around the world.

7　Muki Betser with Robert Rosenberg, op. cit., pp. 165–66.

8　Samuel M. Katz and Ron Volstad, *Israeli Elite Units Since 1948* (Botley, Oxford: Osprey Military, 1988), p. 50.

9　Yonni Netanyahu died from injuries sustained in the raid on Entebbe.

10　Lonny Rafaeli was named by Lally Weymouth in "Israel's 'Lone Wolf,'" *Washington Post,* November 10, 1999.

11　Quoted by Andy Goldberg, "Peres Calls up Warrior Barak to Win Election," *Sunday Times,* May 26, 1996.

12　Filmed interview in Hebrew with Muki Betser. The lax security is astonishing given that Israel had launched a penetrative military strike to kill Fatah leaders less than two months previously, when helicopter-borne soldiers had crept into refugee camps at Baddawi and Nahr el Bared and lain in wait to attack an expected high-level terrorist summit (the summit was cancelled at the last moment).

13　Muki Betser with Robert Rosenberg, op. cit., p. 170.

14　Filmed interview in Hebrew with Muki Betser.

15　Rumors that Nasser was found with two naked women, who were both asked to dress and leave before Nasser was killed, appear to be completely unfounded.

16　Salameh was interviewed by Nadia Salti Stephan, for Beirut's *Monday Morning Magazine* 5, no. 202, April 26–May 2, 1976.

17　Muki Betser with Robert Rosenberg, op. cit., p. 172.

18　Stewart Steven, *The Spymasters of Israel* (New York: Macmillan, 1980), p. 273.

19　Ibid.

20　Shahak succeeded Ehud Barak as the Israeli chief of staff in 1995.

21　The PDFLP was an offshoot from the Popular Front for the Liberation of Palestine, led by Dr. George Habash, which had in turn split from the PLO.

22　Muki Betser with Robert Rosenberg, op. cit., p. 158.

23　Lebanese press reaction quoted in ibid., p. 175.

24 Following quotes from filmed interview in Hebrew with Muki Betser.

25 Quoted by Christopher Dobson, *Black September* (London: Robert Hale & Company, 1975), p. 131.

26 David B. Tinnin with Dag Christensen, *The Hit Team* (Boston and Toronto: Little, Brown and Company, 1976), p. 95.

27 Boudia is alleged to have attacked the refinery with Thérèse Lefebvre, a French physiotherapist who fell in love with him.

28 This and following quotes from filmed interview with Ankie Spitzer.

29 Interviews with Israeli sources, and Dan Raviv and Yossi Melman, *Every Spy a Prince* (Boston: Houghton Mifflin, 1991), p. 188.

30 Her comments were reported in *Monitin* 113, February 1988.

31 Filmed interview with Jamal Al-Gashey.

32 This and following quotes from filmed interview with the widow of Adnan Al-Gashey.

33 Israeli intelligence source.

34 Peter Taylor, *States of Terror* (London: BBC Books, 1993), pp. 42–46. Taylor interviewed Lebanese intermediary and wealthy businessman Mustafa Zein for his television series, as well as Salameh's first wife Um Hassan, and a former CIA case officer he calls "Alan," who, he says, became the Agency point man for contact between the CIA and Salameh. Based on this information, Taylor's interviews appear to be the most reliable source of information on these early meetings between the Red Prince and U.S. intelligence. The evidence shows that the CIA tried to recruit Salameh on at least two occasions, each time showing a staggering lack of tact or respect for the wealthy Palestinian. The first is thought to have been in December 1970, at the Cavalieri Hilton in Rome, when Mustafa Zein rented suites 18–21 with Yasser Arafat's approval so that both sides could meet and talk freely.

35 Ibid., p. 43.

36 Interview by Nadia Salti Stephan, op. cit.

37 Another version of events, however, suggests that Salameh had already left the hotel by the time Mossad learned of his presence in Paris.

38 David B. Tinnin with Dag Christensen, op. cit., p. 128.

39 Dagny Bring, a nurse, interviewed twenty years later by Neil Grant from the BBC. (Source: Peter Taylor, op. cit., p. 40.)

40 More information on this case can be found in the transcript of the judgement of Norway's Eidsivating Criminal Court, case number 182/1973, February 1, 1974.

11 The Red Prince

1   Interviews with an Israeli intelligence source, and David Halevy and Neil C. Livingstone, "Biog: Noriega's Pet Spy," *Washington Post,* January 7, 1990.

2   In his eagerness to talk, "Dan" allegedly revealed more than just details of the Lillehammer debacle. He even explained to the Norwegians how he had played a pivotal role in the mysterious 1968 disappearance of drums of uranium oxide from a ship called *Scheersberg A.* The uranium had been smuggled to Israel and used by the military for atomic research and development.

3   The Norwegian police did not get any help from their own national intelligence services, which seemed to be less concerned with solving the murder of an entirely innocent man than with helping to spare the Israeli government's blushes.

4   "Sylvia" was later accused of involvement in the Rome murder of Wael Zwaiter in October 1972. In 1981, the Italian government asked Norway to extradite her to face charges but never seriously pursued the former agent.

5   Interview with an Israeli intelligence source, and David Halevy and Neil C. Livingstone, op. cit.

6   Christopher Dobson, *Black September* (London: Robert Hale & Company, 1975), p. 162.

7   Excerpts from testimony of Abu Daoud before the military prosecutor on February 15, 1973. Amman radio report of confession broadcast on the Amman Home Service, 16.00 GMT, 24 March 1973, and published in the *BBC Summary of World Broadcasts, Part 4: The Middle East and Africa,* Second Series ME/4255, March 27, 1973.

8   Ibid.

9   Hussein's gamble sent shock waves through the Palestinian movement, sending militants back to Lebanon who wanted to reclaim their positions within the PLO, which caused confusion and animosity.

10 James Adams, *The New Spies* (London: Pimlico, 1995), p. 144.

11 Salameh used Koranic law to justify taking more than one wife.

12 Many Arabs and dispassionate observers might describe the Irgun as a terrorist organization.

13 David Halevy and Neil C. Livingstone, op. cit.

14 Peter Taylor, *States of Terror* (London: BBC Books, 1993), p. 45.

15 The Lebanese government conducted a lengthy investigation into the Israeli operation under the stewardship of Mohammed Ali Sadeq, a senior investigating judge, whose report was published on February 11, 1980. "Erika Chambers" arrived in Beirut carrying a British passport, no. 25948, issued on May 30, 1975.

16 David Halevy and Neil C. Livingstone, op. cit.

17 For more details of the immediate aftermath of the explosion, see Edward Cody, "Bomb Kills Palestinian on Israeli Wanted List," *Washington Post*, January 23, 1979.

18 Raymond Carroll with Ron Moreau and Milan J. Kubic, "Death of a Terrorist," *Newsweek*, February 5, 1979.

19 This and following details from David Halevy and Neil C. Livingstone, op. cit.

20 Raymond Carroll with Ron Moreau and Milan J. Kubic, op. cit. With Salameh dead the CIA lost their star contact in the Middle East. Largely on the back of his connections with Salameh, Robert Ames had risen up through the ranks of the CIA, and even after his death rose still further and eventually became personal adviser on the Middle East to U.S. Secretary of State George Shultz. But Salameh's death was still a terrible blow to American involvement in the Middle East. They had no one higher up the tree than Salameh. Robert Ames was eventually killed when a suicide bomber wiped out most of the American embassy in Beirut in 1983, killing at least forty people, including all but two of the CIA's agents in Beirut. It was a disaster from which the agency took years to recover.

21 Angus Deming with Charles Mitchelmore and Milan J. Kubic, "A Terrorist Cross Fire," *Newsweek*, January 24, 1977.

22 John A. Conway, "Money Talks," *Newsweek*, February 7, 1977.

23 Angus Deming with Charles Mitchelmore and Milan J. Kubic, op. cit.

24 Edward Cody, op. cit.

25 Dispatches, "Israelis, Carter Denounce Paris' Release of Arab," *Washington Post*, January 13, 1977.

26 John Vinocur, "French Protests," Associated Press, January 13, 1977.

27 Angus Deming with Charles Mitchelmore and Milan J. Kubic, op. cit.

28 Dispatches, "Israelis, Carter Denounce Paris' Release of Arab," *Washington Post*, January 13, 1977.

29 Dispatches, "Abu Daoud Offers to Go to Munich to Clear Self," *Washington Post*, January 16, 1977.

30 Details were revealed in the *Berliner Morgenpost*, a West Berlin–based newspaper, July 15, 1990; further details published in "Paper Says Palestinian Terrorist Living in East Germany," Associated Press, July 15, 1990.

31 Reinhard Hellmann was interviewed by East Germany's ADN news agency in July 1990; details published in "East Germany Admits Having Sheltered Abu Daoud," Associated Press, July 16, 1990.

32 This and following account and quotes from John O. Koehler, *STASI* (Boulder Colorado: Westview Press, 1999), pp. 363–67. An excellent study of the repressive East German secret police by a veteran correspondent.

33 *Wanted: The Secret behind the 1972 Olympic Assassinations*, a film by Wilfried Huismann.

34   Krzysztof Burnetko, "Polish War Against Terrorism," interview with General
      Slawomir Petelicki, commander of the Operational Manoeuvre Reaction
      Group, *Krakow Tygodnik Powszechny,* October 25, 1998.

35   Joan Brecher with Holger Jensen, Milan J. Kubic, and Douglas Stanglin, "A
      Taste of His Medicine," *Newsweek,* August 17, 1981.

36   This and following account from Kryzysztof Burnetko, op. cit.

37   "Reputed Munich Massacre Plotter Shot in Warsaw Café," Associated Press,
      August 5, 1981.

38   Dina Kraft, "Alleged Plotter Says 1972 Olympics Attack put Palestinians on
      the Map," Associated Press, September 5, 1997.

39   "Israel: CIA Tipped Arafat to Assassination Plots in 1970s," Reuters, Novem-
      ber 13, 1998, quoting from an interview with Anderson by David Makovsky,
      published in the Israeli newspaper *Ha'aretz.* There is plenty of evidence to
      support the theory that the Israelis wanted to kill only those who might be a
      threat to them in the future. Amin el-Hindi, for example, who by 1997 was
      the head of Yasser Arafat's General Intelligence Service, has been accused of
      helping to plan the Munich operation, yet he does not appear to have figured
      on the list of targets for assassination. El-Hindi even featured in the PLO del-
      egation during peace talks with Israel in 1993. There can be no doubt the Is-
      raeli government has long believed Amin el-Hindi was involved in the
      Munich operation. At the 1993 peace talks the Israeli delegation refused to
      participate until he was removed — specifically because of unsubstantiated al-
      legations that he was involved in Munich. In June 1997 the Zionist Organiza-
      tion of America finally began a campaign to have el-Hindi extradited to the
      U.S. to face trial for Munich, on the grounds that David Berger held dual
      U.S.-Israeli citizenship.

40   Yariv was interviewed for *States of Terror,* BBC Television, 1993. The text of
      the interview was published in Peter Taylor, op. cit., pp. 15–28.

41   Information on Abu Iyad based on interviews and "Obituary of Salah Kha-
      laf" (Iyad's real name), *Daily Telegraph,* January 19, 1991; Karma Nabuisi,
      "Obituary: Abu Iyad," *Independent,* January 18, 1991; "Abu Iyad: Obituary,"
      The Times, January 16, 1991; Sharon Waxman, "PLO Says Arab Once Linked
      To Iraqi-backed Group Killed 3," *Washington Post,* January 16, 1991; and
      Charles Richards, "Defending a Palestinian State of Mind," *Independent,* July
      26, 1989.

42   Tony Walker, "PLO Orders Death of Bodyguard Assassin," *Financial Times,*
      April 8, 1991.

43   For more on the attack, see William Branigin, "Official of PLO Critically
      Hurt in Murder Attempt," *Washington Post,* July 26, 1979.

44   Jonathan C. Randal, "Assassination of PLO Aide Raises Many Questions,"
      Washington Post, July 10, 1992.

45   However, if the Wrath of God team were the unit tracking Bseiso, they may
     have learnt of his plans to travel to Paris — which he decided just four days
     before his death — by tapping the phones of senior Palestinians. Some sources
     also suggest that Mohammad Sadeq, a communications specialist and radio
     operator at the PLO communications center near Tunis, who is also alleged to
     have been a spy for Mossad, may have passed Bseiso's location to the Israelis.
     Sadeq was later arrested by the PLO. (Source: interview with an Israeli intel-
     ligence source. For further information see several reports in the Tunisian
     daily newspaper *El-Chorouk,* around November 11, 1993.)

46   Jonathan C. Randal, op. cit.

47   Ibid.

48   Abu Nidal (real name Sabri al-Banna) split from Fatah in 1973 and was sen-
     tenced to death in absentia by a Fatah Revolutionary Court in 1974; when
     Arafat later sought a political settlement with the Israelis, Nidal became one of
     his most bitter critics. Bseiso's killing also seemed to spark off a small war be-
     tween Arafat and Nidal, during which dozens of Palestinians on either side
     were quietly assassinated. When Mahmoud Khaled Eintour (a.k.a. Abu Ali Ma-
     jed), the alleged head of the assassination branch of Nidal's Fatah Revolution-
     ary Council faction, was arrested in southern Lebanon in February 1995, there
     were rumors that it was in retaliation for his role in the death of Bseiso three
     years previously. For those wanting more information on the feud, see the run-
     ning commentary from the Associated Press, notably between September 1992
     and June 1993.

49   For example, see "PLO Leader Arafat Promises to Avenge Official's Killing,"
     Associated Press, June 10, 1992.

50   Ibid.

51   Filmed interview with Abu Daoud.

52   William Drozdiak, "Senior Aide to Arafat Slain in Paris," *Washington Post,*
     June 9, 1992. Another factor that may have hastened Bseiso's demise was the
     continuing desire of Mossad to discourage senior Palestinians from getting too
     close to Western intelligence services. Bseiso was the third senior Palestinian
     acting as liaison officer between the PLO and the West to be killed, after Ali
     Hassan Salameh and Abu Iyad. Bseiso had already held meetings in Spain with
     the CIA, and had been due to meet officials from the French DST the morn-
     ing after he was killed. Murdering him was a brutal but effective way of warn-
     ing French and other Western spies not to get too close to Israel's enemies.
     Confusingly, however, another explanation for Bseiso's murder may be that Is-
     raeli intelligence passed information about Bseiso's location through a double
     agent to the Abu Nidal Organization in the knowledge he would then be as-
     sassinated. Not only would the move have prevented direct Israeli involve-
     ment on the ground, but it still enabled General Saguy to allege Bseiso was

involved in Munich, and for the government to claim "credit" for the death of another Palestinian terrorist.

12 The Cover-up

1   Netty C. Gross, "They Died a Second Time," *Jerusalem Post,* July 17, 1992.
2   This and all following quotes from filmed interview with Ankie Spitzer.
3   "All I was focused on was trying to raise my baby and trying to deal with the situation of being in a relatively foreign country [Israel] by myself, and most of all being without Andre, which was the main problem." (Source: ibid.)
4   This and following quotes from filmed interview with Pinchas Zeltzer. Zeltzer points out that in most countries in the world a person who is injured can go to court and seek a legal redress. "This is exactly what the families have decided to do in this case." (Source: filmed interview with Pinchas Zeltzer.)
5   Netty C. Gross, op. cit.
6   Filmed interview with Ilana Romano.
7   "Grounds of the Appeal," filed by the relatives of the Israeli athletes, quoting lawyer Pinchas Zeltzer.
8   Filmed interview with Ankie Spitzer and "Grounds of the Appeal," filed by the relatives of the Israeli athletes, quoting annex B 3–10.
9   Ibid.
10 Netty C. Gross, op. cit.
11 Ibid.
12 Filmed interview with Pinchas Zeltzer.
13 This and following quote filmed interview with Ankie Spitzer.
14 Yosef Harmelin, the head of Shin Bet, angrily protested that blame should not be pinned on the shoulders of that solitary individual. Harmelin threatened to resign if the sacking was pushed through. But Golda Meir insisted, the official left Shin Bet, and Harmelin kept his job. The new head of the Shin Bet's Protective Security Branch was Avraham Shalom, who had been the deputy leader of the mission to kidnap the Nazi Adolf Eichmann. Pinhas Koppel and his team of investigators also took testimony from Zvi Zamir, and some sources claim the commission of inquiry was angered by his version of events. Zamir apparently admitted that Mossad had received a warning prior to the Munich attack that a PLO unit of unknown size was flying into Europe from the Middle East for some unidentified terrorist attack, but the warning was so vague as to be virtually useless. There was, concluded Zamir, nothing to suggest terrorists were targeting the Olympic Games. (Source: Ian Black and Benny Morris, *Israel's Secret Wars: A History of Israel's Intelligence Services* [London: Warner Books, 1996], pp. 271–72.) The contents of the Koppel Report will remain secret until 2002, under an Israeli thirty-year

secrecy rule, but sources who have seen the report state that it contains no great revelations.

15   Eric Marsden, "Israeli Security Men Dismissed," *The Times,* October 17, 1972.

16   Filmed interview with relative.

17   Netty C. Gross, op. cit.

18   Filmed interview with Ankie Spitzer.

19   This and following account and quotes in ibid.

20   Dudley Doust, "Special Report on the Olympics: Obsession for Truth and Understanding," *Sunday Telegraph,* March 24, 1996.

21   This and following quotes from filmed interview with Ankie Spitzer.

22   Filmed interview with Pinchas Zeltzer. When permission was finally granted for the Israelis to view the files, Zeltzer knew he had to move quickly: "I hired the services of a German colleague to help me with the German and all the procedures. And then I asked here in the embassy in Tel Aviv; I said that I was going to the Ministry of Justice in Bavaria and I would come on a certain day, that I would like to be received by the head of the office and to receive all the documents. It was arranged, and when I arrived in Munich I was accompanied by a German professor of law, who is a very prominent lawyer in Munich. And we were promised all of the documents. Of course, they made some more difficulties and we didn't receive them the same day, but we saw all the documents. And I counted the files, and after a few days we received all the documents for reviewing and copying." It was a mammoth task.

23   Filmed interview with Ankie Spitzer.

24   This and following quotes from filmed interview with Manfred Schreiber. He also said: "And in addition to that, there was the question of Germany's burden [because of its Nazi past], hence its restrictions on the use of force from a legal, political and psychological point of view, which we all supported at the time. And one had to stand by the convictions that one had at the time."

25   Other German officials believe policing at the Games was completely inadequate. Ulrich Wegener, aide-de-camp to Hans-Dietrich Genscher in 1972, is scathing of the security precautions in place in the Olympic Village. He claims to have had a "bad feeling" from early on in the Games "because there was only a very limited security." (Source: filmed interview with Ulrich Wegener.)

26   Early copy of "Grounds of the Appeal," filed by the relatives of the Israeli athletes and prepared by Israeli lawyers. Israeli officials privately admit they also underestimated the danger to their athletes at Munich. "At that time we were prepared for, and almost expected, attempts to send letter or parcel bombs to our athletes in Munich," said a senior Israeli intelligence source. "We also accepted there might be attacks on Israeli interests at Munich airport or else-

where in Europe. But to the best of my knowledge we did not consider the possibility of a direct assault on the Olympic Village."

27 T. A. Sandrock, "Interpol Were Told to Expect Attack at Olympics," *Daily Telegraph,* September 6, 1972.

28 Ronald Payne, Duff Hart-Davis, and Peter Birkett, "Munich's Shattered Dream," *Sunday Telegraph,* September 10, 1972.

29 Ibid., quoting the testimony of Hein-Peter Gottelt, Arno Thomas, Karl Weber, all in the Leitz-file StA 1 of the investigation record, chapter "Kontaktpersonen, Postbeamte," LKA-report (annex K 8, p. 29). Rumors initially swept through police ranks that there were up to 21 "crazed Arabs" ranged against them.

30 Ibid., quoting the testimony of Siegbert Hans Hahn, Leitz-file StA 1 of the investigation record, chapter "Kontaktpersonen, Postbeamte" Siegbert Hans Hahn, N. Britz.

31 Ibid., quoting investigation records Bd. III interrogations, p. 908–1, Harry Valérien, as a witness; also the special edition of the *Bild-Zeitung,* from September 5, 1972.

32 Ibid., quoting testimony of Anneliese Graes (investigation records Bd. III interrogations, p. 694–4), as a witness.

33 Ibid., quoting LKA-report (annex K 8, p. 87, last paragraph), Kriminalinspektor Nachreiner, as a witness.

34 Ibid., quoting the testimony of Manfred Schreiber (annex K 30, p. 31, paragraph 2, lines 4–7) as a witness — he knew the number of terrorists because of his own observations.

35 Ibid., quoting the testimony of Dr. Wolf and the marksmen 1, 2, and 5, LKA-report (annex K 8, p. 66).

36 Ibid., quoting the testimony of Manfred Schreiber (annex K 8, p. 32).

37 "Grounds of the Appeal," filed by the relatives of the Israeli athletes.

38 Ibid.

39 Some sources suggest at least three marksmen were needed per terrorist, making a minimum requisite number of twenty-four.

40 "Grounds of the Appeal," filed by the relatives of the Israeli athletes, quoting testimony of Dr. Wolf (annex K 14, p. 4).

41 Ibid., quoting marksman 7 (investigation records Bd. III interrogations, p. 682).

42 Testimony of Manfred Schreiber to the official Bavarian pre-criminal investigation into the Munich crisis.

43 In a conversation with a senior German police commander present at Fürstenfeldbruck on the night of the disaster, Ankie Spitzer claims he said to her: "'Look, I'm very glad that they decided at the last moment to abandon the plane because there might have been many more victims if they would

have stayed.' I looked at him, I said, 'Yes, but that was their job, right, wasn't it? They are the policemen.' So he said, 'Yes, but I looked into their eyes and I saw young guys and they wanted to live,' and I said to him, 'They wanted to live! Don't you think that Andre Spitzer wanted to live? Did you look into his eyes when he was sitting there in the helicopter bound by hand and feet . . . Did you ask yourself if he wanted to live?'"

44 Filmed interview with Ankie Spitzer.

45 Filmed interview with Walther Tröger.

46 Manfred Schreiber refutes any suggestion German snipers may have shot some of the Israelis, even by accident: "There was firing, from inside the helicopters too, which led to the accusation that the hostages had been killed by German bullets. The Palestinian side was very quick to make that accusation. But both the university's forensic medical department and other reports from experts clearly refuted [the allegation] that Israelis had been hit by German bullets." (Source: filmed interview with Manfred Schreiber.)

47 Filmed interview with Jamal Al-Gashey. He added: "I should say that the person who decided to implement the military option by ambushing us, that person is responsible for all the deaths, Palestinian and Israeli alike. The German government are the ones who are to blame, for caving in to Israeli demands that we all be killed. If they had allowed us to leave, everyone, Israelis and Palestinians, would have survived."

48 Filmed interview with Abu Daoud.

49 Filmed interview with Ankie Spitzer.

50 Ibid.

51 Filmed interview with Pinchas Zeltzer.

52 Ibid.

53 Filmed interview with Heinz Hohensinn. The police snipers were expected to shoot over a distance of between fifty and seventy-five yards, depending on their positioning and the location of the target. "Even a mediocre marksman is not allowed to miss [at] such a distance," note the lawyers for the relatives of the dead athletes. At this range a precision marksman (according to German police regulations) has to be able to hit a five-deutsch-mark coin; an experienced marksman has to be able to hit a circle with a diameter of four inches. (Source: "Grounds of the Appeal," filed by the relatives of the Israeli athletes.)

54 Filmed interview with Ulrich Wegener. One of the main effects of Munich was the immediate creation of elite antiterrorist units by several governments and antiterrorist weapons by arms manufacturers. The government of Hong Kong set up their Special Duty Unit in 1974 after a post-Munich investigation, while German arms company Heckler & Koch began development of what became the $10,000 PSG1 semiautomatic sniper rifle — capable of continuous quick and accurate shooting. The Munich massacre "prompted many

countries to rethink their entire approach to combating international terrorism," states Brian Sullivan of Heckler & Koch, USA. The German government created the GSG-9 unit within days of Munich. Under the leadership of Ulrich Wegener, who has since become something of a legend in Germany, GSG-9 has since participated in numerous antiterrorist operations. The unit's best known mission was the October 18, 1977, "takedown" of four terrorists who hijacked a Lufthansa 707 and took it to Mogadishu airport in Somalia. At 12:05 A.M. a GSG-9 unit, supported by two British Special Air Services (SAS) soldiers acting as "observers," forced their way into the plane with the help of British stun grenades, shot one female terrorist dead and severely wounded another. As passengers were being evacuated, another male terrorist was cut down by automatic weapons fire, before Wegener himself is said to have shot the fourth and final terrorist several times in the head. After Munich the French created the Groupe d'Intervention de la Gendarmerie Nationale within the Gendarmerie Nationale to take on anyone tempted to try a similar attack within France, while in Britain the legendary SAS regiment began channelling new resources into counterrevolutionary warfare training (or CRW, as it became known among practitioners). Strangely, however, the American government under President Nixon took little action, and merely created a new Inter-Departmental Working Group on terrorism headed by Secretary of State Henry Kissinger. Nixon was apparently reassured by the FBI and police chiefs that their officers could handle any similar hostage scenario.

55 Robert Mahoney, "Mossad's Norway Bungle Still Haunts Israel," Reuters, January 8, 1996.

56 Ibid.

57 Dafna Linzer, "Israel Should Pay Compensation for Mistaken Assassination," Associated Press, January 3, 1996.

58 *New York Times* Service, "Israel, Admitting Nothing, to Compensate a Victim's Family," *International Herald Tribune,* January 12, 1996.

59 Speaking on Norwegian television, quoted in ibid. But it was not until November 1997 that the Norwegian government finally decided it should consider taking action against one of the alleged leaders of the Wrath of God team that assassinated Bouchiki: the legendary Israeli agent "Mike." The Norwegians had suddenly realized they were running out of time if they were ever to secure a conviction against the man, because their statute of limitations on the crime was due to expire in July 1998. But they still wavered, and it was not until February 1999 that Lasse Qvigstad, the Oslo state attorney, quietly let his colleagues know he had decided that he did not have enough evidence to prosecute "Mike" for his alleged role in Bouchiki's death. The case against "Mike," said Qvigstad, should be closed forever. From the comfort of his retirement, the seventy-one-year-old Polish-Russian Jew must have

breathed a careful sigh of relief. Other, more trivial court cases relating to Munich have also finally been resolved in recent years. "Dan," who was sentenced to five years in jail in 1974 for his role in Bouchiki's killing, was released in 1975. In 1998 he tried to sue Norway for compensation for an accident he suffered in the prison carpentry workshop. "Dan" sliced off the top of one finger and claimed he suffered continuous pain which prevented him from doing normal office work. The Norwegians, who had concluded in 1977 that "Dan" had not shown due care when he was using a carpenters' plane and had failed to wear protective gloves, rejected the claim.

60　Filmed interview with Pinchas Zeltzer.

61　A member of the German negotiating team, speaking off-camera to a member of the *One Day in September* film production team.

62　Hohensinn did, however, solicit and secure payment of DM 2,000 for his testimony.

63　Interview with a legal source who requested anonymity.

13 The Survivors

1　Netty C. Gross, "They Died a Second Time," *Jerusalem Post,* July 17, 1992.

2　This and following quotes from filmed interview with Schlomit Romano.

3　This and following quotes from filmed interview with Anouk Spitzer.

4　Filmed interview with Alex Springer.

5　This and following quote from filmed interview with Mayo Springer.

6　Dudley Doust, "Munich: The Gunfire Still Echoes Today," *Daily Telegraph,* February 29, 1992.

7　Ibid.

8　This and following quote from filmed interview with Ankie Spitzer.

9　Filmed interview with Anouk Spitzer.

10　Netty C. Gross, op. cit.

11　This and followings quotes and account from filmed interview with Anouk Spitzer.

12　This and following quotes from Doust, op. cit.

13　Filmed interview with Anouk Spitzer.

14　Netty C. Gross, op. cit.

15　Ibid.

16　Filmed interview with Ilana Romano.

17　Shmuel Lalkin, for example, the head of the Munich delegation, was involved with the families of those who died "from the first day," and still meets them regularly. "In some families, it was the only son that they had," he said. He still sees the families, the parents, getting older and older, year by year. "You cannot disconnect yourself from the families. You are there — more often, less often but . . . you are there with this situation and you keep on . . . knowing that you've been there, you've been saved, very miraculously, but you are there." The pain is constant: "Being the head of this delegation . . . knowing those athletes for so many years before . . . going to that country that we had such bad memories of the Holocaust, of the Second World War . . . starting with a very good atmosphere at the Olympic Games . . . and then this tragedy . . ." He shakes his head in disbelief. "I remember them every day and I'll remember them as long as I live." (Source: filmed interview with Shmuel Lalkin [final quote from Paul Holmes, "Daughter of Munich Victim Hits Out at Silence," Associated Press, July 28, 1992].)

18 Filmed interview with Esther Roth.

19 Dudley Doust, op. cit.

20 "Athletics: Munich Survivor is Still Alive and Walking Tall," *The Herald*, May 29, 1993.

21 Morley Myers, "Olympic Massacre: When Talks Failed," United Press International, September 4, 1987.

22 Filmed interview with Hans-Jochen Vogel.

23 Filmed interview with Zvi Zamir.

24 Filmed interview with Abu Daoud.

25 Abu Iyad with Eric Rouleau, *My Home, My Land* (New York: Times Books, 1981), pp. 106–12. Iyad added defiantly: "As for the slaughter which ended the operation, the West German government must bear a heavy responsibility."

26 Filmed interview with Jamal Al-Gashey.

27 Authorship of this communiqué has also been attributed to George Habash.

28 Abu Daoud agrees. "What a lot of politicians and journalists said was that, regardless of the methods used, the Palestinians did succeed in dragging their cause into five hundred million households who were watching sport and were not interested in politics, forcing them to ask, 'Who are these Palestinians? What are they fighting for? Why did they do this? Why didn't they do that?' It served as a gesture that forced the Palestinian cause to the forefront."

29 Filmed interview with Mahmoud Mohammad Jawad.

30 Filmed interview with Adel Mohammad Jawad.

31 Bruce Hoffman, *Inside Terrorism* (London: Victor Gollancz, 1998), p. 71.

32 Ibid., p. 75.

33 Peter Jennings, who was the ABC Middle East correspondent at the time of the Munich Olympics, makes the point that it was the first time television crews at Munich were able to simply aim their cameras at a spot (the Israeli building) and let the story unfold. "In this day and age now the whole world can share it. I like to remind people that in 1901 at Queen Victoria's funeral in Westminster Abbey the only people who knew what was going on were

the people in the Abbey. Ninety-seven years later when Diana the Princess of Wales was buried, same gun carriage, same horses, same Anglican service, several hundred million people shared in it, that's how the century's changed." (Source: filmed interview with Peter Jennings.)

34 Irwin Arieff, "Paris Bars PLO Guerrilla who Planned Munich Attack," Reuters, May 3, 1999. There are significant obstacles in the way of full reconciliation between men like Abu Daoud and the Israelis. Not least because in June 1999, German police finally issued an arrest warrant for Abu Daoud, with Manfred Wieck, Munich's chief prosecutor, alleging he was an accessory to murder for planning the 1972 hostage-taking, a fact that Abu Daoud has not exactly sought to hide in interviews for the film on which this book is largely based.

35 While working in Palestinian areas Ankie has talked at great length with victims on the other side of the fence: "I speak to mothers who lost their sons to the Israelis and I speak to wives who lost their husbands and who are in the same situation as I am." She has even met and worked with Um Jihad, the widow of senior PLO official Abu Jihad, who was "was very much instrumental in what happened in Munich," and was killed by an Israeli hit team in Tunis in April 1988. "This is really in the spirit of Andre . . . this is what he would have wanted," she said. "He wouldn't have wanted me to take revenge, he would have wanted me to try to understand and that's what I'm doing." Despite her suffering Ankie has hope for the future: "Only by explaining it to one another and by trying to understand the other side will we some day maybe finish this conflict. I hope very much that this will be the case because it's impossible to live with hate in your heart and it is impossible to live with neighbors that you hate." (Source: filmed interview with Ankie Spitzer.)

36 This and following quotes from filmed interview with Jamal Al-Gashey.

37 Mahmoud Mohammad Jawad, brother of the Black September guerrilla Khalid Jawad, who was shot in the face at Fürstenfeldbruck, also speaks movingly of the suffering of the Israeli relatives. "I sympathize with the wrong they have suffered," he said. Khalid's brothers still live in southern Lebanon, another brother lives in Berlin. They still dream of a Palestinian homeland. (Source: filmed interview with Mahmoud Mohammad Jawad.)

38 Filmed interview with Hajja Hamid and her husband.

39 Ibid.

40 Filmed interview with Alex Springer.

41 Anouk's hopes for a peaceful future are tinged with lingering anger. She is bitter that Jamal Al-Gashey has remained hidden in the shadows for so long "to protect his daughter": "That makes me very angry, obviously, and I don't think she has more of a right than I do to a father." (Source: filmed interview with Anouk Spitzer.)

42 This and following quotes from filmed interview with Schlomit Romano.

Acknowledgments

Although this book grew out of research conducted for a documentary film of the same name, it includes details of events not covered in the film and uses research for which the team behind the film is not responsible. But while the book and the film are separate projects, I would like to offer thanks to all in the film production who have tirelessly investigated the Munich tragedy.

On a personal note I would like to thank all those who were prepared to be interviewed for this book, but particularly R.A., S.P., and J. for their advice. Beth Morgan, my parents Alan and Cynthia, my brother James, Lucy Brandon and Michael Hall, all read various drafts of this book, suggested improvements and deletions, and generally kept me afloat. Other friends, family, and colleagues also helped and supported me while I was researching and writing, for which I am tremendously grateful.

Thanks also to Robert Kirby, Catherine Cameron, and Maria Dawson at Peters, Fraser & Dunlop in London. At Arcade in New York, Richard and Jeannette Seaver have been most kind and thoughtful, as has their colleague Greg Comer. At Faber & Faber, my editor Julian Loose and his colleague Luke Vinten offered unstinting support and guided me along the way. Others at Faber, including Charles Boyle, Amabel Gee, and Toby Faber, have also been closely involved with the book, and I am deeply grateful to Lesley Levene for her work on the proofs.

My thanks to everyone.
Simon Reeve

Bibliography

Abu-Sharif, Bassam, and Uzi Mahnaimi. *Best of Enemies.* New York: Little, Brown and Company, 1995.

Adams, James. *The New Spies: Exploring the Frontiers of Espionage.* London: Pimlico, 1995.

Amdur, Richard. *Moshe Dayan.* World Leaders — Past and Present Series. New York: Chelsea House Publishers, 1989.

Antonius, George. *The Arab Awakening: The Story of the Arab National Movement.* London: Hamish Hamilton, 1945.

Barnaby, Frank. *Instruments of Terror: Mass Destruction Has Never Been So Easy . . .* London: Vision, 1997.

Bar-Zohar, Michael. *Spies in the Promised Land: Iser Harel and the Israeli Secret Service.* Translated by Monroe Stearns. Boston: Houghton Mifflin, 1972.

Bar-Zohar, Michael, and Eitan Haber. *The Quest for the Red Prince.* London: Weidenfeld and Nicolson, 1983.

Betser, Colonel Muki, with Robert Rosenberg. *Secret Soldier: The True Life Story of Israel's Greatest Commando.* London: Pocket Books, 1997.

Black, Ian, and Benny Morris. *Israel's Secret Wars: A History of Israel's Intelligence Services.* London: Warner Books, 1996.

Brandt, Willy. *My Life in Politics.* London: Hamish Hamilton, 1992. Originally published under the title *Erinnerungen,* Berlin (Propyläen, 1989).

———. *People and Politics: The Years 1960–1975.* New York: Little, Brown and Company, 1978. Originally published under the title *Begegnungen und Einsichten* (Hamburg: Hoffmann & Campe Verlag, 1976).

Butt, Gerald. *The Arabs, Myth and Reality.* London: I. B. Tauris & Co., 1997.

Cattan, Henry. *Palestine, The Arabs and Israel: The Search for Justice.* London: Longmans, Green and Co. Ltd., 1969 (proof copy).

Cooley, John K. *Green March, Black September: The Story of the Palestinian Arabs.* London: Frank Cass, 1973.

Coote, James, and John Goodbody. *The Olympics 1972.* London: Robert Hale & Company, 1972.

Coulson, Danny O., and Elaine Shannon. *No Heroes: Inside the FBI's Secret Counter-Terror Force.* New York: Pocket Books, 1999.

Dayan, Moshe. *Moshe Dayan: Story of My Life.* New York: Da Capo Press, 1992.

Deacon, Richard. *The Israeli Secret Service.* London: Sphere Books, 1984.

Demaris, Ovid. *Brothers in Blood: The International Terrorist Network.* New York: Charles Scribner's Sons, 1977.

Dimbleby, Jonathan, with photographs by Donald McCullin. *The Palestinians.* New York: Quartet Books Inc., 1979.

Dobson, Christopher. *Black September: Its Short, Violent History.* London: Robert Hale & Company, 1975.

Dobson, Christopher, and Ronald Payne. *The Carlos Complex: A Pattern of Violence.* London: Hodder and Stoughton, 1977.

———. *The Never-Ending War: Terrorism in the 80s.* New York: Facts on File, 1987.

———. *The Terrorists: Their Weapons, Leaders and Tactics.* New York: Facts on File, 1979.

Drath, Viola Herms. *Willy Brandt: Prisoner of His Past.* Radnor, Pennsylvania: Chilton Books, 1975.

Eisenberg, Dennis, Uri Dan, and Eli Landau. *The Mossad: Inside Stories.* New York: Signet Books, 1979.

El-Kikhia, Mansour O. *Libya's Qaddafi.* Gainesville: University Press of Florida, 1997.

Elon, Amos. *The Israelis — Founders and Sons.* New York: Pelican Books, 1983.

Farsoun, Samih K., with Christina E. Zacharia. *Palestine and the Palestinians.* Boulder: Westview Press, 1997.

Follain, John. *Jackal: The Secret Wars of Carlos the Jackal.* London: Weidenfeld and Nicolson, 1998.

Gee, John. *Unequal Conflict: The Palestinians and Israel.* New York: Interlink Publishing & Group, 1998.

Goldschmidt, Arthur. *A Concise History of the Middle East,* 5th ed. Boulder: Westview Press, 1996.

Groussard, Serge. *The Blood of Israel: The Massacre of the Israeli Athletes, The Olympics, 1972.* Translated by Harold J. Salemson. New York: William Morrow & Company, Inc., 1975. Originally published under the title *La Médaille de Sang.* Paris: Editions Denöel, 1975.

Guttmann, Allen. *The Games Must Go On: Avery Brundage and the Olympic Movement.* New York: Columbia University Press, 1984.

Hadawi, Sami. *Bitter Harvest: A Modern History of Palestine.* Buckhurst Hill, Essex: Scorpion Publishing, 1990.

Hart, Alan. *Arafat: A Political Biography.* Indianapolis: Indiana University Press, 1989 (the U.S. edition of Hart's book, *Arafat: Terrorist or Peacemaker?*).

————. *Arafat: Terrorist or Peacemaker?* London: Sidgwick & Jackson, 1984.

Hipler, David K. *Arab and Jew: Wounded Spirits in a Promised Land.* New York: Times Books, 1986.

Hiro, Dilip. *Inside the Middle East.* London: Routledge & Kegan Paul, 1982.

Hirst, David. *The Gun and the Olive Branch: The Roots of Violence in the Middle East.* London: Faber & Faber, 1977.

Hitti, Philip K. *The History of the Arabs.* London: Macmillan, 1937.

Hoffman, Bruce. *Inside Terrorism.* London: Victor Gollancz, 1998.

Hohenemser, Herbert (Chairman of the Arts Committee), Klaus Bieringer (Head of the Cultural Program), and Martin Volkmann, eds. *Olympic Summer: The Official Cultural Program for the Games of the XXth Olympiad Munich 1972.* Munich: Atlas Verlag und Werbung, 1972.

Ignatius, David. *Agents of Innocence.* London: Star, 1989.

Iyad, Abu, with Eric Rouleau. *My Home, My Land: A Narrative of the Palestinian Struggle.* Translated by Linda Butler Koseoglu. New York: Times Books, 1981.

Jonas, George. *Vengeance: The True Story of a Counter-Terrorist Mission.* London: Collins, 1984.

Katz, Samuel M. *Israeli Special Forces.* Osceola, Wisconsin: Motorbooks International, 1993.

Katz, Samuel M., and Ron Volstad. *Israeli Elite Units Since 1948.* Botley, Oxford: Osprey Military, 1998.

Khaled, Leila, as told to George Hajjar. *My People Shall Live: Autobiography of a Revolutionary.* Toronto: NC Press Ltd., 1975.

Koehler, John O. *STASI: The Untold Story of the East German Secret Police.* Boulder: Westview Press, 1999.

Langer, William L., ed. *An Encyclopaedia of World History, Ancient, Medieval and Modern.* London: Harrap/Galley Press, 1987.

Laqueur, Walter. *The Road to Jerusalem: The Origins of the Arab-Israeli Conflict.* New York: Macmillan Press, 1968.

Livingstone, Neil C., and David Halevy, in cooperation with the Ethics and Public Policy Center, Washington, D.C. *Inside the PLO: Covert Units, Secret Funds, and the War Against Israel and the United States.* New York: William Morrow & Company Inc., 1990.

Mackey, Sandra. *Passion and Politics: The Turbulent World of the Arabs.* New York: Dutton, 1992.

McNab, Tom. *Olympic Games, Munich 1972: A Guide.* Leicester, England: Knight, 1972.

Mandell, Richard D. *The Olympics of 1972: A Munich Diary.* Chapel Hill and London: University of North Carolina Press, 1991.

Mansfield, Peter. *The Arabs.* London: Pelican, 1987.

Meir, Golda. *My Life.* New York: Dell Publishing, 1975.

Melman, Yossi. *The Master Terrorist: The True Story Behind Abu Nidal.* New York: Adama Books, 1986.

Mercer, Derrik, Editor-in-Chief. *Chronicle of the 20th Century.* Harlow, Essex: Longman, 1989.

O'Ballance, Edgar. *Language of Violence: The Blood Politics of Terrorism.* San Rafael, California: Presidio Press, 1979.

———. *No Victor, No Vanquished: The Arab-Israeli War, 1973.* Novato, California: Presidio Press, 1997.

O'Brien, Conor Cruise. *The Siege: The Saga of Israel and Zionism.* London: Weidenfeld and Nicolson, 1986.

O'Brien, William V. *Law and Morality in Israel's War with the PLO.* New York: Routledge, 1991.

Ostrovsky, Victor, and Claire Hoy. *By Way of Deception: The Making and Unmaking of a Mossad Officer.* New York: St Martin's Press, 1990.

Payne, Ronald. *Mossad: Israel's Most Secret Service.* London: Bantam Press, 1990.

Peres, Shimon, with Arye Naor. *The New Middle East.* New York: Henry Holt and Co., 1993.

Prittie, Terence. *Willy Brandt: Portrait of a Statesman.* New York: Schocken Books, 1974.

Pryce-Jones, David. *The Face of Defeat: Palestinian Refugees and Guerrillas.* London: Quartet Books, 1974.

Raviv, Dan, and Yossi Melman. *Every Spy a Prince.* Boston: Houghton Mifflin, 1991.

Reische, Diana. *Arafat and the Palestine Liberation Organisation.* New York: Franklin Watts, 1991.

Rubin, Barry. *Revolution Until Victory? The Politics and History of the PLO.* Cambridge: Harvard University Press, 1994.

Said, Edward W. *The Question of Palestine.* New York: Random House (Vintage Books), 1980.

Sarwar, Ghulam. *Islam: Beliefs and Teachings.* London: The Muslim Educational Trust, 1984.

Schoenberg, Harris Okun. *A Mandate for Terror: The United Nations and the PLO.* New York: Shapolsky Publishers, 1989.

Senn, Alfred E. *Power, Politics, and the Olympic Games.* Champaign, Illinois: Human Kinetics, 1999.

Sharabi, Hisham. *Governments and Politics of the Middle East in the Twentieth Century.* Princeton: D. Van Nostrand, 1962.

———. *Palestine Guerrillas: Their Credibility and Effectiveness.* Beirut: The Institute for Palestine Studies, 1970.

Smith, Colin. *Carlos: Portrait of a Terrorist.* London: Sphere Books, 1976.

Sterling, Claire. *The Terror Network: The Secret War of International Terrorism.* New York: Berkley, 1982.

Steven, Stewart. *The Spymasters of Israel.* New York: Macmillan, 1980.

Stevenson, William, with material from Uri Dan. *90 Minutes at Entebbe.* New York: Bantam Books, 1976.

Taslitt, Israel I. *Soldier of Israel: The Story of General Moshe Dayan.* New York: Funk and Wagnalls, 1969.

Taylor, Peter. *States of Terror: Democracy and Political Violence.* London: BBC Books, 1993.

Thomas, Gordon. *Gideon's Spies: Mossad's Secret Warriors.* London: Macmillan, 1999.

Thompson, Thomas L. *The Mythic Past: Biblical Archaeology and the Myth of Israel.* New York: Basic Books, 1999.

Tinnin, David B., with Dag Christensen. *The Hit Team.* Boston and Toronto: Little, Brown and Company, 1976.

Tophoven, Rolf. *GSG-9: German Response to Terrorism.* Koblenz: Bernard & Graefe Verlag, 1985.

Wallechinsky, David. *The Complete Book of the Olympics.* New York: Penguin Books, 1988.

Wels, Susan. *The Olympic Spirit: 100 years of the Games.* London: Harper-Collins, 1996.

Yallop, David. *To the Ends of the Earth: The Hunt for the Jackal.* London: Jonathan Cape, 1993.

Further Reading

Aburish, Said K. *Arafat: From Defender to Dictator.* Bloomsbury Publishing, 1998.

———. *A Brutal Friendship: The West and the Arab Elite.* Dunne Books, 1998.

Alexander, Yonah. *Middle East Terrorism: Current Threats and Future Prospects.* International Library of Terrorism, Vol. 5, G. K. Hall & Company, 1994.

Alexander, Yonah, and Dennis A. Pluchinsky. *European Terrorism Today and Tomorrow.* Brassey's, 1992.

Becker, Jillian. *The PLO: The Rise and Fall of the Palestine Liberation Organisation*. St. Martin's Press, 1984.

Bell, J. Bowyer. *A Time of Terror: How Democratic Societies Respond to Revolutionary Violence*. Basic Books, 1978.

Ben-Yehuda, Hemda. *The PLO, 1964–1980: Dynamics of Transnational Politics*. Gordon & Breach Science Publishing, 1997.

Bickerton, Ian J., and Carla L. Klausner (contributor). *A Concise History of the Arab-Israeli Conflict*. Prentice Hall, 1995.

Cattan, Henry. *To Whom Does Palestine Belong?* Institute for Palestinian Studies, 1967.

Cobban, Helen. *The Palestinian Liberation Organisation: People, Power, and Politics*. Cambridge University Press, 1985.

Crenshaw, Martha, ed. *International Encyclopaedia of Terrorism*. Fitzroy Dearborn, 1997.

Daoud, Abu, with Gilles Du Jonchay. *Palestine: From Jerusalem to Munich, from Munich to Jerusalem*. Arcade Publishing. New York (to be published).

El Shazly, Saad. *The Arab Military Option*. American Mideast Research, 1986.

Feldman, Fred, and Georges Sayad. *Palestine and the Arabs' Fight for Liberation*. Pathfinder Press, 1991.

Finkelstein, Norman G. *The Rise and Fall of Palestine: A Personal Account of the Intifada Years*. University of Minnesota Press, 1996.

Gilbert, Martin. *Atlas of the Arab-Israeli Conflict*. Oxford University Press, 1993.

──────. *Israel: A History*. William Morrow, 1998.

──────. *The Atlas of Jewish History*. William Morrow & Company, 1993.

Glubb, Sir John Bagot. *Britain and the Arabs: A Study of Fifty Years 1908 to 1958*. Hodder & Stoughton, 1959.

Gowers, Andrew, and Tony Walker. *Behind the Myth: Yasser Arafat and the Palestinian Revolution*. Interlink, 1991.

Gresh, Alain. *The PLO: The Struggle Within; Towards an Independent Palestinian State*. Zed Books, 1985.

Guyatt, Nick. *The Absence of Peace: Understanding the Israeli-Palestinian Conflict*. St. Martin's Press, 1998.

Herzog, Chaim. *The Arab-Israeli Wars: War and Peace in the Middle East*. Random House, 1984.

Inbari, Pinhas. *The Palestinians between Terrorism and Statehood*. Sussex Academic Press, 1995.

Kiernan, Thomas. *Arafat: The Man and the Myth*. Norton, 1976.

Laffin, John. *Fedayeen: The Arab-Israeli Dilemma*. Cassell, 1973.

Laqueur, Walter. *Israel-Arab Reader: A Documentary History of the Middle East Conflict.* Citadel Press, 1969.

Mishal, Shaul. *The PLO Under Arafat: Between Gun and Olive Branch.* Yale University Press, 1986.

Nasr, Kameel B. *Arab and Israeli Terrorism.* McFarland & Company, 1997.

Nassar, Jamal Raji. *The Palestine Liberation Organization.* Praeger, 1991.

Neff, Donald. *Warriors for Jerusalem.* Simon and Schuster, 1984.

O'Neill, Bard E. *Revolutionary Warfare in the Middle East: The Israelis vs. the Fedayeen.* Paladin Press, 1974.

Peretz, Don. *Israel and the Palestine Arabs.* Middle East Institute, 1968.

Petran, Tabitha. *Syria: A Modern History.* Ernest Benn, 1978.

Polk, William R. *The Arab World.* Harvard University Press, 1980.

Rodinson, Maxime. *Israel and the Arabs.* Pelican, 1969.

Rubenberg, Cheryl. *The Palestine Liberation Organisation: Its International Infrastructure.* Institute of Arab Studies, 1983.

Rubin, Barry, Joseph Ginat, and Moshe Ma'Oz, eds. *From War to Peace: Arab-Israeli Relations 1973–1993.* New York University Press, 1995.

Safran, Nadav. *Israel: The Embattled Ally.* Belknap Press of Harvard University Press, 1978.

Sayigh, Rosemary. *Palestinians: From Peasants to Revolutionaries.* Zed Press, 1979.

Schiff, Zeev. *A History of the Israeli Army 1870–1974.* Straight Arrow Books, 1974.

Schleifer, S. Abdullah. *The Fall of Jerusalem.* Monthly Review Press, 1972.

Segal, Jerome M. *Creating the Palestinian State.* Lawrence Hill Books, 1989.

Segev, Tom, trans. Arlen Neal Weinstein. *1949: The First Israelis.* Henry Holt, 1998.

Sela, Avraham. *The PLO and Israel: From Armed Conflict to Political Solution, 1964–1994.* St. Martin's Press, 1997.

Shahak, Israel, and Edward Said. *Open Secrets: Israel Foreign and Nuclear Policies.* Pluto Press, 1997.

Sharabi, Hisham. *Palestine and Israel: The Lethal Dilemma.* Pegasus, 1969.

Shemesh, Moshe. *The Palestinian Entity 1959–1974: Arab Politics and the PLO.* Frank Cass, 1996.

Tessler, Mark. *A History of the Israeli-Palestinian Conflict.* Indiana University Press, 1994.

Toubbeh, Jamil. *Day of the Long Night: A Palestinian Refugee Remembers the Nakba.* McFarland & Company, 1997.

Usher, Graham. *Palestine in Crisis: The Struggle for Peace in Political Independence after Oslo.* Pluto Press, 1997.

Wallach, Janet, and John Wallach. *Arafat: In the Eyes of the Beholder.* Birch Lane, 1997.

Whitelam, Keith W. *The Invention of Ancient Israel: The Silencing of Palestinian History.* Routledge, 1997.

Yari, Ehud. *Fatah.* A. Levin-Epstein Ltd., 1970.

Yonah, Alexander. *Terrorism: PLO Connection.* Crane Russak & Company, 1989.